Marxian Totality

Historical Materialism Book Series

The Historical Materialism Book Series is a major publishing initiative of the radical left. The capitalist crisis of the twenty-first century has been met by a resurgence of interest in critical Marxist theory. At the same time, the publishing institutions committed to Marxism have contracted markedly since the high point of the 1970s. The Historical Materialism Book Series is dedicated to addressing this situation by making available important works of Marxist theory. The aim of the series is to publish important theoretical contributions as the basis for vigorous intellectual debate and exchange on the left.

The peer-reviewed series publishes original monographs, translated texts, and reprints of classics across the bounds of academic disciplinary agendas and across the divisions of the left. The series is particularly concerned to encourage the internationalization of Marxist debate and aims to translate significant studies from beyond the English-speaking world.

For a full list of titles in the Historical Materialism Book Series available in paperback from Haymarket Books, visit: www.haymarketbooks.org/series_collections/1-historical-materialism.

Marxian Totality

Inverting Hegel to Expound Worldly Matters

Kaveh Boveiri

Haymarket Books
Chicago, IL

First published in 2024 by Brill Academic Publishers, The Netherlands
© 2024 Koninklijke Brill NV, Leiden, The Netherlands

Published in paperback in 2025 by
Haymarket Books
P.O. Box 180165
Chicago, IL 60618
773-583-7884
www.haymarketbooks.org

ISBN: 979-8-88890-543-2

Distributed to the trade in the US through Consortium Book Sales and Distribution (www.cbsd.com) and internationally through Ingram Publisher Services International (www.ingramcontent.com).

This book was published with the generous support of Lannan Foundation, Wallace Action Fund, and the Marguerite Casey Foundation.

Special discounts are available for bulk purchases by organizations and institutions. Please call 773-583-7884 or email info@haymarketbooks.org for more information.

Cover art and design by David Mabb. Cover art is a development of *Painting 16, Rhythm 69 (William Morris Block Printed Pattern Book, with Hans Richter Storyboard, developed from Richter's 'Rhythmus 25' and Kazimir Malevich's film script 'Artistic and Scientific Film – Painting and Architectural Concerns – Approaching the New Plastic Architectural System')*. Paint and wallpaper on canvas (2007).

Printed in the United States.

Library of Congress Cataloging-in-Publication data is available.

This book is dedicated to Danny Goldstick, for being Danny

∴

Contents

Acknowledgements IX

Prologue 1

1 **Two Misconceptions of Totality** 4
  1 The Atomist-Rationalist Conception of Totality 4
  2 The Organicist and Organicist-Dynamic Conception of Totality 11
  3 Conclusion 14

2 **On Hegel's Totality** 17
  1 Totality in the Doctrine of Being 17
  2 Totality in the Doctrine of Essence 18
  3 Totality in the Doctrine of Notion 21
  4 Conclusion 26

3 **On Lukács's Totality** 29
  1 Conclusion 39

4 **On Kosík's Totality** 41
  1 Totality: Concrete and Pseudo-concrete 42
  2 Totality and Objectivity 47
  3 *Objekt-Gegenstand*: Marx's Distinction 48
  4 Objectivity in Kosík: Conceptual-Lexical Discussion and Its Implications 50
  5 Praxis, Labour, Care, and Totality 57
  6 History and Totality 64
  7 Factor Theory, System, Structure, and Totality 68
  8 Criticism of Kosík 70
  9 Conclusion 75

5 **Marxian Totality Seen through His Works** 78
     A Note on the Difficulty and the Strategy Adopted 79
  1 Prelude – The Poem and the Letter to His Father: Marx, a Diver in Search of the *Sache selbst* in Life in the Street 81
    1.1 *Methodology-Logic* 82
    1.2 *Praxis in Methodology* 83
    1.3 *Dialectics and Mathematics* 84

2 Marx in the Laboratory: *Economic and Philosophical Manuscripts of 1844* 86
  3 Prototype-Genesis: Totality in the *German Ideology* and the 'Theses on Feuerbach' 91
  4 Totality in Oscillation: The *Grundrisse* 98
     4.1 Introduction to the *Grundrisse* 99
     4.2 The Chapter on Money in the *Grundrisse* 106
     4.3 The Chapter on Capital in the *Grundrisse* 111
        4.3.1 The Production Process of Capital 112
        4.3.2 The Circulation Process of Capital 113
        4.3.3 Capital as the Fruit-Bearer: Transformation of Surplus Value into Profit 115
     4.4 Conclusion 120
  5 Totality in Categorial Movement: *Capital* 122
     5.1 *Categorial Movement in Capital Volume I* 123
        5.1.1 The Opening Passage of *Capital* Volume I 123
        5.1.2 Categorial Movement in *Capital* Volume I 128
     5.2 *Categorial Movement in Capital Volume II* 132
     5.3 *Categorial Movement in Capital Volume III* 136
     5.4 Conclusion 141
  6 Conclusion 142

6 **The Relationship between the *Grundrisse* and *Capital* and between the Method of Enquiry and the Method of Exposition** 144
  1 The Roots of the Thesis of a Rupture in Marx's Works 145
  2 The Idea of a Rupture between the *Grundrisse* and *Capital* 148
  3 The Alternative Reading 151
  4 Conclusion 162

Epilogue 166

Appendix 1: Rereading of a Passage from the French Edition of First Volume of *Capital* Edited by Marx 169
Appendix 2: Some Passages of *Capital III*, in Original for Further Verification 171
Appendix 3: Note on Translation 177
Bibliography 178
Index 201

Acknowledgements

When I am asked when I began my project on Marx, I typically answer when I was a toddler! At that age Kaveh was taken to demonstrations against the Shah in Masjed Soleiman, during the last days of the Iranian revolution of 1979. Consequently, the question arises as to how I can thank all those who have, in one way or another, played roles in the development of this lifetime project, which does not stop here. The answer is straightforward: I can't! The safest way would probably be to alphabetically list some names, as far as I can think of them – this remains, undoubtedly, a non-exhaustive list.

Professor Yves-Marie Abraham let me audit his seminar on Degrowth (Décroissance) in autumn 2016, and hence put me in touch with problems on the ground relating to current capitalist society and possible practical and immediate actions.

Professor Andreas Arndt permitted me to participate in his two seminars on Hegel at Humboldt Universität zu Berlin in 2014–15, which deepened my knowledge of Hegel, and gave me this opportunity to discuss my project with him. He also commented on an earlier version of the Chapter on the relationship between the *Grundrisse* and *Capital*, during the conference 'Materialistische Dialektik: Marx Lektüren im Dialog', organised in Freie Universität in Berlin in October 2015.

Professor Joseph Berkovitz very patiently and kindly helped me to improve my first papers on philosophy of science in general and philosophy of economics in particular.

Professor Andy Blunden gave me the opportunity to discuss the basic thoughts leading to this project, particularly in Marxist epistemology – since 1990! As a dear colleague in the Marxists Internet Archives (MIA), of which Andy is the secretary, he has always been a source of inspiration and exemplar of assiduousness and solidarity.

Martina Chumova kindly and patiently checked all the terms in the Czech language in the Chapter 'On Kosík's Totality' and corrected mistakes and typos as I finalised this text.

Professor Di Giovanni kindly elaborated on some complexities in Hegel's methodology.

The late Professor Mahmoud Ebadian, with whom I took the first serious steps of dialectical thought, encouraged me in my translations and made me familiar with the texts of Hegel and Marx in their original language. His encyclopedic knowledge of the ancient Iranian and European languages, on the one hand, and his deep knowledge of European philosophy, on the other, also helped me to broaden and deepen my intellectual competence. He also let me discuss with him, on numerous occasions, his own translations, particularly of Karel Kosík and Hegel.

My comrade Danny Hayward, the editorial co-ordinator of the Historical Materialism Series in Brill, meticulously read the whole text and asked for clarifications when necessary. His contribution became more meaningful when I heard later that he was doing all this during the period that his partner and our dear comrade Marina Vishmidt was in a terminal stage of a long illness. Along with Danny, I would also like to thank all my colleagues of the HM Series and also Brill.

Professor Stephen Houlgate patiently clarified some technical points of the Hegel-Marx relationship regarding method.

Professor Martin Jay insightfully elaborated on the complexities of totality from a Marxian standpoint as they pertain to contemporary capitalism.

Professor Ivan Landa has clarified several points regarding Kosík's terminology and also read the relevant chapter of the current book, assisting me with my references to the Czech.

Professor Karim Mojtahedi generously permitted me, more than once, to participate in his seminar on Hegel held at University of Tehran during the years 1997–99.

Since 2000, Doctor Khosrow Parsa has helped me to familiarise myself with the scientific discussions in general and the relationship between evolution and Marxism in particular from a materialist point of view.

Professor Milan Prucha, Professor Emeritus at the Freie Universität Berlin, was of great help not only in clarifying different passages in Kosík's book *Dialektika Konkrétního*, by elaborating on the nuances of the original text in Czech, but also in discussing the relationship between Hegelian and Marxist dialectics.

Professor Paul Sabourin, whom I have known since 2012, discussed my monograph on many different occasions since its germinal stage.

Professor Tony Smith kindly read and commented on a paper related to this monograph. One of the most well-known figures in debates concerning Marx's methodology, he has exerted an invaluable influence on my project – one that goes beyond the present text.

The late Professor Abolghasem Zakerzadeh kindly permitted me to participate in his seminars on Hegel and Kant at the University of Shahid Beheshti in Tehran in 1998–99.

Michael Zibell not only read and edited a shorter version of Chapter 6 of this monograph, published in the proceedings of the abovementioned conference in Berlin, but also, with his decades of profound engagement in philosophy and theology in general and German philosophy in particular, enhanced my philosophical thought.

I also need to thank my comrades in the union of the lecturers at our university (Syndicat des chargées et chargés de cours de l'Université de Montréal – SCCCUM), and also Northcliffe Educational Foundation for their inestimable support.

To four persons, however, I am particularly indebted:

The first is my supervisor, the late Professor Yvon Gauthier. If Professor Gauthier had not accepted the supervision of an earlier version of this work in the second year of my PhD in 2013, I cannot just envisage how I could have accomplished this project. His profound knowledge of Hegel's philosophy, on the one hand, and his gigantic mastery of analytic philosophy and philosophy of science, on the other, invigorated this work even before he accepted me as a PhD candidate.

Professor Frieder Otto Wolf, whom I first met at a conference on Althusser and Benjamin in Potsdam in 2011, paved my way for a scholarship at Freie Universität Berlin in 2014–15, where I had the opportunity to discuss my project step by step and regularly, participating in his own courses and seminars as well as those of many others in Berlin.

Professor Marianne Kempeneers accepted me as her teaching assistant and gave me the opportunity to be exposed directly to the students of sociology in her course *Marx et Marxismes* in the department of sociology at Université de Montréal. In my lifetime as an elderly student, enrolled in six universities in four languages, and exposed to an extensive number of Marxist scholars in several countries in the world, I have *never* seen anyone with the ability of Professor Kempeneers to expound sophisticated concepts in Marxist thought with such enviable lucidity; this remains an ever-unachievable goal for me. In the following year, 2016, she also supported my candidacy to teach the same course. Teaching this course and being challenged by the earnest students who participated in it helped to concretise my somewhat remote theoretical and abstract discussions on Marx's methodology and connect it to social contexts.

Niloo, my comrade-partner, supported me with all the means possible during this project and before. I cannot imagine how one can be simultaneously a comrade and a *muse*: Niloo is! Without her support, particularly with my poor health, which has been affected by both chronic and acute diseases, the current monograph could not have been accomplished. During this period, she has also been the guardian who made me concentrate notwithstanding all my weaknesses, who made me proceed faster when I was unnecessarily slow, and more slowly when I was too fast! This is even more meaningful once I mention she has done all this with her master's and PhD project waiting to be accomplished! If this monograph is to be thought of like a child, then it represents a shared delivery, with all the pangs and pains divided between Niloo and me.

This monograph is dedicated to Danny Goldstick, the source of both theoretical and practical inspiration.

It is needless to add that notwithstanding all the support I had, the shortcomings of this work are uniquely mine.

Prologue

Marx is recognised as the most important thinker of our epoch, not only by a public medium like the BBC (1 October 1999), but also by more science-oriented sources such as *Nature* (6 November 2013). A survey made by the Arts & Humanities Citation Index for the period 1993 to 2000 puts Marx's works as the first among the ten most cited sources – the Bible comes fifth! We do not, however, witness the positive effect of his standpoint in our daily life; much worse, parts of the self-proclaimed left take conflicting positions on major issues – the question of whether the United Kingdom should leave EU, the question of participation in the 2017 US elections, or the more recent conflict between Russia and Ukraine are just a few examples. That there should be some theoretical agreement that could provide social-practical orientation seems evident. It is equally needless to emphasise the need for some common general methodological agreements on which these particular theoretical agreements rely. It has been argued that Marx's ambition was to theorise the capitalist mode of production as a totality, instead of offering a prescription for how that totality might be 'corrected'. The fulfilment of this ambition has been left to other writers who came after him.[1] The current work follows that path. This book has as its aim to introduce some common theoretical ground by showing a methodological dialectical consistency on the conception of totality in Marx's works: between the works of the young and the mature Marx on the one hand, and between two works by the mature Marx, namely the *Grundrisse* and *Capital*, on the other.

It is therefore composed of three parts. Following a broadly recognised classification suggested by the Czech philosopher Karel Kosík in his book *The Dialectic of the Concrete*, published in 1966, Chapter 1 of the first part sets the scene by discussing two misconceptions of totality. The first section of this chapter evaluates the first misconception of totality (the atomist-rationalist conception which prioritises the parts over the whole) through a detailed elaboration of the work of the best representative of this misconception, namely Ludwig Wittgenstein's *Tractatus Logico-Philosophicus*. The second section examines the second misconception (the organicist and organicist-dynamic conception of totality, which prioritises the whole over the parts) by examining the work of Schelling and Othmar Spann. The demonstration of the shortcoming of these two misconceptions leads the discussion to the second chapter, where

---

1   Jameson 2011, p. 3.

the Hegelian conception of totality is discussed. This is done by analysing the treatment of totality by Hegel in the work where he discusses this conception in the greatest detail, namely the *Science of Logic*. It will be shown that his account from the chapter on Being to the chapter on the Absolute Idea does not overcome the closedness of the totality of his system and leaves no room for the human subject or for future and conscious transformation of social reality. The third chapter deals with the first representative of Marxist philosophy to emphasise the importance of totality, Georg Lukács. His attempt to propose a reading of Marxist dialectics is shown to suffer from some important shortcomings. Not only does he not adequately criticise the closedness of Hegel's system, but he endorses it. What is more, by hypostasising the whole against its parts, his account remains ultimately close to the second misconception of totality discussed in Chapter 1. Responding to such shortcomings is the bedrock of the fourth chapter, where Karel Kosík's own conception of totality is evaluated. Through an extensive analysis of Kosík's *Dialectics of the Concrete* with reference to the text in Czech, it will be shown that his multifaceted account is the most rewarding in the existing Marxist literature. Nonetheless, his project suffers from two main shortcomings. The first is that he does not textually show how Marx's conception of totality is differentially nuanced in the different moments of his intellectual development. I try to address this first lacuna in the fifth chapter, in Part II, which in turn contains five sections that trace the complex development which Marx's account of totality goes through. In section i., through an examination of Marx's letter to his father and also one of the poems he wrote in 1837, it is shown that some characteristics of the later conception of totality exist even in these two pieces written by the nineteen-year-old Marx. This claim is then developed further in section ii., where it is shown how Marx approaches more closely the later conception of totality and neighbouring concepts in the *Economic and Philosophical Manuscripts of 1844*. In iii., this is shown to be even more developed in the work Marx and Engels wrote jointly, the *German Ideology*, and also in Marx's 'Theses on Feuerbach'. Although the prototype-genesis of the eventual conception can be seen here, for a detailed discussion of totality one has to wait for section iv, which considers Marx's most extensive discussion of the conception of totality, which is found in the *Grundrisse*. Oddly enough, that characteristic, the dialectical language of the *Grundrisse*, along with explicit reference to totality, does not make it the best representative of Marx's viewpoint on this subject. On the contrary, the conception of totality is shown to oscillate between the main two chapters of the book, the Chapter on Money and the Chapter on Capital. For the paramount example of Marx's treatment of totality, it is necessary to turn to the examination of *Capital*, where the Marxian totality is shown to exhibit totality via categorial movement, albeit with hardly any direct reference to this by name. The analysis of this movement is presented in section v. While several studies have discussed the conception of totality, hardly any have fully considered its development in Marx's works. With this, the examination of Marx's treatment of the conception of totality in Marx's works is accomplished. Although I hope that by this point the work has already made a new contribution to the existing literature on Marxian methodology, it does not stop there. Chapter 6, in Part III, addresses the second lacuna in Kosík's account. The point is that, although Kosík underlines the necessity of distinguishing the method of inquiry and the method of exposition, he does not recognise this distinction in Marx's works. By referring to the last two sections of Chapter 5, this last chapter of the book advances a response to the longstanding problem in Marxist literature about the relationship between the method of inquiry and the method of exposition. It will be argued that, contrary to what Alex Callinicos[2] and Jacques Bidet[3] claim, there is no rupture between the *Grundrisse* and *Capital*; rather, the former is an example of the method of inquiry, while the second exemplifies the method of exposition. It will be established that these two are related to each other as two moments embraced in the overall method of investigation.[4]

---

2 Callinicos 1978, 2014.
3 Bidet 1984, 2004, 2005.
4 This book-length discussion deals with totality from a methodological point of view. It draws on the previous works in the literature, but has some distinctive features. For readers interested in the broader literature on the topic, I here add a few brief remarks about some of the more significant contributions in this earlier literature.
   John E. Grumley's *History and Totality* (1989) has only a short chapter on Marx, and even there he does not show the different moments of Marx's conception of totality. Although Furio Cerutti writes at the beginning of his book *Totalità, Bisogni, Organizzazione: Ridiscutendo 'Storia e coscienza di classe'* (1980) that the book is not limited to discussing Lukács, it remains to a large extent within the framework of Lukács's conception of totality, which is discussed in a separate chapter here. Fred Moseley's *Money and Totality* (2015), the most recent book on the conception of totality in relation to money, does not have as its aim the development of an account of totality as such, of methodological problems in general, or the relationship between the method of inquiry and the method of exposition in particular. Martin Jay's now classic *Marxism and Totality: The Adventures of a Concept from Lukács to Habermas* (1984), as its subtitle implies, is more an account of the *adventures* 'totality' has gone through than a focused investigation of the problem of totality; moreover, it ends with the hope that another work might elaborate further on the concept of totality itself – a task which this book has hopefully accomplished, at least in part.

CHAPTER 1

Two Misconceptions of Totality

Before turning in the following chapters to the dialectical conception of totality and its complexities and subtleties, in this chapter I briefly overview two other conceptions of totality, which should rather be considered misconceptions.

To begin with, let us quote the passage where Karel Kosík gives his classification in full:

> Three basic concepts of the whole, or totality, have appeared in the history of philosophical thinking, each based on a particular concept of reality and postulating corresponding epistemological principles:
> (1) the *atomist-rationalist* conception, from Descartes to Wittgenstein, which holds reality to be a totality of simplest elements and facts;
> (2) the *organicist and organicist-dynamic* conception which formalizes the whole and emphasizes the predominance and priority of the whole over parts (Schelling, Spann);
> (3) the *dialectical conception* (Heraclitus, Hegel, Marx) which grasps reality as a structured, evolving and self-forming whole.[1]

This passage constitutes the guiding line of this book. Each of the two sections of this chapter elaborates on one of the first two conceptions. Sentences 1 and 2 are each turned into a section. The rest of the book will elaborate on the third conception.

1 The Atomist-Rationalist Conception of Totality

According to Kosík, the atomist-rationalist conception, of which two representatives are Descartes and Wittgenstein,[2] considers reality to be a totality of the simplest elements and facts. In this conception, we have the ontological predominance of the parts over the whole, where parts determine the whole they compose. The whole, regardless of the parts, is just a proto-whole, an

---

1 Kosík 1976, p. 24.
2 One may add Leibniz: 'And there must be simple substances, because there are compounds; for the compound is nothing else but a cluster or aggregate of the simple [things]' (Leibniz 1881, p. 11, my translation).

ensemble of the uncombined parts, which turns into the whole through the mediation and determination of the parts. Put differently, insofar as a whole is not constructed *ab extra*, it comes into being through the mediation and the determination of its parts.

In referring to Wittgenstein, Kosík has in mind, of course, the early Wittgenstein of the *Tractatus*.[3] Here, I first elaborate on the conception of totality through its critical analysis in the *Tractatus* and through the analysis of what Kosík ascribes, without any further elaboration, to this category; I then criticise a Tractarian conception of totality that goes beyond what Kosík invokes in his book, still according to a dialectical conception.

The opening passages of *Tractatus* imply the notion of totality: 'The world is all [*alles*] that is the case' and then 'The world is the totality [*Gesamtheit*] of facts, not of things' (§1).[4] Totalities are not over and above the facts, and the uncompounded facts [*Sachverhalten*], and the relationship between facts and statements of facts, is the primary question of *Tractatus*. It has been argued that Wittgenstein takes the relationship between facts and sentences as being analogous to a 'phonograph record–sound recorded' relationship.[5] The same relation exists also between a sentence and what it is composed of; that is, the meaning of its components determines the meaning of the sentence. This is equally true of the world and its components as of atomic facts: the complete description of the world hinges on the description of all atomic facts. The nature of this determination is such that the totality is determined by the individual facts. Through this method of construction or generation, as Bertrand Russell puts it,[6] the totality of propositions is constructed through atomic propositions. The totality is then built up through amalgamation of the blocks. This is also how objects, potentially recurrent experiential universals, form atomic facts, the totality of which is the world (§ 2.04). Similarly, the immediate combination or concatenation of names builds up an elementary proposition (§ 2.421).

Wittgenstein then introduces the hierarchy of the components of the world, namely, *Tatsachen*, *Sachverhalten*, and facts. The world is composed of *Tatsachen*, *Tatsachen* are composed of *Sachverhalten*, and *Sachverhalten* are com-

---

[3] The discussion presented here regarding Wittgenstein's conception of totality may be criticised on the ground that, for instance, the logical independence discussed here does not really mean independence. Such a sweeping criticism would, nonetheless, make an elaboration on Kosík's view barren.
[4] All the quotations from the *Tractatus Logico-Philosophicus* (Wittgenstein 1922) refer to the text by numbered proposition. Translations are modified when necessary.
[5] Moore 2005, p. 91.
[6] Wittgenstein 1922, p. 4.

posed of facts (§ 4.2211). We also have a hierarchy of propositions: the one that entails says more than the one that is entailed; it is, so to speak, richer. This determination by the parts imputing themselves to the wholes is reiterated in a work that appeared several years after *Tractatus*. There it is claimed that the logical form of each entity is determined by its two determinants: the sentence, along with the mode of projection which projects reality into the sentence.[7] Hence we have a bottom-up building of propositions. This demarcates the hierarchy of parts over wholes. This determination and superiority of parts over the whole is also asserted on other occasions: if a proposition has no sense 'it is only because we have failed to give sense to some of its constituent parts' (§ 5.4733).[8] The constituent parts of a proposition thus make a proposition sensed or senseless, possessed of a sense or lacking one. Through the meaningfulness of names and the sensefulness of elementary propositions, the scaffolding of the world is presented by logic; we also thus know how it is connected with the world (§ 6.124).

After this brief sketch of the notion of totality in *Tractatus*, in which we take our cue from Kosík's scanty reference to the first conception of totality, in what follows I attempt to distinguish the Tractarian totality from a dialectical one.

To begin with, it should be noted that Wittgenstein's view does not totally lack any hint of a dialectical picture of totality. As if he himself were aware of the problem of a static picture of reality or the world, he makes statements such as the following: 'One name stands for one thing and another for another thing, and they are connected together. And so, the whole [*Ganze*] like a living picture [*lebendes Bild*], presents the atomic facts' (§ 4.0311). There is still a second case where a point similar to a dialectical conception of totality is found in *Tractatus*: In § 5.2 we read that the structures of propositions possess internal relations to one another [*internen Beziehungen*]. Some things are thus in connection with other things. This, along with the previous point – namely, that the whole gives a living picture of the parts – is the moment at which the *Tractatus* acquires an at least apparently dialectical aspect (pace Kosík). Nonetheless, these points will be shown not to be watertight.

From a dialectical standpoint, one central problem with the *Tractatus* is not that the parts determine the whole (the view criticised by Kosík as a reduction) but the fact that there is no room for change. In the only places where Wittgenstein talks about change [*Verwandlung*], the word 'replace' will do just as well; for example, instead of 'change a constituent part of a proposition into a vari-

---

7 Wittgenstein 1929, p. 169.
8 This entails that the propositions do have parts. This standpoint has been challenged recently by Goldstick (2020), who argues that propositions do not have parts, and hence have no forms.

able' (§ 3.315), we may say 'replace a constituent part of a proposition with a variable'. The similarity between death and world that Wittgenstein proposes is also illuminating in this respect. In neither, he claims, do we witness change [*ändern*] but only cessation [*aufhören*], a halt (§ 6.431). The essence of a sentence also cannot be altered without altering its sense (§ 4.465). Furthermore, although we read that in the proposition 'The truth or falsity of propositions does make some alteration in the general construction of the world' (§ 5.5262), reality is restricted to two alternatives: yes and no (§ 4.023). The polar binary world of Wittgenstein's book does not leave room for a dialectical conception of totality that considers incessant change as an essential characteristic of reality. As a result, the whole issue of the dialectical sense of totality, that is, what comes in between, change, incessant becoming, the *mors immortalis*,[9] in relation to which the apparent fixity of objects is but a mere abstraction, as well as the transformation of quantity into quality, is left out.[10] Put differently, such a reading overlooks the fact that continuous change involves more – indeed infinitely more – than two different states of affairs, and take changes in reality as jumps from one state to another.

In the *Philosophical Investigations*, however, Wittgenstein's position changes. In this book, regarding the relation of death and life, he to some extent endorses the well-known and much discussed dialectical dictum of the transition from quantity into quality:

> And so, too, a corpse seems to us quite inaccessible to pain. – Our attitude to what is alive and to what is dead, is not the same. All our reactions are different. – If anyone says: 'That cannot simply come from the fact that a living thing moves about in such-and-such a way and a dead one not', then I want to intimate to him that this is a case of the transition 'from quantity to quality'.[11]

This should not be taken to mean that I believe Wittgenstein remains loyal to a dialectical conception of totality, or for that reason to dialectics in general.

Another flaw in *Tractatus* seen from a dialectical standpoint is the absence of *interconnectedness*, another characteristic of a dialectical conception of totality. Instead, we witness the mutual *disconnectedness* of facts in *Tractatus*, notwithstanding the passage (§ 4.0311) where Wittgenstein claims that he wants to preserve a living picture of reality. Take the following proposition for instance:

---

9   Marx 1977, p. 130.
10 Compare § 5.153: 'An event occurs or does not occur, there is no middle course'.
11 Wittgenstein 1958, I, § 284.

'For each item can be the case or not the case, while everything remains the same' (§ 1.121). This is reiterated in § 2.061: 'Atomic facts are independent of one another'. Once totalised, this mutual independence, according to which each element can be true or false independent of whether the others are true or false, impedes an organic interconnection between the whole and the parts. This is in polar opposition to a dialectical conception of totality, according to which there is an organic relationship between the whole and the parts, and between the parts. This is a principal flaw in Wittgenstein's conception of the totality, but one on which Kosík does not elaborate.

Still another shortcoming that stems from Wittgenstein's prioritising of the parts over the whole is found in the priority he gives to the internal qualities of objects, in contrast to the co-occurrences, sequences, etc. of objects. According to Wittgenstein, this is, in contrast to external qualities of the objects, the determinant of the object, and these internal qualities are what enable us to know an object (§ 2.01231). This demarcation of inner and outer qualities is also different from a dialectical conception of totality, according to which things are taken to be processes in inseparable relationship with each other, and a sharp demarcation between inside and outside is baseless.[12]

One may also add Wittgenstein's understanding of senseless pseudo-propositions (§ 4.1272, § 5.535). Although he maintains that mathematical propositions, for instance, are also pseudo-propositions, since they are mere equations (§ 6.21), they are not senseless. The example he gives of propositions that are in fact pseudo-propositions but also nonsensical [*sinnlos*] is interesting. As is well known, 'in itself', 'for itself', and 'for us' are crucial dialectical terms not only in Hegel but also in Marx. In the aforementioned article, he gives the following example as a senseless pseudo-proposition: 'The Real, though it is an *in itself*, must also be able to become a *for myself*.'[13] Seen from a dialectical perspective this becomes more peculiar when Wittgenstein takes this to be as senseless a pseudo-proposition as 'Red is higher than green'!'[14]

To all this one may add the mystical character of the Tractarian conception of totality. Although Wittgenstein defends language in the name of reality, and in this sense distinguishes himself from Kant, who defends language in the name of appearance,[15] the *Tractatus*'s conception of totality still retains a

---

12 One corollary of adopting such a standpoint is avoiding the dichotomy, or sheer demarcation, of endo-consistence and exo-consistence, as put forward by Deleuze and Guattari 2005, p. 130.
13 Wittgenstein 1929, p. 162.
14 Ibid.
15 Glouberman 1980, p. 20.

strong hint of mysticism that leaves the totality of what is in the world indescribable.[16] Regarding this mysticism, Russell says that it stems from Wittgenstein's doctrine of pure logic. According to this doctrine:

> the logical proposition is a picture (true or false) of the fact, and has in common with the fact a certain structure. It is this common structure which makes it capable of being a picture of the fact, but the structure cannot itself be put into words, since it is a structure of words, as well as of the fact to which they refer.[17]

The unutterability of the structure of the possible picture given of the world is the germ of the mysticism of the *Tractatus*, which turns objects into pseudo-concepts: to say 'x is an object' is to say nothing.[18] If this is so, then the generality and construction elaborated on by Russell are not general enough to talk about things in general or about the world in its totality; being able to do so, according to this approach, necessitates our going outside the world – which is impossible.[19] Wittgenstein's mysticism is probably best expressed in § 6.45: 'The contemplation [*Anschauung*] of the world sub specie aeterni is the contemplation of the world as limited whole [*begrenztes Ganzes*]. The feeling [*Gefühl*] of the world as a closed whole is the mystical [*das Mystische*]'.

This mystical consequence also has its roots in the fact that according to Wittgenstein the boundaries of logic and of the world coincide. You cannot know anything beyond the boundary, nor can you know as a whole what is within the boundaries, because to do so you have to be able to view the totality from outside. As we will see in what follows, Kosík responds to this dilemma by ascribing some characteristics to totality that permit us to know the totality without having to know all its details, but rather through the contradictions and the mechanism of the totality.

The only two candidates in human knowledge that seem, on the face of it, endorsable by *Tractatus* are logic and natural sciences. As to logic, its propositions are tautologies, and since they are analytic, they are uninformative, they say nothing (§ 6.1), and they show only the formal properties of language

---

16 As we will see in Chapter 4, this is totally absent there.
17 Russell in Wittgenstein 1929, p. 7.
18 Wittgenstein 1929, p. 5.
19 A comparison with Kosík is here remarkable: the subtitle of his book – *A Study on Problems of Man and World* – indicates a different path: for according to Kosík, talking about the world in its totality not only is possible, but does not necessitate viewing it from a standpoint outside the world.

and the world (§ 6.12); therefore, they do not give knowledge. As to the natural sciences, Wittgenstein introduces one superstition and one delusion. The superstition is related to the belief in a causal nexus (§ 5.1361), which is also the problem of change elaborated on in the previous passages. The illusion is to believe that the laws of nature explain natural phenomena (enunciating the laws merely states the phenomena, and, like a tree stump, bears no explanation); this is at the basis of whole modern view of the world (§ 6.371).

Both cases are then enmeshed with strong, unutterable solipsism, the indescribability which is concomitant with mysticism. That the world is my world brings the self into philosophy. The borders of my world are the borders of the particular language I understand. The limits of my world, my microcosm and the limits of my language are coincident. The reality is coordinated with this solipsistic I, the metaphysical, philosophical subject that lies not in the world but in its limit, and is not a part of the world (§ 5.62).

Wittgenstein makes use of a paradoxical pun by logically describing the totalities that are logically indescribable; he thus provides us with sentences that are 'strictly nonsensical according to the very doctrine that they propound'.[20] This is of course the paradoxicality that he admits at the end of the book; nonetheless, those totalities remain 'the subject-matter of his mysticism'.[21]

If the criticism presented here is correct, then it follows that what Wittgenstein calls 'the totality' has hardly anything to do with the totality but is just the sum total of the components of it. That totality will then remain an illegitimate totality,[22] because the colossal number of individual facts is determined empirically.[23] This position was criticised by Kosík, who reminds us that the facticity of facts, to use his phrase, is not their reality, it is not per se revealing, unless facts and totality are seen in dialectical relationship to each other. Put differently, neither totality nor reality ensues from the sum total of the facts. It may not be wrong to say that to the Wittgensteinian dictum 'of what one cannot speak, one must be quiet', a dialectical conception of totality would respond – and that this might be akin to what the German sociologist Norbert Elias means when he says that 'of what one cannot speak, one would search'.[24] But before going into the details of such a conception, let us first turn to the second conception of totality in Kosík's classification.

---

20   Anscombe 1959, p. 162.
21   Wittgenstein 1922, p. 7.
22   Sullivan 2000, p. 175: 'the totality of facts is an obvious example of an illegitimate totality'.
23   This is further developed in Glouberman 1980.
24   Elias 1991, p. 215. (My translation.)

2   The Organicist and Organicist-Dynamic Conception of Totality

'[T]he organicist and organicist-dynamic conception', according to Kosík, 'formalizes the whole and emphasizes the predominance [*pantsví*] and priority of the whole over parts (Schelling, Spann)'.[25] Here I attempt to develop the merely fragmentary references to Schelling and Spann as found in the *Dialectics of the Concrete*.

Schelling holds that nothing can be known in its isolation and singularity, 'but rather only in its context and as part of a great, all-encompassing totality'[26] and as one of the characteristics of the philosophical science of the era. While this is partially correct, this conception goes further and holds that what predominates is the whole and that the whole is determinative of the parts. As examples, one may recall the predominance of the genotype over the parts of the phenotype, or the avalanche over its component snowballs. This pre-existence or existential priority of the whole over the parts reflects a tendency in this conception to hypostasise the whole over the parts, leading to emergentism[27] – the view that under certain highly specific conditions, life, consciousness, will, etc. are produced, without the governing law of such production being in turn explicable on the basis of more general laws. Similarly, based on this conception of totality, the proto-parts change into parts through the mediation of the whole. Along the same lines, while each part presupposes the existence of all the other parts, the existence of the parts hinges upon the existence of the whole: beyond presupposing any other part, each part, in consequence, presupposes the existence of the hypostatised whole. A simple analogy may be helpful here. Take you and all the cells of your body. According to this conception, the cells of which you are composed all came into existence later than you did. Such a conception does not realise that the You at time T_1, let's call it Y_1, constitutes the sum total of your cells, let's call it $\sum C_1$ and is constituted by them, in the same way that You at T_2, that is, Y_2, constitutes and is constituted by the sum total of your cells, that is, $\sum C_2$.

After stating his admiration for an unexplored characteristic of Schelling's thought, that is, his treatment of nature as the unity of product and productivity in his early writings, Kosík quotes him to highlight the presence even here of the principal flaw of Schelling's approach, that is, the hypostasising of the

---

25   Kosík 1976, p. 24.
26   Schelling 2007b, p. 150.
27   And in passing it should be added: in contradistinction with the transformation of quantity into quality – a distinctive characteristic of a dialectical conception of totality. This will be further developed in the following chapters.

whole over, or at the expense of, the parts: 'Inasmuch as all parts of an organic whole carry and support each other, *this whole must have existed prior to its parts. The whole is not inferred from the parts, but the parts had to spring from the whole*'.[28]

In other passages, Schelling introduces totality in close relationship with identity. Both totality and identity are what generate perspectives. Viewed from the perspective of totality, the Universe is God; viewed from the perspective of identity God is Universe.[29] What is more, the expression of totality is limited to human beings, because unlike animals their expression is not limited to particularity.[30]

With that said, a distinction is to be drawn with regard to Schelling's discussion of totality that is absent in Kosík's discussion. While totality is introduced as the product of 'the apposition of plurality to unity and the apposition of unity to plurality',[31] according to Schelling this is true only about relative totalities. 'God', for instance, as an absolute identity, is also immediately 'absolute totality, and vice versa',[32] but in this absoluteness there is not multiplicity; instead there is only simplicity. Nonetheless, if it is the mega-totality in which and through which all relative totalities, complex as they are, find their existence as well as their cognisability or intelligibility, then oddly enough all these relative totalities that are complex find all this in what is itself not complex but simple! Hence, any existence of the individual outside the absolute totality is the result of mere arbitrary separation.

What is more, true totality seems to be found more in mythology than in philosophy. Here Schelling introduces the subject matters that lie outside the reach of philosophy, and to which it does not have any relation. The first are the things without any essential actuality to themselves; the second group comprises things that are corrupt and distorted, since only the original things have meanings in philosophy; and a third matter in which philosophy cannot find and know itself is that which is boundless, that is, without end. But mythology as the true totality, as 'the original product of the consciousness striving to restore itself', is self-completing and self-conclusive, 'something complete, something held in certain limits, a world for itself'. The fourth set of things

---

28 Schelling 1927b, p. 279 (quoted in Kosík 1976, pp. 34–35, emphasis added).
29 This is developed in Schelling 1989, p. 15. Such enunciations suggesting non-identification, one may add, could permit Hegel to ridicule Schelling's Absolute, drawing an analogy between this term and a night in which all cows are black (Hegel 1980, p. 22).
30 Cf. Schelling 1989, p. 183: '[Animals] appear as particular precisely because they do not express the totality, which appears only in human beings'.
31 Schelling 1980, § 41, p. 227.
32 Schelling 1989, p. 24.

opposed to totality are the things that are dead and stagnant, but mythology as 'the highest human consciousness' overcomes its contradictions and proceeds based on its immanent laws.[33]

A few points are noteworthy regarding this discussion. One is the difficulty that this conception faces in understanding the totality discursively. The reason for this is that totality for Schelling, as for Spinoza, implies a certain spatiality, but this spatiality is to be in harmony with infinite absolute totality. The impossibility of this synthesis makes it such that any 'discursive understanding's conceit of totality is a lie'.[34] The same difficulty is also seen in Othmar Spann, another figure who commits to this conception of totality, since for him too the concept of the world as a whole lies beyond man's reach.[35] This standpoint is targeted by Hegel in the *Phenomenology of Spirit*: as the coming-to-be of science, this book, Hegel says, does not have the smallest similarity with 'the rapturous enthusiasm which, like a shot from a pistol, begins straight away with absolute knowledge, and makes short work of other standpoints by declaring that it takes no notice of them',[36] and neither does it endorse revelation, as is the case in Schelling's *Positive Philosophy*.

The second point, hinted at previously, is that Kosík ignores the distinction Schelling draws between relative and absolute totality. For instance, Schelling writes: 'Relative totality does not subsist in itself, but only the absolute totality does'.[37] To say that only the wholes exist and the existence of parts is dependent on the existence of the wholes means that even *relative totalities* are dependent on the absolute totality; it is this totality for which all the simultaneity of all potencies holds, which is not true about relative totalities. This absolute, unconditioned totality, or God, is the one to which all existence belongs.[38]

The third point regarding Kosík's discussion of Schelling is that he ignores the fact that Schelling *does* actually approach the third classification at one point in his philosophy, namely, his philosophy of art. Take the following passage as an example: 'They [god figures] necessarily constitute a world in their own turn collectively, one in which everything together is *mutually determined*, an organic whole, a totality, a world'.[39] Although pre-eminence is still ascribed

---

33   Schelling 2007a, pp. 154–55.
34   Vaught 2008, p. 247.
35   Spann 1939, xv: 'The concept of world as a whole is not attainable by human knowledge' (my translation).
36   Hegel 1977, p. 16.
37   Schelling 2012, p. 167, § 26.
38   Schelling 1927b, p. 148.
39   Schelling 1989, p. 41 (emphasis added).

to the whole, as can be seen, the point that there are nonetheless some roles for the parts is recognised here.

Such a misconception regarding totality is attributed to Marx by some contemporary thinkers. This is the case with Paul Paolucci, for instance, who in his book *Marx and the Politics of Abstraction* writes:

> Sociologists as a group accept the principle, as famously expounded by Durkheim, that when we add the parts of society up they collectively result in a whole that is greater than the sum of these parts. Marx – while he does agree the whole is larger than the sum of its parts – *starts with assuming that a whole already exists and then inquires into what sort of parts does empirical evidence allow us to carve*. In Durkheim's approach, and by extension mainstream sociology, parts exist first and the way we put the parts together for study constitutes the whole. For Marx, the whole exists *first* and it is our job to discover, through research, what parts comprise its most important relations and processes.[40]

While Paolucci rightly criticises the first conception of totality presented here, he does not go farther than the endorsement of the Schellingian-Spannian standpoint criticised by Kosík. What Marx invokes is a totality in which the whole and the parts have a dialectical relationship in that they co-constitute each other. The word 'first' underscored by Paolucci and ascribed to Marx cannot be accommodated by the particular conception of dialectics that will be developed in the following chapters. This 'first' is a reiteration of the 'prior' we earlier saw in Kosík's passage in which he specifies a dialectical approach.

3 Conclusion

But before turning to the following chapter let us review some of the sociopolitical implications of these two conceptions. While it may not be difficult to infer an asocial atomistic individualism from an atomistic conception of totality, the upshot of which is on the one hand the non-existence of society,[41] as articulated by Margaret Thatcher, and on the other the right to pursue individual happiness as found in the American Constitution, neither is it difficult to see how the second conception of totality leads to despotic regimes in gen-

---

40   Paolucci 2011, p. 56.
41   Thatcher 1987.

eral and fascism in particular. If the whole is to be prioritised over the parts not only epistemologically but also ontologically, with generalisation, the same may be said about a society and the individuals composing that society. Would it then be too far-fetched to infer that one consequence of such an approach would be the endorsement of despotic regimes? Although this may not be explicit in Schelling, Karl Polanyi insightfully demonstrates such a relationship in the doctrine of the Austrian philosopher Othmar Spann, another proponent of such a conception. In 'Othmar Spann, the Philosopher of Fascism', Polanyi highlights the 'Master-key role' that the conception of totality plays in Spann's endorsement of Fascism. If single ideas, single facts, and single individuals are taken to be the articulations of totalities in these different realms – namely, cognition, existence, and society – and causation is also to be gotten rid of, as argued by Spann, the riddle of his endorsement of Fascism would be explained. In *Der wahre Staat*, Spann develops the elements of the predominance of whole, nation, society, etc. over individuals, and advocates 'the model of a non-democratic, hierarchical, and corporatist state as the only truly valid political constitution'.[42] Nonetheless, Polanyi finds a 'functional and corporative organization of society' more adequate to its essential nature, in contrast to what can be a consequence of the atomistic conception, in which isolated individuals independent of one another are society's basic constituents. But the question would be: What forces us to put ourselves to commit to this inevitable binary choice between individualistic laissez-faire of capitalism on the one hand, and the endorsement, even a partial one of the kind made by Polanyi, of the corporative society, in the illusion that it can be simply functional, rather than outright fascistic or despotic?[43]

This is one of the pivotal questions of this book. The answer lies, I believe, in adopting a Marxian conception of totality that avoids the dilemma presented here, as well as several other pitfalls that will be presented in the following chapters. Such a Marxian conception of totality will be full developed by the end of this book. By adopting such a conception of totality one can look forward, with Marx, to the day when 'human progress [will] cease to resemble that hideous pagan idol who would not drink the nectar but from the skulls of the slain'.[44]

---

42   Tudor. Spann did not realise that such an approach can affect his own individual life: he was expelled from the party owing to minor disagreements. See Klemperer 1968, pp. 204–5.
43   Polanyi 1934, p. 7. Polanyi's short text does not explicitly endorse the dialectical conception of totality presented in this book.
44   Marx 1979, p. 222.

With this note, and after the development of the two phrases by Kosík introduced at the beginning in this chapter into a brief clarificatory overview, we turn to the third conception of totality, that is, the dialectical conception. This is one of the bedrocks of the work at hand. In the next chapter, we will undertake a discussion of Hegelian totality, examining its relation to the Marxian dialectical conception. And by examining Kosík's third classification – the dialectical approach to totality – we will find that the misunderstanding of this dialectical conception is not limited to non-Marxist thinkers, but that there are also Marxist thinkers who have failed to appreciate it – as was the case with Paolucci's reading, hinted at above.

CHAPTER 2

On Hegel's Totality

Having briefly elaborated on what Kosík presents as the characteristics of the two misconceptions of totality, in this chapter we will introduce the dialectical conception of totality. As Kosík remarks: 'The dialectical conception [of totality] (Heraclitus, Hegel, Marx) ... grasps reality as a structured, evolving and self-forming whole'.[1] Examining this version of totality in Hegel's *Science of Logic* is the objective of this chapter.[2]

Hegel's conception of totality in turn may be thought of as a response to the Kantian conception of totality. For Kant, totality falls under the group of the categories of quantity: allness and totality. It comes after unity and plurality, and according to him it is plurality taken as unity.[3] Notwithstanding this apparent dynamism, it has, like all the other of Kant's eleven categories, a fixed place in the table of categories – a conviction that Hegel does not share.

I attempt to limit the discussion of Hegel's totality to *The Science of Logic*. In addition to feasibility, there are several important reasons for this: *The Science of Logic*, known as 'the only real candidate for the role of strict dialectical proof',[4] is the work in which totality is the most extensively elaborated.[5]

1 Totality in the Doctrine of Being

Hegel discusses totality mainly after the Doctrine of Being. The reason is not difficult to grasp when we remember that the categories in the following book (namely, the Doctrine of Essence) are the result of mediation and are realised through reflection, which is absent in the Doctrine of Being. Essence is thus Being mediated by its self-negation. Owing to this characteristic, what we have before the Doctrine of Essence is an 'unmediated and presupposed

---

1 Kosík 1976, p. 24. This is a slightly modified version of a chapter published in Ferrer et al. 2020. I would like to thank Editora Fundação Fênix and Diego Ferrer for their kind permission.
2 All the references to these works, unless otherwise specified, come from Hegel 1969b and 1969c.
3 Kant 1968, B111, p. 154.
4 Taylor 1995, p. 225.
5 And, one may add, most frequently referred to – more than three hundred times!

totality',[6] a 'totality of indifference',[7] 'indifferent totality',[8] 'the totality being for itself',[9] 'formal totality',[10] and a 'negative totality'.[11] Totality, the all-sided contradiction, the result of unity being posited as totality, posits itself as a 'self-sursuming contradiction'[12] and passes over to Essence. In so doing, it overcomes its being just an empty name,[13] its formality, its being negative, and its indifference. We may say roughly that we have the sursumption of the presupposed totalities through determination. At the transition moment of Being to Essence, this amounts to sursumption of the outsideness or externality of the former and its passage to the latter. In order for totality to posit itself, each determination has to have a double transition: forwards to the determination that comes after it, and backwards to the determination that comes before it. This double transition is presented as of the utmost importance to scientific method in general.[14] If there are these two transitions, the categorial movement entailing the determination of the totalities is not unidirectional.[15]

2 Totality in the Doctrine of Essence

It is in coherence with the discussion of the previous section that at the beginning of the Doctrine of Essence, Hegel speaks of the *return* of Being in its totality into Essence and (at the end of the *Logic*) of a *return* to the beginning.[16] The complex act of the subject matter [*Sache selbst*] conditions itself, and at the same time it posits its conditions as ground against itself.[17] To step into existence, the *Sache selbst* must have all its conditions at hand, which is tantamount

---

6   Hegel 1969b, p. 457.
7   Hegel 1969b, p. 449.
8   Hegel 1969b, p. 444.
9   Hegel 1969b, p. 146.
10 Hegel 1969b, p. 445.
11 Hegel 1969b, p. 457.
12 Hegel 1969b, p. 451. For a discussion on the translation of *Aufhebung* see Appendix III.
13 Hegel 1969b, p. 450.
14 Hegel 1969b, p. 384.
15 Cf. McTaggart, who speaks of the succession of categories 'from one [category] to another because the admission of the first as valid requires logically the admission of the second as valid' (McTaggart 1999, p. 140; see also p. 6). The result of a non-linear reading of determination – different from McTaggart's account, which is introduced as an alternative here – is found in the very end of the *Science of Logic* (Hegel 1969c, p. 573).
16 Hegel 1969c, pp. 21, 572.
17 Hegel 1969c, p. 119.

to its totality being posited as the groundless immediacy; 'then the scattered manifoldness recollects itself in the Thing itself'.[18]

Although Hegel refers to whole and part and to their relationship on numerous occasions in the *Logic*, he allocates a particular part of the Doctrine of Essence to this theme.[19] This is, according to Hegel, the first moment of essential relationship, where both sides, so to speak, simultaneously and mutually condition and presuppose each other. This first moment is followed by the second moment of the essential relationship – that is, force and its externalisation – then by the third moment of the internal and external relationship. The reflected independence is here brought about through the reflection of the unmediated independence in itself. Each side is a moment posited by the other side and in negative unity with it.

Part and whole are both here existing, reflecting, and in immediate independence, but their being posited in isolation is just a moment of their negative unity. The whole makes the independence of the plurality of the parts, and the parts are the realisation or instantiation of the whole, since they are merely the means of the manifestation of the whole. Their independent reflected totality is in fact relative, and this relativity is the product of the mediation of each in the other.[20] Through this negation, the parts are the same as the whole, but only insofar as they are parts of that whole; similarly, the whole is the same as the parts merely as the whole of the parts. While in Hegelian terminology the parts are the same as the whole considered 'as partitioned whole' [*als geteiltem Ganze*],[21] one may say by generalisation that the whole is the same as the parts considered as the 'wholified parts' [*als geganzte Teile*]. Thus, the primary negative unity, in which the immediacy of each side is mediated through the other, is developed into reflective identity [*Reflexionsidentität*], or 'reflected unity' [*reflecktierte Einheit*].[22]

The parts have the whole as one of their moments in themselves.[23] There is nothing in the parts that is not in the whole, and vice versa.[24] While the part in

---

18 Hegel 1969c, p. 122. My translation of the last part of the sentence ('so *erinnert* sich diese zerstreute Mannigfaltigkeit an ihr selbst') is different from that of George di Giovanni: '... then this scattered manifold *internally recollects* itself' (Hegel 2010, p. 416). There are two reasons for this: 1. 'internally' is added; and 2. Hegel says *an ihr*. Without this, 'recollects itself' would be enough; with this, it is not.
19 Hegel 1969c, pp. 166–72.
20 Such an approach, taking into consideration both parts and whole in treating Hegel's work in general, is highlighted by Stephen Houlgate (Houlgate 2006, pp. 4ff.).
21 Hegel 1969c, p. 169.
22 Hegel 1969c, p. 170.
23 See Hegel 1969c, p. 168.
24 Hegel 1969c, p. 169: 'Es ist nichts im Ganzen, was nicht in den Teilen, und nichts

its stance before being for itself seems to be differentiated from the whole, once it is for itself the part *is* the whole.[25] This relationship is an inseparable identity in which the whole is the reflected identity and the parts are the various pluralities of the whole. The whole is also the starting point of the parts, and so too the parts are the starting point of the whole; each is in this way in essential relationship with the other through self-negation, or with itself through negation of the other, and each then collapses into the other. In doing so, each side constitutes both itself as well as the other side as the foundation [*Grundlage*] of this relationship, and each is both conditioned [*bedingte*] and conditioning [*bedingende*]: 'This relationship is therefore the immediate contradiction and sursumes itself in the very relationship'.[26] This contradiction, which is no more than the opposing tension in this relationship, which is immediately independent and relative, leads to the next moment.

The distortedness of the isolated consideration of parts and whole is not just an epistemological question, in which parts are not fully *understood* without considering the whole they constitute, and also the whole is in turn not a comprising whole unless seen as the whole of the parts. The relationship between them is rather an ontological one, in which the differentiation and functioning of each hinges upon the existence and differentiation of the other. Each of them, both part and whole, also has its independence through the other. The part is independent as an independent part of a whole; the whole, in turn, is independent as a whole comprising the parts. Each finds its independence through the mediation of the other – that is, through *inter*dependence.

In the Doctrine of Essence, the immediate totality as the illusion-totality or pseudo-totality – in the form of 'being for itself',[27] 'negative being',[28] 'being closed in itself',[29] and merely 'formal being'[30] – is propelled through negation to make 'the totality of existence'.[31] It is dichotomised into the two completely

---

in den Teilen, was nicht im Ganzen ist'. One can legitimately rebut that there is of course something in the whole that is not in its parts, namely, their mode of combination. The reason is that the same parts can be combined in different ways, thus constituting differing wholes, and those parts had it in them to combine in that way into the whole. At this point, Hegel's discussion is silent about such a question.

25 Hegel 1969c, p. 172.
26 Hegel 1969c, p. 167: 'Dies Verhältnis ist daher der unmittelbare Widerspruch an ihm selbst und hebt sich auf'.
27 Hegel 1969b, p. 146.
28 Hegel 1969b, p. 457.
29 Hegel 1969b, p. 373.
30 Hegel 1969b, p. 445.
31 Hegel 1969c, p. 132.

expelling and dissimilar but also complementary worlds of the appearing and the essential: the *world that is in and for itself* [*die an und für sich seiende Welt*] and the apparent or phenomenal world [*die erscheinende Welt*]. While their independence brings along the construal of the former by the whole and the latter by the parts, their relationship puts each in the illusion [*Schein*][32] and identity of both of these worlds.[33] Both the independent wholes of existence – where the apparent and phenomenal world is the ground for the world that is in and for itself, and the world that is in and for itself is the ground for the apparent or phenomenal world – are the expression of the world of which each is a moment. The contradictory unity of the pseudo-totality of the Doctrine of Being hence differentiates itself by relating itself to the differentiated moment of itself that is the product of its negation and its realisation through externalisation.

This externalisation and differentiation, in which the totality or the *Sache selbst* itself is limited to the determination of form, has to internalise [*erinnern*] this differentiation.[34] However, this cannot be done in the Doctrine of Essence, in which the totality is mainly reflective. This propels this negativity to sursume 'the totality-less multiplicity of form and content determinations'.[35] To free itself, the negation is propelled from the mediated but still incomplete totality in the Doctrine of Essence to the completed [*vollendete*] totality in the Doctrine of Notion.

3   Totality in the Doctrine of Notion

In the Doctrine of Notion, Hegel first introduces the general characteristic of the *Science of Logic*: it is the formal science of absolute formalness, which is in itself totality, and in its absolute formalness has its content or reality, and thus constitutes the pure idea of truth.[36] Since the notion itself is the totality, it may not be wrong to say that all the different forms of the totalities introduced and sursumed one after another are the precursory introductions to the totality as notion to be developed, enlightened.[37] Nonetheless, since every determined

---

32   I have translated the word *Schein* as 'illusion.' George Di Giovanni chooses 'shine' in his translation of *The Science of Logic* (Hegel 2010, p. 341).
33   Hegel 1969c, pp. 166–7.
34   Hegel 1969c, p. 181.
35   Hegel 1969c, p. 193: '[D]ie totalitätslose Mannigfaltigkeit der Form und Inhaltsbestimmungen'.
36   Hegel 1969c, p. 265.
37   Hoffmeister 1932, quoted in Kosík 1976, p. 34: 'The German word *entwickeln* is a translation

notion is empty and contains only the 'one-sided determination'[38] – notwithstanding its being the richest and the most concrete moment in comparison with the previous determinations – and their totality as well, notion is thrust towards judgement.[39]

Each of the components of judgement – namely, subject and predicate – in and by itself is the totality of the notion, but a partial totality. The movement of judgement towards the predicate – that is, the development [*Entwicklung*] of the judgment in the predicate – brings along the judgement, which is 'the reality of the Notion' [*Realität des Begriffes*].[40] The judgement itself in this more developed moment, that is, judgement of notions, leads to the syllogism through the restoration of the notion in the judgement, and hence gives the unity and the truth of both of these moments, namely, notion and judgement. As the most fully posited notion, syllogism becomes the reasonable, but in reason the determined notions are posited in their totality; 'therefore not only is syllogism reasonable, but all that which is reasonable is syllogism'.[41] In this way, the syllogism turns into the objective nature of the *Sache selbst*.[42]

In his discussion of syllogism, Hegel introduces an unprecedented point. Whereas according to Aristotle, finding the middle term in a syllogism (that is, the recognition of a minor term that is subject to a major term through a middle term) is identical to what all questions search for,[43] Hegel's *Logic* shows that what is really arduous and of the utmost importance is the recognition of the fluid character of the onto-logical middle term. Therefore, Hegel's statement in this section that 'what is mediated is itself the essential moment of its mediators, and each moment is as the totality of the mediated',[44] is valid for the whole scenario in this book in general and his particular treatment of totality.[45]

Through this process, the extremes and the middle are in an organic relation, rather than static entities put into motion.[46] In other words, organic-

---

of the Latin *explicatio* and means "unfolding", clear structuration of a whole that had been dark, muddled and mysterious'.

38   Hegel 1969c, p. 28.
39   Hegel 1969c, p. 295.
40   Hegel 1969c, p. 310.
41   Hegel 1969c, p. 351.
42   Hegel 1969c, p. 354.
43   At *Posterior Analytics* II.3, 90a35, we read: '[T]hat everything we seek is a search for a middle term is clear' (Aristotle 1975, p. 54).
44   Hegel 1969c, p. 400.
45   This general characteristic is demonstrated by Yvon Gauthier (2010, pp. 19–22) in the context of the *Phenomenology of Spirit*.
46   Compare Yvon Gauthier's view (2010, pp. 77), according to which injecting the dynamic

dialectical motion is inherent in them. In this respect, in Hegel's statement that different types of syllogism represent the stages [*Stufen*][47] of the completion or concretisation of the middle term, these stages should be read as moments [*die Momente*],[48] determined and being determined by the moments preceding and following them. This is how the middle term will be posited as totality.[49] While each term taken individually is partial and one-sided, it overcomes this partiality and one-sidedness by being the totality of all moments. This is accomplished not merely by transposing its place in the syllogism, but by the possibility stemming from its inherent contradiction; hence the dialectics that inherently makes such role-taking possible. Put differently, the dialectical nature of the formal syllogism lies in its inherent contradiction.[50] To be the one-sided and abstract moment of singularity, particularity, or universality is a deficiency that must be overcome if the content is to be represented through syllogism. It is in this way that each moment overcomes its merely partial totality to engender a 'fulfilled totality'.[51] This makes it necessary for the notion to overcome the syllogism with its inherent deficiency (because it remains a subjective that is not objectified) and to objectify itself in objectivity. This objectivity is the *Sache selbst* that is now in and for itself.[52]

Although in its unity, Objectivity is the returned totality of the notion,[53] this does not mean that it is so at the beginning of Objectivity. For without passing through all the intermediary moments of Objectivity it cannot gain its unity. The first of these moments is mechanism. The totality is here the object in the form of the universality of the reflected being in its manifold that is not determined particularity. But because of this it has the determinacy of its totality outside it: an outside that is necessarily endless.[54] But this endless,

---

      aspect into Aristotelian syllogistics is a main feature of Hegel's contribution in the history of logic and philosophy.

47 Hegel 1969c, p. 400.
48 Marx and Engels both insist on this notion of *das Moment*. See Engels and Marx 1978, p. 29: 'Übrigens sind diese drei Seiten der sozialen Tätigkeit *nicht als drei verschiedene Stufen zu fassen*, sondern eben nur als drei Seiten, oder um für die Deutschen klar zu schreiben, drei "Momente", die vom Anbeginn der Geschichte an und seit den ersten Menschen zugleich existiert haben und sich noch heute in der Geschichte geltend machen.' See also Marx and Engels 1976, p. 43.
49 Hegel 1969c, p. 401.
50 Hegel 1969c, pp. 376–7.
51 Hegel 1969c, p. 377.
52 Hegel 1969c, p. 401.
53 Hegel 1969c, p. 409.
54 Hegel 1969c, pp. 410–12.

undetermined determinism, which regards objects as enclosed totalities,[55] cannot lead to anything but formal totality.[56]

To overcome this deficiency, Hegel introduces the notion of mechanical process. In this way, the unhindered continuity of the determinacy will be introduced.[57] Nonetheless, this continuity of objects does not overcome their being still external to one another, even when absolute mechanism is introduced to overcome this deficiency. This necessitates overcoming mechanism, to be sursumed by an alternative in which a higher unity, as a less formal and more content-laden state of totality, may be introduced, and that of the mechanical object – this 'indifferent totality'[58] – is to be sursumed.

In its effort to overcome its decentralisedness, this insurmountable individuality in which the objects remain external to one another, and in order to attain inner totality, the mechanical object gives its place to the chemical object, and hence we witness the introduction of chemism. In chemism this indifference and outsidedness of the objects in relation to each other is overcome. Hence, chemism is introduced by Hegel as the first negation of the indifferent objectivity and also the externality or outsidedness of the determinateness; however, it is still unleashed insofar as it is still immediately dependent on the objects and their outsidedness.[59] This interdependence of the chemical objects still leaves some outsidedness in chemical totality in place, which cannot be surmounted in chemism itself, since a chemical object remains without a goal. The latter, the notion itself in its existence, according to its form in itself an endless totality, and the truth of both mechanism and chemism, cannot be introduced in chemism but only in the third moment of objectivity, namely, teleology. With this, self-determination is introduced in this moment as motion.

Whereas in judgement, the notions, as totalities, are related to one another, in a syllogism the judgements, as totalities, are in turn posited as extremes in a dynamic way, in which each in turn takes the place of the middle term. The formation [*Bildung*] of each higher totality, notion, judgement, and syllogism is through its realisation. Syllogism, having gone through objectivity in the forms of mechanism, chemism, and teleology, has in the last moment the goal according to its form and as a totality that is in itself endless.[60] The totality concretised in this process becomes at this moment immediately identical

---

55   See Hegel 1969c, pp. 413–14.
56   Hegel 1969c, pp. 412–13.
57   Hegel 1969c, p. 416.
58   Hegel 1969c, p. 422.
59   Hegel 1969c, p. 434.
60   Hegel 1969c, p. 439: '[D]er Zweck ist seiner Form nach eine in sich unendliche Totalität'.

with objectivity. Nonetheless, the intertwined and unresolved tension within the identity of this concrete totality – that is, its being immediately objective on the one hand, and being immediate only through sursuming mediatedness on the other – leads to Idea [*Idee*].[61] Hegel's dictum that there is nothing in the part that is not in the whole and vice versa, finds its unsurpassed repercussion in the section on the Idea, where each of the moments is essentially the totality of all the other moments.[62] Immaterial, subjective totality is hence developed into objective totality through notions in which the *Objekt* itself is no more than the totality of the notions.[63] As a result, it is not entirely right to say that Hegelian logic, as a processual totality, goes through *Erinnerung*, that is, internalisation or 'inwardising';[64] it is more accurate to say that this process occurs through a complementary internalising-externalising process in which the notion is incarnated through the states of this system.[65]

Attribution of the closedness of Hegel's system has been criticised in the literature. One such case may be read in Houlgate's *The Opening of Hegel's Logic*:

> Hegel has become for many today the quintessential philosopher of 'totality', whose system allows nothing to fall outside it – no 'otherness' or radical 'alterity' – but always aims to 'assimilate', 'absorb', or 'digest' whatever might seek to criticize or resist it and confronts everyone after Hegel with the (possibly impossible) task of trying to 'elude', 'subvert', or 'disrupt' it.[66]

I think two comments are noteworthy regarding this standpoint. First, there are some passages in the *Science of Logic* which are explicitly against such a reading. Take for instance Hegel's statement that the content of the book is 'the exposition of God [as found] in the eternal essence before the creation of the nature and the limited spirit'.[67] Along with some commentators, I think this assertion should be taken seriously.[68] To give another example, Hegel criticises

---

61   Hegel 1969c, p. 461.
62   Hegel 1969c, p. 479.
63   Hegel 1969c, p. 503.
64   See Callinicos 2014, p. 297.
65   This is also confirmed by Hegel (Hegel 1969c, p. 570): 'Each new stage of exteriorization [*Außersichgehen*], that is *further determination*, is also an interiorization [*Insichgehen*], and the greater *extension* [is] the *higher* is *intensity*'.
66   Houlgate 2006, p. 57. I would like to thank Stephen Houlgate for his comments on an earlier version of this chapter presented at the conference A Autobiografia do Pensamento: A Ciência da Lógica de Hegel, held in Coimbra in 2019.
67   Hegel 1969c, p. 44. See Callinicos 2014, p. 71 on this passage.
68   Callinicos 2014, p. 71.

Plato's *Parmenides* not only because it has presuppositions but also because it leaves room for externality (that is, something external to the totality); therefore, although it is dialectical, it remains a dialectic of external reflection.[69] Thus, according to Hegel, Plato here leaves some room for a ἕτερον (other) that comes from outside the totality,[70] instead of giving the inner dialectic of the notions,[71] since Being and the One are differentiated from one another.[72]

4   Conclusion

At the end of the *Science of Logic*, as a step towards the fusion of the true absolute method and the true absolute system,[73] the Absolute Idea attained at the end of *Science of Logic* – that is, the Idea absolutised or the Absolute idealised – is the realisation of the concretisation of totality. It is the exposition of the system of totality that is to overcome the 'night of totality' [*Nacht der Totalität*] introduced in Hegel's Jena writings.[74] The notion, which is not free in the previous moments, finds its absolute liberation at this moment. One may say that here the double transition put forward previously is accomplished: each category is determined by its previous one and also by the one following it. That said, this moment, that is, the Absolute Idea, is still an intermediate step between Absolute Knowledge – the zenith of *The Phenomenology of Spirit* – and the Absolute Spirit – as the pinnacle of the *Encyclopedia* – a moment that is yet to be attained.

Nevertheless, if totality is a *metacategory* present through Hegel's *Science of Logic*, and if the beginning had in itself the concrete totality, then why did Hegel not introduce Being and Idea as equals from the start? The reason lies in his entire dialectical conception: logic must go through all these states to, so to speak, totalise this totality. The determination of Being is through its totalisation-concretisation. Without passing through these states, Being would remain a totality-illusion [*Scheintotalität*] or, in Kosík's language, a pseudo-totality. Before the complete exposition of the determinations culminating in the last chapter, this undifferentiated unity of the Being and Idea could not be posited. Once accomplished, an enriched return to the simple, or immediate

---

69   This constitutes the bedrock of Bertel Ollman's (2003) 'internal relationships'.
70   Hegel 1969b, p. 126.
71   Hegel 1969b, p. 193.
72   Hegel 1969b, pp. 105–6.
73   See Kroeger 1872.
74   Hegel 1986a, p. 30.

unity which was introduced at the beginning of *Logic* becomes possible.[75] In this way, the determination has construed the *Gegenstand* of the logical science in which the content in its universal form can be examined.[76]

In this regard, a standpoint that overlooks the distinction between Whole [*Ganze*] and Totality is not watertight.[77] As we have seen, in Hegel's *Science of Logic* the Whole has a particular (though of course fluid) place. This is not the case regarding totality, and it is for this reason that we introduce it as a meta-category as opposed to a category.[78] Such a standpoint also draws a similarity between Kant and Hegel regarding totality, one that is not really the case. As presented in this chapter, the Hegelian totality is the all-sided bearer of contradictions. Each of the categories can be called totality; and conversely, totality can be thought of as any of the categories. Put differently, what we have witnessed, according to our account, is a complex and multifaceted movement from the chaotic totality to the accomplished totality, in which the particular all-embracing totality amounts to absolute emancipation, for which no immediate determination exists,[79] a movement that is far from a mere repetition.[80]

In the same vein, the attainment at the conclusion of the *Science of Logic* of a fully determined concept does not mean that discourse has thereby come to an end but, on the contrary, that fully self-critical discourse can finally begin.[81] This paves the way for further elaboration as found in the *Elements of Philosophy of Right*, for instance.

But a Hegelian conception of totality, with its *Geist* – its 'unifying essence behind the apparent multiplicity of phenomena'[82] – and with its a priori derivation of categories from pure being, cannot be satisfactory for a Marxian reading. The following chapters aim at providing such a reading, first through the evaluation of two major Marxist thinkers, namely, Georg Lukács and Karel

---

75 Hegel 1969c, p. 572.
76 Hegel 1969c, p. 550.
77 For a case in which such a distinction is overlooked, see Theunissen 1980, pp. 403 ff. and 501.
78 See Houlgate 2006, p. 21: 'The *category of totality* signifies that which is determined to be "all" *rather* than "some"' (emphasis added). Read from Kosík's standpoint, there is a misinterpretation in prioritising the Whole, or All over Parts or Some. Read according to the interpretation presented in this chapter, it mistakenly calls totality a category.
79 Hegel 1969c, p. 573.
80 This idea shared by some commentators goes far back to an earlier interpretation of Hegel's logic. E.g., Calkins 1903, p. 317: '[N]obody can read either the larger Logic or the Logic of the Encyclopedia, without the conviction that what is regarded as progress is often mere repetition'; see also p. 339.
81 Di Giovanni 2013, p. 256.
82 Tilly 1993, p. 304.

Kosík, then through an extensive rereading of Marx's conception of totality in his own works. Lukács seems to be the first to recognise that the problem with Hegel's approach lies in the relation between parts and the whole, put in sociological terms, between man and society: 'Hegel does not depart from the objective truth simply because he seeks to give man an ontologically autonomous form as mind, for social being – whatever it maybe in itself – does actually have an existence which is independent of the individual consciousness of particular men and has a high level of autonomously determining and determined dynamic in relation to individual'.[83] That's why the following chapter discusses his conception of totality.

---

83 Lukács 1978a, p. 25.

CHAPTER 3

On Lukács's Totality

Among the Marxist philosophers who accentuate totality and who see both similarity and also difference between a Marxian conception of totality and a Hegelian one, the Hungarian philosopher Georg Lukács, who provided the first and most extensive discussion of totality after Marx, is undoubtedly the pioneer.

It has been said that in attributing a pivotal importance to totality, 'Lukács announced a new paradigm in the history of Marxist theory, whose exploration was to occupy western Marxists for the next half century'.[1] Here I examine Lukács's works in his Marxist period; the analysis of his pre-Marxist works and the role that totality plays in them is left to another study.[2] In the foreword to the second edition of *History and Class Consciousness*, Lukács writes that restoring the category of totality to the central position of methodology, against other non-revolutionary tendencies, was the great merit of his book. He admits that he was unaware that a similar line of thought had already been developed by Lenin – a result of the fact that Lenin's *Philosophical Notebooks* were not published at the time Lukács' studies were composed.

In this chapter, I first survey the major features Lukács ascribes to totality, concentrating mainly on *History and Class Consciousness: Studies in Marxist Dialectics*, the locus classicus where totality is discussed, but also making reference to his later works. Then I examine some of the criticisms of Lukács and try to see whether they can be answered on the basis of his own work. Finally, I criticise Lukács according to my own view.

Lukács's treatment of totality is manifold and intricate. He introduces totality as a category against the primacy of economic motives,[3] according to which changes in the economy automatically lead to social revolutions; he takes it to be 'the decisive difference between Marxism and bourgeois thought'[4] and 'the bearer of the principle of revolution in science'[5] – the science of the proletariat in contradistinction to bourgeois science. The revolutionary nature of prolet-

---

[1] Jay 1977, p. 118.
[2] For a study that covers different periods of Lukács's works regarding totality, see Grumley 1989.
[3] Lukács 1971a, p. xx.
[4] Lukács 1971a, p. 27.
[5] Lukács 1971a, p. 27.

arian science is not just due to its content (*Inhalt*)⁶ in opposition to bourgeois society, but is primarily due to its method.

Lukács shares with many Marxist thinkers the view that, for the overthrow of the Hegelian dialectic, 'it was not enough … to give it a materialist twist'.⁷ What is needed, instead, is to adopt the point of view of totality, the core of the Marxian method. Unlike many,⁸ however, he finds the core of this approach to be equally present in Hegel. This common core is owing to Hegel's insight that human activity is what bridges the gap between the cognising producer, or the subject, and the object.

According to Lukács, a genuinely holistic approach of the kind found in Marx puts all the specifications of society into a totalising whole. Those specifications exist in a procedural relation⁹ as in a flux, but this relation also makes this totality understandable. This is such an indispensable conviction for Lukács that '[t]he whole system of Marxism stands and falls with the principle that revolution is the product of a point of view in which the category of totality is dominant'.¹⁰ In a work that was written later, Lukács recognises this in Lenin and quotes him in agreement:

> In order to know an object thoroughly, it is essential to discover and comprehend all of its aspects, its relationships and its 'mediations'. We shall never achieve this fully, but insistence on all-round knowledge will protect us from errors and *inflexibility*.¹¹

A seemingly simple object such as pudding, whose test according to Engels lies in eating it, is itself a social product, and so too when it is seen in its social totality and process is 'the making of the proletariat into a class, the process by which its class consciousness becomes real in practice'.¹² Attaining this truth in practice brings about an objectivity for the proletariat that is not found in

---

6   Lukács 1971a, p. 27: 'Proletarian science is revolutionary not just by virtue of its revolutionary ideas which it opposes to bourgeois society, but above all because of its method'.
7   Lukács 1971a, p. 175.
8   Compare Althusser's discussion regarding the relationship between a Marxian and a Hegelian totality: 'These totalities have in common just: (1) a word, (2) some vague conception of the unity of things, (3) theoretical enemies' (Althusser 2005, p. 208, my translation).
9   Lukács 1970, p. 92. This dual process-relation is later taken up among others by Bertel Ollman (2003, p. 36). In a sense Lukács establishes the field for Ollman's 'Philosophy of Internal Relations'.
10 Lukács 1971a, p. 29. This is also highlighted later in the same book (p. 180).
11 Lukács 1980, p. 33 (Lukács's emphasis).
12 Lukács 1971a, pp. 198–99.

other classes. While members of other classes are also reified, and trapped in their roles – that is, turned into things or objects in social relationships – it is only for the proletariat that it is possible to overcome this reification, and realise the possibility and necessity of radical transformation of the social totality of which it is the self-aware subject-object. This realisation applies both in the sense of recognition and in the sense of bringing it from possibility into actuality. In so doing, the proletariat overcomes the duality of the correspondence theory of truth,[13] the duality between subject and object – since it is jointly the subject and object of history – and practical life, including the cognition of the social world. This duality cannot be overcome, according to Lukács, unless his Marxist reading is adopted.

In the political realm, this orthodoxy is also realised through and translated into 'proclaiming the relation between the tasks of the immediate present and the totality of the historical process'.[14] Lukács links this to what Marx and Engels write in the *Communist Manifesto*:[15] the communists see from this standpoint the common interest of the proletariat worldwide, hence the borderless pursuit of the interest of the proletariat, and secondly the overall, and not just the temporally immediate, pursuit of their interests here and now – spatially and temporally, one may say. Then this counter-isolation of the moment in the movement is achieved by sursumption [*Aufhebung*] of the momentariness and immediacy of the moment.

To see an ultimate antagonism between these two, however, seems inappropriate.[16] Only through seeing an *apparent* contradiction between these two, can the immediate struggles of the working class in their workplaces for wages, working conditions, etc. be dialectically linked to their long-term and wide-scope struggle. Only in this way could Marx say that the 'trade unions are the schools of socialism'[17] for the working class, where they sursume their immediate consciousness into imputed consciousness. The 'emancipation from the here and the now'[18] and the accompanying immediacy of the struggle, is realised by demonstrating their role and relationship to that totality. This is also a program for a struggle against vulgar materialism, vulgar economic determin-

---

13 For an attempt to argue against the correspondence theory of truth from a dialectical perspective, see Boveiri 2016a.
14 Lukács 1971a, p. 24.
15 Marx and Engels 1972, p. 474.
16 Compare Grumley 1989, p. 145.
17 Marx 2000, p. 583.
18 Russell 1956, p. 175: 'I think the essence of wisdom is emancipation, as far as possible, from the tyranny of the Here and the Now'.

ism, utopianism, as well as the thinkers of capitalism who refuse to contextualise the moments in the process, since they take the moments to be isolated, eternal, and haphazard.[19]

Lukács therefore advises us to heed Marx's dictum, namely, that 'the relations of production of every society form a whole', as 'the methodological starting point and the key to historical understanding of social relations'.[20] This is clarified in some passages where Lukács reminds us of Hegel's criticism of mechanism in *The Science of Logic*, while elaborating on the insufficiency of the reciprocal relation between parts taken as inorganic elements as in a machine, in which the parts act and react towards and against one another – since such a conception cannot replace dialectical totality, and illusory conceptions will remain untouched. The result will be mechanistic dialectic and mechanistic fatalism.[21]

The distinctive characteristic of Marxism, according to Lukács, is thus *not* the predominance 'of the economic motives in historical explanation' but the standpoint of totality: 'The category of totality, the all-pervasive supremacy of the whole over the parts is the essence of the method which Marx took over from Hegel and brilliantly transformed into the foundations of a wholly new science'.[22] On occasion, he even equates the development of society and the dialectical totality,[23] in arguing against prioritising any moment of total production, as well as the producer, a prioritisation and separation which is, according to him, one characteristic of capitalism. A revolutionary orientation does not limit itself to the confrontation of the proletariat with capitalism in its entirety but 'above all because of its method'.[24] Hegel's dialectic is thus turned into the *algebra of revolution*.

All this, one may note, is actually an elaboration on Marx's double metaphor in the afterword to the second edition of the first volume of *Capital*: Hegel's dialectic should be turned upside down, and its materialistic kernel taken out from its mystical shell. This is done through the recognition of society as a totality that goes beyond its illusory moments and their abstracting isolation, and

---

19   Here he is reiterating Marx's view: 'Die Roheit und Begriffslosigkeit liegt eben darin, das organisch Zusammengehörende zufällig aufeinander zu beziehen, in einen bloßen Reflexionszusammenhang zu bringen' (Marx 1983a, p. 23).
20   Lukács 1971a, p. 9.
21   Lukács 1970, p. 38.
22   Lukács 1971a, p. 28. In being against 'vulgar economic determinism' Lukács is believed to be on the same page as Marx, Engels, and Lenin, but also Luxemburg and Gramsci. See Thomas 2002, p. 99.
23   Lukács 1971a, p. 175.
24   Lukács 1971a, p. 28.

which also supersedes the bourgeois sciences, such as science of law, national economy, history, by the 'single – unified dialectical and historical – science of the evolution of society as a totality'.[25]

But the method, itself a product of class warfare,[26] boils down to the conception of totality as 'the subordination of every part to the whole history and thought'.[27] The latter also determines both the subject and the object, which is also possible only on condition that the subject can be totality, not only as the subject but also as the object, which is in turn possible only when it – that is, the proletariat – posits itself as a class,[28] and hence gains a genuine subjectivity.[29]

In *A Defence of History and Class Consciousness*, a work written several years after *History and Class Consciousness*, Lukács reiterates the principal points found in the earlier book:

> It is impossible to separate the 'moment' from the 'process'. The subject does not find the object inflexibly and unconnectedly. The dialectical method does not intend either an undifferentiated unity or a definite separation of moments.[30]

In the absence of this particular conception of totality, revolution will be viewed as an isolated moment apart from the process.

According to Lukács, it is not the case that the 'concrete totality is the category that *governs* reality', (as it is implied in the English translation of the text)[31] but that 'the concrete totality *is* the genuine category of *reality*'. This is the conception to which Lukács remains loyal, and although he criticises several points in *History and Class Consciousness* and *The Theory of the Novel*, he explicitly defends an 'objectively unified totality'[32] developed previously.

---

25   Lukács 1971a, p. 28.
26   Lukács 1971a, p. 21: 'The Marxist method is equally as much the product of class warfare as any other political or economic product'.
27   Lukács 1971a, pp. 27–8.
28   Lukács 1970a, p. 56: 'Diesen Gesichtspunkt der Totalität als Subjekt stellen in der modernen Gesellschaft einzig und allein *die Klassen* vor'.
29   Cf. Grumley 1989, p. 148.
30   Lukács, Rees et al. 2002, p. 30. See also Lukács 1971a, p. 9. The difference between such an approach and Žižek's will be discussed later in this book.
31   Emphasis added. This is how the German sentence 'Die konkrete Totalität ist also die eigentliche Wirklichkeitskategorie' (Lukács 1970, p. 71) is translated into English in *History and Class Consciousness*, p. 10. As will be seen in the next chapter, Kosík developed this point extensively.
32   Lukács 1980, p. 31.

That said, the prominence of totality is not limited to a single realm of human activity. Ontologically, reality is the total process,[33] and totality itself the underlying unity.[34] Methodologically, dialectical totality makes the real relationship between ends and means possible, and hence avoids not only the rigid polarity and disconnection between means and ends, but also the prioritisation of either means or ends over the other.[35] Yet totality also plays an essential role in aesthetics: Aesthetically, 'the novel', writes Lukács, 'is the epic of an age in which *the extensive totality of life is no longer directly given*, yet which still thinks in terms of totality'.[36]

After presenting Lukács's viewpoint, we will now see how his views are criticised by others. One of the most recent critiques of Lukács is that of the contemporary Marxist philosopher Lucien Sève, who puts forward several objections. First, he finds the absence of a qualitative distinction between philosophical categories and scientific concepts a major regrettable point.[37] I do not find this criticism a strong one, and it may actually be an illegitimate demand. The Marxian categories are the categories of the critique of political economy, and thus possess simultaneously the characteristics of positive scientific concepts such as money, exchange, distribution, but also more philosophical categories such as essence, appearance, subject, etc. An attempt to demarcate these two mechanically would lead, I believe, either to something like pure economics, or to purely philosophical speculation. Furthermore, such a distinction is not possible owing to the dialectical character of Marx's work in general. This particular characteristic, reprised also as the bat-like[38] characteristic of the Marxian terms, has led many to claim that classical definitions are absent in Marx's works.

Furthermore, Sève criticises Lukács for not accompanying gnoseology with ontology, and thus leaving behind a barren ontology. Here, although Sève is right, as far as I can see, in not finding explicit claims regarding the dialectical relationship between ontology and gnoseology (or epistemology), there are

---

33   Lukács 1980, p. 40.
34   Lukács 1980, p. 32.
35   For a discussion of Hegel's teleology, see Lamb 1992, esp. pp. 173 and 180.
36   Lukács 1971b, p. 56, my emphasis. For further elaboration on totality in literary works, see Cascardi 1992.
37   Sève 2014, p. 96: 'There, there is something else other than the very regrettable absence of precision, namely, the qualitative indistinction between philosophical category and scientific concept'. Oddly enough, in his 1967 article, 'Structural Method and the Dialectical Method', Sève almost entirely leaves out the conception of totality.
38   Pareto 1902, p. 332: 'Marx's words are like bats. One can see in them both birds and mice' (Quoted from Ollman 2003, p. 4). This is developed further by Ollman.

several reasons to think that Lukács's epistemology is actually intertwined with a well-developed theory of knowledge.[39] For instance, he relates social existence and knowledge through the mediation of praxis. This is accomplished, according to Lukács, through the categories of mediation. The moments of totality of the bourgeoisie, invisible or implicit in their immediacy, find their organic relation in the totality through mediation. Such objects, such moments, cannot, to use an imprecise phrase, be assimilated by the consciousness of the proletariat if they are not objectively effective.[40] As a methodological lever, the category of mediation is both subjective and objective.[41] This intertwined character lies in the activity of the proletariat as well: 'The essence of the method of historical materialism is inseparable from the "practical and critical" activity of the proletariat: both are aspects of the same process of social evolution'.[42]

Furthermore, there are still more explicit passages in *History and Class Consciousness* which buttress such an interpretation. Take the following for instance:

> For a problem always makes its appearance first as an abstract possibility and only afterwards is it realized in concrete terms. And it only becomes meaningful to discuss whether questions are rightly or wrongly conceived when this second stage has been reached, when it becomes possible to recognize the concrete totality which is destined to constitute the environment and the path to the realization of the goal in question.[43]

If each problem is then visible just in its abstract possibility, it is owing to its undeveloped ontological status, not having yet attained concrete totality. The intertwinedness of ontology and epistemology – let us call this their *epistemonical* unity[44] – is then recognised. Put differently, concrete totality can be realised by the cognisant subject only once it is ontologically recognisable, that is, once it has passed from abstract status to concrete status.

Sève also accuses Lukács of altering Marx's text in the *Grundrisse*, so that it could match his subject-object identity, this time as regards to the categories.[45]

---

39 As we shall see in the Chapter 4, Kosík avoids completely such a criticism, as he recognises a distinction along with unity between these two realms.
40 Lukács 1971a, p. 163.
41 Lukács 1971a, p. 162.
42 Lukács 1971a, pp. 20–1.
43 Lukács 1971a, p. 296.
44 For an elaboration on this term in relation to Walter Benjamin's works, see Boveiri 2014.
45 Sève 2014, p. 95.

Here is the full text:

> Pour renforcer sa thèse Lukács altère le texte cité: Marx écrit que les catégories ("économiques") "expriment" des "formes d'être": la dualité du concept et de la chose est ainsi respectée; Lukács lui fait dire qu'elles "sont" des "formes d'être" – "existant indépendamment de la conscience pensante" ... –: cette dualité est annulée, d'une façon qu'on n'hésitera pas à dire indéfendable. La conclusion est lourde: il n'est vraiment pas possible de considérer ces Prolégomènes comme un digne achèvement de l'œuvre lukácsienne.

The point is that Lukács changes Marx's original wording, 'die Kategorien daher Daseinsformen, Existenzbestimmungen, oft nur einzelne Seiten dieser bestimmten Gesellschaft, dieses Subjekts *ausdrücken*',[46] into 'Ökonomischen Kategorien *sind* nach Marx "Daseinsformen, Existenzbestimmungen"'.[47] Thus, according to the text as Lukács has it, the claim that 'the economic categories *express* the forms of being' is turned into the claim that 'economic categories *are* the forms of being'. This, I think, cannot be responded to within Lukács's conception of totality, and it is left to one of the Marxists following him, namely, Karel Kosík, to introduce a more nuanced relationship between subject and object instead of their identity *tout court*.

That said, if the human being is taken as subject and nature as object, there are passages in Marx's works in which such an identity is reaffirmed. Indeed, such an identity of subject and object in Marxian thought is not limited to earlier works such as *Philosophical and Economic Manuscripts*,[48] but is also found in the introduction to the *Grundrisse* where Marx emphasises the 'unity which arises already from the identity of the subject, humanity, and of the object, nature – [while] their essential difference is not forgotten'.[49] This is, of course, an identity in difference, which Lukács does not seem to deny either, and in this way stays loyal to non-idealist dialectics, unless he is taken to be a Hegelian idealist.

---

46 Marx 1983a, p. 40.
47 Lukács 1970, p. 136.
48 Marx 1968c, p. 516: 'Daß das physische und geistige Leben des Menschen mit der Natur zusammenhängt, hat keinen andren Sinn, als daß die Natur mit sich selbst zusammenhängt, denn der Mensch ist ein Teil der Natur'.
49 Marx 1983a, p. 21: 'Einheit – die schon daraus hervorgeht, daß das Subjekt, die Menschheit, und das Objekt, die Natur, dieselben – die wesentliche Verschiedenheit nicht vergessen wird'.

These are not the only criticisms that can be directed against Lukács's conception of totality. And although Kosík, as will be seen in the following chapter, considers Lukács's *History and Class Consciousness* an exemplary expression of the dialectical conception, the interpretation that follows casts some doubt on this claim.

The first point is the strong Schellingian vein in his approach towards totality. To discuss this issue, we have to remind ourselves, with reference to the first chapter, that hypostasising the whole over the parts was introduced by Kosík as the characteristic feature of the second conception of totality, that is, 'the organicist and organicist-dynamic conception which formalises the whole and emphasises the predominance and priority of the whole over parts'.[50] Then we see that by the introduction of totality as 'the all-pervasive supremacy of the whole over the parts'[51] Lukács lets his conception fall into the same conception of totality. He repeats the same claim when he says that in dialectical method and the concept of totality we witness 'the subordination of all the parts to the unity of history and thought'.[52] In fact, this implicit dichotomy of the whole and parts, and the prioritising of the former over the latter, is repeated time and again throughout *History and Class Consciousness*.[53] In so doing, notwithstanding all the differences – once more overlooked by Kosík – Lukács's account has an important feature in common with Kosík's second classification, discussed in the first chapter. That said, apart from Lukács's sharing one of the characteristics of the second conception, namely, the hypostasising of the whole, the other characteristic of the second conception of totality introduced by Kosík, namely, the unattainability of the world by the subject and its comprehension, is absent in Lukács's work.

Still, this common feature is not the only shortcoming of Lukács's interpretation. By mythologising the category of totality, he overlooks the importance of other concepts, such as contradiction, categorial movement, etc., and more importantly, the relation between them. The linear determination for which he criticises his opponents, rooted in their economic determinism, is replaced in his own work by the category of totality. Here is an example: 'The category of

---

50 Kosík 1976, p. 24.
51 Lukács 1971a, p. 27.
52 Lukács 1971a, pp. 27–8.
53 Here is another example: 'The category of totality begins to have an effect long before the whole multiplicity of objects can be illuminated by it' (Lukács 1971a, p. 175). To be fair, we have to admit that this is a possible reading of the passage in the Introduction to the *Grundrisse*. This will be elaborated on in Chapter 5.

totality ... determines not only the object of knowledge but also the subject'.[54] This determination, I think, is performed through the action of all the categories in the discussion; moreover, the subject-object dialectically determines the totality as well.

There is yet another significant shortcoming in Lukács's account. Although he recognised the closedness of Hegel's system and its historical character – '[The dialectics should be] nonetheless, no longer in the form of a closed system. Hegel's system, as left for us is a historical matter'[55] – he does not elaborate on the openness of a Marxian dialectic. Furthermore, he does not refute the charge put forward by Bloch regarding the closedness of his conception of totality. In a paper he published after *History and Class Consciousness*, after quoting Bloch,[56] he does not argue that such a totality is open – as Kosík does, as we will see in the following chapter – but instead takes totality to be the 'closed integration'.[57] Regarding this, while I do not find the criticism advanced by some against the claim of closedness or completion of Lukács's standpoint watertight,[58] the claim that because of its shortcoming Lukács's account of totality is 'philosophical mythology'[59] is equally extravagant.

Finally, Lukács also takes totality to be a category; I do not consider this to be precise. As was seen in the Chapter 2, totality is not a category, since to say that it is a category necessitates finding its place in the categorial movement of categories – the movement of categories [*Bewegung der Kategorien*]

---

54   Lukács 1971a, p. 28.
55   My translation of Lukács 1970, pp. 54–5: 'Allerdings: nicht mehr in der Form eines geschlossenen Systems. Das System Hegels, sowie es für uns vorliegt, ist eine historische Tatsache'. The existing translation (Lukács 1971a, p. xiv) is plainly misleading: 'Of course we will no longer expect to discover his achievement in his total system. The system as we have it belongs to the past'.
56   Lukács 1980, p. 22: 'Since Lukács operates with a closed, objectivistic conception of reality, when he comes to examine Expressionism, he resolutely sets his face against any attempt on the part of artists to shatter any image of the world, even that of capitalism. Any art which strives to exploit the real fissures in surface inter-relations and to discover the new in their crevices, appears in his eyes merely as a wilful act of destruction. He thereby equates experiments in demolition with a condition of decadence'.
57   Lukács 1980, p. 31.
58   For such a response, see the entry on Lukács in the *Stanford Encyclopedia of Philosophy* (Stahl 2016): 'As many critics of Lukács have remarked ... this seems to commit Lukács to the view that there can be a complete overcoming of reification resulting in a totally transparent society. However, this interpretation ignores Lukács' insistence that the resistance against reification must be understood as a never-ending struggle'. The major difficulty with this passage is not that Stahl's claim is not reinforced in the pages he refers to: his claim makes the status of the proletariat eternal!
59   Grumley 1989, p. 151.

to use Marx's term – without yet fixing it in its place, as may be done with Aristotle's categories or Kant's table of categories. Once we see that it is impossible to demonstrate its place in the categorial movement, totality turns out to be a concept – or better put, a metacategory, as was suggested in the previous Chapter – rather than a category. Further clarification on this distinction will be given in Chapter 6 of this book.

Conclusion

We have seen that a few erroneous characteristics remain in Lukács's totality. First, it remains closed notwithstanding his efforts, and he did not argue against the accusation in the writings he published after *History and Class Consciousness*. Also occasionally, his conception of totality remains Schellingian, in the sense that we saw in the first chapter regarding the second misconception of totality, for it makes the whole predominant over the parts, though without remaining an idealist conception, as is the case with Schelling's approach. This predominance of the whole over parts is the standpoint to which Lukács remains faithful through and through.

As we have seen, Lukács does admit that 'it was not enough ... to give it [i.e., Hegelian dialectic] a materialist twist';[60] nevertheless, he seems not to have adequately integrated the elements of Marx's approach in this regard. Put differently, he might be said to have overestimated Hegel's role in Marxian dialectic. On one occasion, he sees the subordination of the Hegelian category to logic as nothing 'more than a mere form of appearance of the system'.[61] He also admits that Marx concretises Hegel's idea of evolution 'by *applying it* to social development';[62] but if this is the case, this is not much more than the injection of the sociality of the subject matter into Hegelian dialectics – undoubtedly a complicated twist. In all of this, and notwithstanding a few remarks that suggest the contrary,[63] Lukács seems not to fully see the differences between the two dialectics.

Even the subtitle of *History and Class Consciousness* – 'Studies in Marxist Dialectics' – leaves a lot for later Marxists to develop. This leads us to the following chapter, where we assess the challenges that are left for later Marxists – a consequence of the impossibility of rebutting the claims made against Lukács

---

60   Lukács 1971a, p. 175.
61   Lukács 1978a, p. 47.
62   Lukács 1971a, p. 20 (emphasis added).
63   Lukács 1978a, p. 25.

within the frame of his own thought – and to what extent their responses to these challenges were successful. Among the efforts to develop a more comprehensive conception of totality, the most noteworthy are those made by the Czech philosopher Karel Kosík. The following chapter critically reviews his account.

CHAPTER 4

On Kosík's Totality

It is undoubtedly true that Georg Lukács was the first Marxist thinker to underscore not only the significance of the concrete totality in contradistinction to abstract and formal totality, but also its revolutionary importance;[1] however, the task of providing an extensive and profound account of this conception was left to the Czech philosopher Karel Kosík. In this chapter, I go deeper into Kosík's reading of the dialectical conception of totality, to which I have so far made only passing reference.

In developing his own materialist dialectical philosophy – which he calls 'dialectical rationalism',[2] a dialectical reason that gives 'the universal and necessary process of cognition and of forming of reality'[3] – Kosík emphasises that the primary concern common to all forms of dialectic is the quest for the subject matter, *die Sache selbst*.[4] Given that the subject matter is not manifest and cannot be known immediately through contemplation, discovering it requires both effort and a bypass, a detour [*Oklika*]. The process of this effort and detour consists not just in the comprehension of social reality as concrete reality but also in the formation of this reality through a process of concretisation. To explicate this particular conception, Kosík develops a complex account that is simultaneously a unified but also manifold theory of reality as a whole, and its active cognition through the activity of human beings. His account is thus at once epistemological, historical, and ontological.

Like Marx, Kosík sees contradiction as the central concept of dialectics. If this view is correct, then wherever contradictions can be seen, so too can dialectics; therefore, since contradictions can be seen in nature, so too can dialectics. Where Kosík is innovative is in his elaboration of the interconnec-

---

1 Cerutti 1980, p. 35.
2 Karel Kosík, *Dialectic of the Concrete*, trans. Karel Kovanda and James Schmidt (Dordrecht: D. Reidel, 1976), p. 59. Unless otherwise specified, all references to Kosík's text in English are from this translation.
3 Kosík 1976, p. 60.
4 I am translating the Czech phrase *věc sama* as 'subject matter'; see Kosík 1966, p. 10. The German translator chooses the Hegelian term *Sache selbst*; see Kosík 1986, p. 7. The English translators choose 'thing itself' (Kosík 1976, p. 1). Although this is literally correct, I do not use their translation, to avoid any confusion with the Kantian *Ding an sich*.

tion of totality and contradictions.⁵ As Kosík puts it, 'The process of forming the whole and forming a unity, the unity of contradictions and its genesis, all belong to the dialectical whole'.⁶ Moreover, totality and contradiction are seen as concomitant, and so prioritising one over the other robs them of their dialectical character: 'Without contradictions totality is empty and static; outside totality contradictions are formal and arbitrary'.⁷ In what follows, we elaborate on Kosík's reading of Marxian totality and neighbouring conceptions, then examine the two major shortcomings of his view. These necessitate further discussion in the following two chapters, each of which responds to one of these shortcomings.

1 Totality: Concrete and Pseudo-concrete

In what seems to be a tautology, Kosík writes: 'The dialectics of the concrete totality ... is a theory of reality as concrete totality',⁸ 'a coherent methodological principle'⁹ 'for investigating objective reality'.¹⁰ This is a conception of reality in the most general sense, in which there is no bifurcation between nature and society, but the concepts are not monolithic either – a conception distinct from scientism, or the excessive belief in the power of scientific knowledge and techniques, whose goal is efficiency, or the attaining of the greatest advantage possible with the least consumption of energy. This totalisation-synthetisation-concretisation is also radically distinct from a reductionist approach which Kosík calls the 'method of abstract principle'. This method, which is a constituent of capitalism as a part of its superstructure, does not let us see the process of concretisation (the formation of totality in general), and cannot grasp that it is not the theory but 'the economic reality of capitalism ... that reduces man to the abstraction of the "economic man" really and practically'.¹¹

The contradictory character of totality and its multiple meanings, as well as the richness of reality, are thus left out; the result is instead 'an empty totality which treats the wealth of reality as an irrational "residue" beyond compre-

---

5   What Kosík sees as the interconnection of totality and contradictions is the notion which can be traced back to Marx's dissertation, 1968c, p. 38.
6   Kosík 1976, p. 24.
7   Kosík 1976, p. 30.
8   Kosík 1976, p. 19.
9   Kosík 1976, p. 18.
10 Kosík 1976, p. 22. The details of such a principle, which were left undeveloped by Kosík, will be fleshed out in the chapters to follow.
11 Kosík 1976, p. 87.

hension'.[12] This vacuous or *empty* totality is one outcome of such an approach: this is the totality that does not comprehend how the individual moments are reflected in the whole, and thus excludes the 'appropriation of reality as individual moments, and the activity of analytical reason' in relation to totality.[13] It is found in the Romantics, for instance, whose search for totality renders it void of its vibrancy and fails to grasp the determinacy of relations within totality.

This empty totality, however, is just one type of false totality. Elaborating on the different kinds of false totality will help us to better grasp concrete totality. The second form of false totality is *abstract totality*. Such a totality one-sidedly opposes the whole and the parts; it hypostasises the former against the latter and petrifies it. Totality, thus taken to be a closed whole, is 'without genesis and development, without the process of forming the whole, without structuration and destructuration'.[14] In attributing a higher reality to the whole, this conception ignores the inputs into its genesis and the process by which the structure of the whole is formed.[15]

The third type of false totality is *bad totality*. This is the misconception which replaces the real subject with a mythologised subject; as a result, 'social reality is intuited only in the form of the object, of ready-made results and facts, but not subjectively, as objective human praxis'.[16] In divorcing human activity from the product of that activity, autonomous structures are taken to play a social role without any involvement of actual people. Social reality is then the sum total of the structures in the society that reciprocally influence each other. The result is thus not real-historical objectivity but a fictitious-fetishistic objectivity. Kosík also shows how the epistemological aspects of such a misconception of totality entail the political shortcomings of such a response: if reality is graspable only in chunks, each change will be limited to those chunks, and an orientation towards revolutionising reality as a whole is out of the question. If capitalism in its totality is beyond our grasp, so *a fortiori* is revolutionising it in its entirety.[17]

---

12 Kosík 1976, p. 28.
13 Kosík 1976, p. 31.
14 Kosík 1976, p. 31.
15 As we saw in Chapter 3, this is what Lukács's account comes close to doing. Another pitfall of such a conception of totality is taking reality as an immutable totality, which is certainly not found in Lukács.
16 Kosík 1976, p. 31. This does not mean that the erroneous counterpart of this account is not possible: understanding social reality subjectively also consists in understanding social reality as ready-made *subjective* results and facts.
17 Politically, the alternative standpoint has its roots in the 'objective experience of social reality', namely, the view that the dynamics of the commitment to left politics 'are not derived from the reading of the "Marxist classics", but rather from the objective experi-

All these are possible responses to what Kosík takes to be the cardinal question in Marxism, namely: What is reality? This question comes before the question of whether reality can be known; put differently, one has to know what question about reality is involved before one can consider the possibility or impossibility of knowing the answer. The category[18] of concrete totality is introduced as a response to this question. Reality is taken to be concrete totality. Let us call the components of reality *facts*. What then is the relationship between facts and reality? One possible response would be to take reality to be the sum of all the facts that constitute reality. If this is correct, then since there are too many facts, properties, and aspects for us to be able to take them all into account and newer ones appear at each stage of inquiry, we cannot *envisage* reality as a totality, but only parts of it. *A fortiori*, we can never *know* reality in its totality, but only partially and within horizons that may converge towards reality but never *are* reality.[19]

It may be argued that only divine omniscience could know all of reality completely and perfectly. To respond to such an argument, instead of adopting a summative, additive view about reality, Kosík first admits that reality in its absoluteness – that is, the world – is neither exhaustible by human beings nor reducible to human knowledge. To this effect, three characteristic features are introduced as related to reality. Since it is 'structured', totality is not a chaotic whole, but is made up of parts that are organised and interrelated. However, though this view turns the heap of facts into a structured form, it does not necessarily entail life or even motion, since static structures can easily be envisaged, as by Parmenides, for instance. To avoid this, a second feature is introduced: reality is an evolving whole. This gives dynamism to reality: it is not 'given once and for all'.

So far, the Kosíkian conception of totality is similar to what Hegel would call mechanism or chemism, since in both of these cases there is a dynamic whole that is structured. However, although reality is shown to be a dynamic whole once it is posited as evolving, it is still void of its genesis or original evolution, that is, the process by which it is formed and what it turns into; hence, this account still fails to account for the coming into being and evolution of

---

ence of social reality and the way in which one isolated cause or issue, one specific form of injustice, cannot be fulfilled or corrected without eventually drawing the entire web of interrelated social levels together into a totality, which then demands the invention of a politics of social transformation' (Jameson, 1990, p. 251).

18   It will be seen in the next chapter on the Marxian conception of totality that the introduction of totality as a 'category' is imprecise, as was the case with Hegel's conception seen in Chapter 2.

19   Similar argument is developed in Boudin 1993, pp. 24–30.

reality. To meet this requirement, a third feature comes into play: reality is a self-forming whole. This last feature, the expression of the law of the transformation of quantity into quality, explicates the formation of novelty in totality. Here Kosík reiterates what Marx says in *Capital* when he draws an analogy between natural changes and the phenomena in his subject of exposition:[20] in both cases, merely quantitative changes lead to qualitative differences. Considered this way, facts, or the encoded realities, are decoded: the essence of the phenomenal is known through phenomena, and reality is the unity of phenomena and essence. What such an account of dialectical totality is about then, on the side of the human being, may be described as the process of decoding facts. This entails that we should avoid seeing facts as merely mediated or merely unmediated entities: grasping the *Sache selbst* is the process of penetrating into facts by putting them into a dialectical relationship with one another. If we may expound grasping the *Sache selbst* and penetrating into it as the apprehension of its intrafactuality, then we may say that this is achieved only through interfactuality.[21]

This grasping simultaneously sursumes the process of what wrongly introduced itself as the concrete when it was only *pseudo-concrete*, and this in three respects: ideas, things, and conditions. Before seeing how this world of the pseudo-concrete is to be sursumed, let us first see what the characteristics of the world of the pseudo-concrete are. The world of the pseudo-concrete, according to Kosík, is 'the world of fictitious intimacy, familiarity and confidence within which man moves about "naturally" and with which he has his daily dealings'.[22] The fact that human beings are usually able to meet their routine needs presents a world to them in which things are regular, permanent, immediate, and self-evident. This world includes external phenomena detached from their essence, the world of manipulation (the same as the unsophisticated praxis at the level of ideas, as ideological appearances of things), the ideological forms of such a routine praxis, and the world of static objects. The world of the pseudo-concrete is thus the world of solid, isolated,

---

20 See Marx 1976, p. 423: 'Here, as in natural science, is shown the correctness of the law discovered by Hegel, in his *Logic*, that at a certain point merely quantitative differences pass over by a dialectical inversion into qualitative distinctions'. This will be further discussed in Chapter 5.

21 The introduction of the term 'interfactuality' is a development of a passage in the Afterword to the second edition of *Capital* Volume I: 'A critique of this kind will confine itself to the confrontation and comparison of a fact, not with ideas, but with another fact'. Marx 1976, p. 101.

22 Kosík 1976, p. 2.

and static objects that are also ideology-driven: not only are they seen as solid, isolated, and static, but they are also idea bearers, not concept bearers.

The standpoint of concrete totality entails the process of sursuming the pseudo-concrete.[23] If we adopt the view that social reality, the only existent reality for a human as a social being, is the construction of the social human being, we will see how ontology and gnoseology are intertwined, while avoiding Hegelianism, and also how social reality, natural reality, and their cognition are intertwined.[24] This is the result of discovering praxis, and indeed revolutionary praxis, in this new concept of reality. This reformulation of the standpoint introduced by Marx and Engels in *The German Ideology*,[25] *inter alia*, does not involve a reduction of nature to social life, but emphasises the fact that any interaction with nature on the side of human being, which is always, so to speak, an active act of praxis, is always in a social milieu.

Let us elucidate this with an example. If there is something that is so unknown to us, and so different from all that we know in the already existing known totality, that it cannot even be called a case for cognition, then that thing, until it is socially acquired and interacted with, does not exist for our cognition, but only in itself. Talking about its existence entails some minimum level of praxis, social integration, and interaction with it, even at the level of sensation, in which case it is no longer merely a case of cognition detached from human sociality.[26] If it is a case of cognition, its being such a case entails that we are already in the process of interaction with it. Before that, without any minimal influence on us, it is no-thing for us, since it remains outside of the procedural life of the *Sache selbst*. On this account, however, the dynamicity of totality, its inherent dialectics, is not to be taken to be injected into the substance; rather, it *is* the substance.[27]

---

23 This will be discussed below when the role of praxis is further elaborated in this chapter.
24 Cf. Jameson, 2016, p. 77: 'No philosophical or aesthetic synthesis between these dimensions [i.e., history and nature] is attainable'.
25 See for example, the following passage from *The German Ideology* (Marx and Engels 1976, p. 39): '[Feuerbach] does not see that the sensuous world around him is not a thing given direct from all eternity, remaining ever the same, but the product of industry and of the state of society; and, indeed [a product] in the sense that it is an historical product, the result of the activity of a whole succession of generations, each standing on the shoulders of the preceding one, developing its industry and its intercourse, and modifying its social system according to the changed needs. Even the objects of the simplest "sensuous certainty" are only given [to] him through social development, industry and commercial intercourse'.
26 Kosík 1976, p. 31: 'All degrees of human cognition, sensory or rational, as well as all modes of appropriating reality, are activities based on the objective praxis of mankind, and are consequently in some degrees connected with in some way by all other modes'.
27 According to one interpretation, the introduction of a dynamic aspect into Aristotelian

2   Totality and Objectivity

So far, we have seen that Kosík defends the view that reality as totality is knowable and representable. He thus takes a position that is radically different from what is thought to be common in postmodernism in general,[28] but also from standpoints which try to retain totality while refuting reality.[29] A question then naturally arises: What is the relationship between this account of reality and objectivity? Kosík's account of the relationship between totality and objectivity is key, since when he defends objectivity, what is taken to be the 'opium of Marxism,'[30] he criticises those who fail to take social reality as a 'search for what it is objectively, i.e., concrete totality'.[31] This section and the two following this attempt to answer this question.

To begin with, it should be noted that reality is grasped through the complementary functions of pre-predicative cognition and predicative cognition, where understanding prior to predication is immediate cognition, and understanding through predication is mediated cognition. The former is the understanding that everybody has prior to any explication; the latter is the result of argumentation or explication. Neither the immediacy of cognition nor its mediacy brings about by itself such a status; rather, they do so conjointly; this is what is intended by their complementarity role. Limiting oneself to immediacy leads to vegetative, pre-predicative cognition, or to a search for intellectual intuition as found in Schelling; limiting oneself to mediacy leads to the positive sciences or to Wittgenstein's claim that the merely cognitively important is science, and philosophy has no task beyond clarification and remains a discipline full of tautologies. An overarching cognition is thus either unnecessary or limited to the clarification of scientific claims. Although modern science – say since Galileo – has taught us that intuitive inferences and mere observations are not always trustworthy, there are cases whose truth is to be pre-predicatively adopted and then confirmed through experience.

---

syllogistics is a main feature of Hegel's contribution in the history of logic and philosophy; see Gauthier 2010, p. 69.

28   While 'All of postmodernism ... concurs that even if totality exists it would be unpresentable and unknowable' (Jameson 1990, p. 248).
29   This is the standpoint developed by Žižek (2002) in his introduction to a selection of Lenin's writings, and will be further criticised in this book.
30   Jacoby 1981, p. 8.
31   Kosík 1976, p. 76.

In Marx's mature works we find both reliance on observation[32] and the untrustworthiness of mere observation.[33] Taken in abstraction, these claims seem contradictory, but once conjoined with Kosík's account they reveal their dialectical significance. Taking such a standpoint is in a sense a response to the classical problem put forward by Sextus Empiricus:[34] there are cases whose truth is to be accepted *a priori*, that is, non-empirically. One such belief is the existential-ontological-historical primacy of existence over cognition.[35] Although Kosík may be taken as an ontology-first theorist of truth, according to whom truth depends on being, in contradistinction to an explanation-first theorist of truth,[36] his understanding of the role of the subject means that this attribution cannot be made without qualification. We will examine this further in what follows.

3   *Objekt-Gegenstand*: Marx's Distinction

As is recognised in the literature, Hegel distinguishes between the terms *Gegenstand* and *Objekt*,[37] which are used interchangeably in normal spoken German. Marx also distinguishes between these two terms.[38] The distinction later

---

[32]   See Marx 1976, p. 247: '[W]e do not need to look back at the history of capital's origins in order to recognize that money is its first form of appearance. Every day the same story is played out before our eyes'.

[33]   Compare the two following passages: Marx 1976, p. 433: 'A scientific analysis of competition is possible only if we can grasp the inner nature of capital, just as the apparent motions of the heavenly bodies are intelligible only to someone who is acquainted with their real motions, which are not perceptible to the senses'. Marx 1968f, pp. 206–7: 'It is ... [a] paradox that the earth moves round the sun, and that water consists of two highly inflammable gases. Scientific truth is always paradox, if judged by everyday experience, which catches only the delusive appearance of things'.

[34]   Sextus Empiricus 1976, p. 163: 'In order to decide the dispute that has arisen about the criterion, we have need of an agreed-upon criterion by means of which we shall decide it; and in order to have an agreed-upon criterion it is necessary first to have decided the dispute about the criterion. Thus, with the reasoning falling into the circularity mode, finding a criterion becomes aporetic; for we do not allow them to adopt a criterion hypothetically, and if they wish to decide about the criterion by means of a criterion we force them into an infinite regress'.

[35]   This should be taken generally and dialectically, however, as will be developed in what follows.

[36]   For a further discussion on this distinction (though in a different context), see Asay 2020, particularly Chapter 3, 'The Truth Making Relation'.

[37]   See Inwood 1992, pp. 203–5.

[38]   This distinction is not recognised in all interpretations, even those which defend objectivity. See, for example, Goldstick and Cunningham 1978.

turned into one of the bedrocks of Cultural Historical Activity Theory (CHAT) in the USSR.[39] Before elaborating on Kosík's position on the relationship between objectivity and totality, I first give an interpretation of Marx's first thesis on Feuerbach, where this distinction can be seen quite explicitly. Since the nuances of the text are not fully detectable in English, I quote the text in German:

> Der Hauptmangel alles bisherigen Materialismus (den Feuerbachschen mit eingerechnet) ist, daß der Gegenstand, die Wirklichkeit, Sinnlichkeit nur unter der Form des Objekts oder der Anschauung gefaßt wird; nicht aber als *sinnlich menschliche Tätigkeit*, Praxis; nicht subjektiv. Daher die *tätige* Seite abstrakt im Gegensatz zu dem Materialismus von dem Idealismus – der natürlich die wirkliche, sinnliche Tätigkeit als solche nicht kennt – entwickelt. Feuerbach will sinnliche – von den Gedankenobjekten wirklich unterschiedne Objekte: aber er faßt die menschliche Tätigkeit selbst nicht als *gegenständliche* Tätigkeit. Er betrachtet daher im 'Wesen des Christenthums' nur das theoretische Verhalten als das echt menschliche, während die Praxis nur in ihrer schmutzig jüdischen Erscheinungsform gefaßt und fixiert wird. Er begreift daher nicht die Bedeutung der 'revolutionären', der 'praktisch-kritischen' Tätigkeit.[40]

This thesis in fact argues against a dual anti-reductionist standpoint. On the one hand, it is directed against the materialists who reduce *Gegenstand* to *Objekt*, and hence deprive the former of its active, real, and subjective characteristics, but also against the idealists, who underscore the active side of the *Gegenstand* but cannot stay loyal to this standpoint. According to this thesis, however, it is imperative that human praxis, which is the characteristic of all social life, be taken objectively. It is thus suggesting a materialism that stems from this dual critique. It should be noted that the whole thesis actually suggests a distinctive Marxian materialism; this is important in order to avoid a misreading that suggests going beyond materialism and idealism,[41] a view that does not bear scrutiny, even based just on the actual text of the other theses. Such a new materialist standpoint supplies a political characteristic for a materialist philosophy, one which, unlike intuitive materialism, does not find

---

39   For further elaboration on this, see Blunden 2017.
40   Marx 1978e, p. 5.
41   Cf. Jameson 2016, p. 79: 'The ontology that wishes to escape ideological imprisonment in either idealism or materialism can only do so by foretelling the inevitable temptations of both and using them against each other in a permanent tension that cannot be resolved'.

in civil society a satisfactory form of social totality and wants instead a 'humanised society' – or formulated differently, a 'socialised humanity'.[42] Whereas here Marx highlights the active side of human praxis, Kosík, without any direct reference to this thesis, refines it in a more dialectical manner by underscoring its intertwined double function: registering and projecting, fact-finding and planning, reflection in the sense of mirroring, but also projection. But before getting into that in the following section, let's first see in detail his treatment of objectivity.

4   Objectivity in Kosík: Conceptual-Lexical Discussion and Its Implications

After briefly considering the nuances introduced by Marx regarding the difference between *Gegenstand* and *Objekt* and its derivations, I now return to Kosík to see how he deals with these nuances and what his particular contribution is. In addition to this nuanced objectivity – and also subjectivity – Kosík introduces what may be called *objectuality* (he makes use of the corresponding adjective 'objectual'). In objectuality, what is grasped has the appearance of objectivity without being really objective.

To avoid losing sight of this nuance through translation, let us first make a lexical review of Kosík's conception with reference to the original Czech text. The classification of terms may be schematically illustrated, as shown in the two tables below, the result of a thoroughgoing search of the whole text. The first table shows the terms for 'object', 'objective', and 'objectivity', as used in German more or less until Kant, together with Kosík's rendering of the terms in Czech and their English translations.

'Object' and Its Derivations

Czech	German	English
objekt	*Objekt*	Object
objektivní	*objektiv*	Objective
objektivita	*Objektivität*	Objectivity
objektivace	*Objektivierung*	Objectivation

---

42   Theses 9 and 10 in Marx 1978, p. 7.

The particular nuance pointed out before, found in Hegel, Marx, and Kosík (with differences which go beyond the purpose of this chapter), is reflected in Table 2. In the third column, and for ease of discussion, I have added an asterisk to the terms to mark the difference. From now on, all the Czech or German terms which lose their nuance in English are marked in this way.

Object* and Its Derivations

Czech	German	English
předmět	Gegenstand	object*
předmětné	gegenständlich	objective*
předmětnost	Gegenständlichkeit	objectivity*
zpředmětnění	Vergegenständlichung	objectification

It remains to be shown how this nuance is reflected in the text. I limit examples to one or two.[43] Kosík uses *předmět* and its derivatives when he wants to attribute objectivity* to 'praxis' (C94/E76), including when he highlights its being *human* praxis (C42/E31); 'material praxis' (C50/E40); 'practical human world' (C51/E41); the 'subject' (C47/E37; C58/E47); *realita* (real objectivity*) (C42/E30), inhuman ('human') *objektivita* (C85/E70); when he wants to ascribe *objektivita* to 'social reality' (C42/E30) or when he wants to talk about the historical, fictitious, or fetishistic reality of *objektivita* (C42/E30); 'activity' (C92/E74, C144/E125); 'doing' (C142/E122; C145/E126).

When he wants to attribute objectivity to *objektivita* he uses 'objective' (C50/E40), but when he is qualifying human praxis, he uses 'objective'*: 'The world of human praxis is objective* – human reality in its genesis, production and reproduction'. (C51/E40)

The objectivity* of labour stems, on the one hand, from the fact that the result of labour has a duration, it is 'a cycle of activity and duration movement and objectivity'* (C141/E122), and on the other hand, from the fact that it is a manifestation of man as a practical being, that is, as an 'objective* subject' (C141/E122) a subject with an objective* existence with thoughts about objects.*

---

43 In-text references to Czech and English versions are to Kosík's *Dialektika konkrétního: Studie o problematice člověka a světa* (Kosík 1966) and to the English translation by Karel Kovanda and James Schmidt, *Dialectic of the Concrete* (Kosík 1976). All page numbers referring to the text in Czech are preceded by C; their counterpart numbers in English are preceded by E.

There is no way to dispense with objectification: 'The existence of objectified artifacts is a prerequisite of history, i.e., of continuity in human existence' in which the 'tool is a reasonable mediation between man and the object' (C141/E122–3). Through the process of objectification of man in labour, man not only realises itself but also tears the object* out of the context in which it existed before this process.[44]

So far, we have focused on cases where 'object'* and its derivatives are used to qualify other concepts or are qualified by them. Now we turn to those that are qualified by 'object' and its derivatives. When Kosík wants to set something over against the subject, like an opposition between matter and spirit, etc., he usually uses 'subject' and 'object' (C154/E137) for example, when he wants to talk about the subject-object relationship (C47/E37, C96/E79). This is also the case when he wants to counterpose the two worlds, namely, the world of objectivity and the world of subjectivity (C72/E59), when he wants to counterpose the dialectics of the subject with its counterpart (C85/E70), or when the former metamorphoses into the latter (subjective into objective; C65/E53); for example, in an objectual world, man, a subject, sinks to the level of an object, a tool, or a machine (C83/E68). It is noteworthy that he uses not the word *předmět* but *objekt* (not 'object*' but 'object' in our clarification), the reduction to which is reprimanded by Marx in his first thesis on Feuerbach (see 3 above). As a result of this metamorphosis, the real reality is reduced to 'the objective world of things and of reified human relationships,' and 'having lost control over the material world he had created, man loses reality itself as well' (C83/E68). As one might expect, the same adjective, 'objective', is used together with 'alienation' (C85/E70). This is equally true when he discusses the 'sense' (meaning) generally, including the objective sense of facts (C38/E26), the significance of facts (C37/E25), 'content' (C37/E26, C42/E30), 'function' (C42/E30), 'substance' (C165/E146), 'spirit' (C165/E146), 'laws' (C47/E37), 'Being' (C50/E40), the transindividual role of the individual (C48/E38), 'mechanism' (C64/E52), 'change' (C80/E65), and 'ground' (C72/E59).

When Kosík takes reality independently – for instance, when talking about the changes that it undergoes (C49/E39), or when it is to indicate how its objectivity is transformed into the world of the pseudo-concrete with only an appearance of reality – he uses the same term 'objective' (C67/E54). In reference to praxis, however, he uses 'objective,'* whereas when he uses it independently, he uses 'objectivity' (C156/E138); this is equally true when he wants to talk about the objectivity of a social context (C65/E53) or a transindividual context (C65–6/E53).

---

44 Kosík 1976, p. 122.

Another noteworthy point regarding the themes to which Kosík ascribes objectivity is a difference from Marx regarding truth. Unlike the adjective Marx uses for truth in the second thesis, namely, *gegenständlich*,[45] Kosík uses *objektivní* (objective) (C33/E22, C99/E82). Interestingly enough, this objective truth, the result of objective* praxis, as far as cognition (C37/E26) is concerned, is the result of cognition to which objectivity is ascribed. The knowledge is also qualified by the word 'objective' (C78/E89), and likewise for 'the reason of an objective observer' (C163/E144). Moreover, all this carries with it an objective criterion, or measure (C119/E104, C79/E64). Once more, interestingly, the objectivity of laws is called *objektivita* (objectivity) (C47/E37) and the investigation or exploration needed to find such laws is also qualified with the same term (C47/E37, C128/112), as well as for formations (C128/E112), and the objective course of things (C133/E116). This objective attribution also confirms the dual primacy of existence. This is in a sense a sign of a defence of objectivity in the already recognised sense of the term, whereas for what is investigated we have an object* of investigation (C150/133).

As far as I can tell, there are only two cases in the whole book where the two terms are used interchangeably. When Kosík discusses the object of manipulation, he refers to it as both *object** (C49–50/E40) and *object* (C49/E40, C153/E136). This is equally true when he wants to use adjectives for relations or relationships: they can be either *objective** (C156/E138) or *objective* (C48/E38).

To elucidate further my reading of Kosík's distinction between *Objekt* and *Gegenstand* and their derivations, let us review the senses that the word 'object' can have in English. In English the word 'object' can mean: (1) the grammatical object, that is, the object of a proposition. In 'I saw John', for instance, 'John' is the grammatical object of the sentence; (2) the purpose aimed at, as in 'The object is to replace capitalism with socialism'; (3) a thing, as in the phrase 'a pile of miscellaneous objects'. Up to here, all the senses are used equally in common English. But 'object' can also be used for (4) what is intended, as in 'object of scorn' or 'object of hatred'.[46] There is yet another sense, (5) which distinguishes that which is the result of the activity of human being from the most inactive forms of being, such as observation, or pure contemplation. (All man-made things you see around while reading this passage fall under this class.) It is the fourth and fifth senses that are the focus of our discussion. The introduction of the concept Object* here is intended to present a dialectical version of the

---

45   Marx 1978, pp. 5–7.
46   This clearly incorporate Husserl's intentionality into the discussion. This had been done before Kosík by another Marxist philosopher to whom Kosík refers, namely, Tran (2012, esp. pp. 82–104).

homogeneity of the historical subject and object*. This in turn makes possible the knowledge of the object* in all its varieties (praxis, labour, history, etc.) by the subject.[47]

In the discussion of the part-whole relationship, one problem is how and why a part of the whole is representative of the whole. The response is that each part is representative of the whole insofar as the whole is an organism of which it is a part. What makes a part representative of the whole is that it is a cell[48] of the whole. Thus, the whole *is* and *is not* in the part. It is in the part as a cell of the whole; it is not in the part in the sense that this part constitutes only a part of the whole.

Where then is the absolute whole or absolute totality? Absolute totality is reality in its totality: in one sense it is ungraspable as a whole in its totality, but in another sense it is graspable as a whole in its totality. This involves a particular dialectic between absolute totality and relative totality. In treating of the relative totalities, given the relationship between them and the absolute totality, it is the absolute totality that is grasped.

This is equally true of objectivity. Objectivity should not be ascribed to the absolute totality as what is over and above the relative totalities. The objectivity ascribed to the relative totality is simultaneously the same objectivity ascribed to absolute totality.[49] This can be better grasped when compared with Hegel's discussion of the finite and infinite. The infinite is not over and above the finite. The absence of a transcendent infinite over and above the finite in Hegelian philosophy, once searched for from a Marxian standpoint, is the relationship between absolute totality and relative totality. Nature as the absolute totality does exist, and one may say that a proof regarding its existence is not dealt with in Marx's works, at least not as a major issue. Yet cognition of the absolute totality is possible and occurs in every aspect of human praxis, including sensation. There is no unbridgeable chasm or insurmountable wall between absolute and relative totality. In this regard, the similarity with a mathematical limit is correct so long as one affirms that what is being achieved through a process is the

---

47 Cf. Gadamer 2006, p. 218.
48 It may be asked whether, according to this account, a cancerous cell is representative of the organism. Given that death, or for that reason, any qualitative transformation of the whole is an inherent characteristic of a dialectical totality represented by all its parts, the response is affirmative.
49 A comparison with a passage from Lenin, referred to in the previous chapter, is interesting here: 'In order to know an object thoroughly, it is essential to discover and comprehend all of its aspects, its relationships and its "mediations". We shall never achieve this fully, but insistence on all-round knowledge will protect us from errors and inflexibility'. Lenin 1976, p. 130, quoted in Lukács 1980, p. 33.

limit itself, not its horizons – the distinction insightfully accentuated by Kosík. What is given to us in each step is not the horizons, aspects, or partial images of the absolute totality, but the absolute totality relatively.

The rather tedious lexical elaboration developed above in order to unravel Kosík's account regarding the relationship between object, object,* and the related conceptual distinctions, helps us to better grasp the conceptual distinction at the basis of his criticism of some Marxist thinkers. He criticises Marcuse, for instance, for identifying two statuses that emerge from such a distinction, namely, objectivation and objectification, 'which renders the author vulnerable to subjectivism and introduces chaos and inconsistency into elaborating the problem of labor',[50] so that his standpoint 'cannot objectively appreciate Marx's contribution'.[51] Nonetheless, Kosík does not see an absolute distinction between objectified and objectivised praxis, since he also sees a connection between them. He does not stop at quoting what Marx says in the *Grundrisse* – 'All production is objectification of the individual'[52] – but adds objectivation, and while he criticises Marcuse for *identifying* them, he himself sees the 'interconnection of objectified and objectivized praxis'.[53]

Kosík's technical usage of the term 'objectification' is thus different from the way this concept is used in, for example, contemporary feminist discussion,[54] where objectification means turning a person (in this case a woman) into an object, a concept with a merely negative connotation. According to Kosík, so long as labour is a transformation of the subject into an object, which brings along with it reification, it is negative, but so long as it is the subject of concrete labour, that is, so long as it transforms nature into what is useful and its use, it is inevitable. In this sense, not only is it positive, but it is also the principal mode of human existence in the form of praxis. Praxis itself, however, taken broadly, is concomitant with human existence, which is inevitably social: our looking at the world is active-social. This does not entail, however, that its revolutionary character, in the sense of the coincidence of the environment and self-change, necessarily entails a social-radical transformation and substitution of 'is' for 'ought'. This latter transformation may be better described as reification. To objectivise, by contrast, is to render things objective, and hence to correct a biased account. In the same vein, says Kosík, 'the subject is already constitutively permeated with an objectivity which is the objectification of

---

50   Kosík 1976, p. 131.
51   Ibid.
52   Kosík 1976, pp. 114, 226.
53   Kosík 1976, pp. 145–146.
54   MacKinnon 1987, p. 50.

human praxis' (C58/E47). In humanising nature and in objectifying (realising) meanings, man forms a human world (C140–1/E122). Given that labour *is* the process of objectification (C156/E138), it is through labour that man is objectified and the object humanised (C140/E122).

A misconception here turns praxis, which 'in Marx's philosophy had made possible both objectivation and objective cognition, and man's openness toward being ... into social subjectivity and closedness: man is a prisoner of socialness' (C121/E106). This is done in dialectical social theory and is criticised by Kosík, because in adopting this 'Man is *walled in* in his socialness' (C121/E106). In contrast, Kosík sees the evidence for human's social character not only through being nothing without an object*, but particularly in that a human being establishes his reality in objective* activity (C85/E70). Kosík explains the relationship between social products and the social subject as follows: 'Without a subject, these social products of man would be senseless, while without means and objective* creations, the subject would be a mere specter' (C86/E70).

A reference to Marx's sixth thesis on Feuerbach is helpful here. Whereas Marx writes that 'the essence of man is the ensemble of his social relations', Kosík, while confirming this, reformulates his viewpoint as follows: 'The essence of man is the unity of objectivity* (*předmětnost*) and subjectivity' (C86/E70). But the same unity can apparently be equally ascribed to the *Idee* in Hegel.[55] If so, then Kosík could easily be criticised for falling into a kind of idealism, unless he proposes an alternative reading. For the time being, it is important to emphasise with the help of the lexical analysis above that Kosík does not use 'objectivity', but 'objectivity*'. This is the objectivity* which is equally 'the constitutive element of labor' (C141/E122). This unity is then human objectivity*, or an objectivity* enriched with the subjectivity of the human being. Kosík's approach is here different from an *objectivist* one, if by that term one understands not the approach which simply seeks to combat bias, but one that tends to obliterate the role of the individual subject and 'flees the subjective as if it were the threat it may be'.[56]

---

55 See the entry for 'Objektivität' in the *Hegel-Lexikon*: 'The Idea is the unity of subjectivity and objectivity' (Onnsach 2006, p. 340, my translation). Cf. Inwood (1992, p. 205): 'The Absolute Idea ... is ... both subject and object'.
56 Jacoby 1981, p. 9; see also p. 144.

5 Praxis, Labour, Care, and Totality

Whereas objectivity, even a non-comprehensive and relativised one, is thought by some contemporary philosophers to be attainable against 'our ideas – whether immediate actions or developed prejudices', because we are reflective thinkers,[57] Kosík shows that objectivity with all its nuances is possible through our social praxis. This is what we turn to now.

In Kosík's words, the 'objective* social reality' that is the result of human praxis is the twofold 'metamorphosis of the objective* into the subjective and of the subjective into the objective*'.[58] Since it is the 'active center in which human intentions are realized and laws of nature discovered', it 'unites causality and purposiveness'.[59] In paraphrasing the point found in Marx's eighth thesis on Feuerbach, that all social life is essentially practical, Kosík equates being with praxis, stressing the significance of objective praxis as Marx's most important discovery. Thus conceived, it is that through which the problem of the mode of comprehension of oneself and nature is solved, a problem that could not be solved either by consciousness or by matter, but only by praxis directed at the Subject matter [Sache selbst].

Since the *Sache selbst* is the goal of dialectic, a distinction is to be drawn between two aspects of the *Sache selbst*: its idea and its concept, that is, its abstract aspect and its concrete aspect.[60] These constitute two different levels of human praxis.[61] Routine, utilitarian praxis grasps the idea of the subject matter [*Sache selbst*], whereas dialectical thinking – where dialectic is a certain cognitive activity engaged in by dialectically minded inquirers – grasps its concept. The former sees facts as detached entities, and the representation of the activity of the individual is thus limited to two states. First, (1) 'care' [*Sorge*], 'the world in the subject,'[62] is the entanglement of the subject in the society; it is praxis in its derived and reified form. Secondly, (2) 'procuring' [*Besorgen*] is the phenomenal aspect of depersonalised praxis limited to manipulation represented as fragmented operations in the form of abstract labour; it is both the

---

57 Burbidge 2013, p. 89: 'Objectivity in our thinking develops out of our ability to reflect on our thoughts and consider them on their own terms'.
58 Kosík 1976, p. 71.
59 Ibid.
60 To associate ideas with phantoms is not unprecedented in the literature. Cf. *L'avare* by Molière 1971, p. 67: 'Ces chevaux ne sont plus rien que des idées ou des fantômes, des façons des chevaux'. This is important to note, because the sense of idea advanced here is not the same as Hegel's *Idee* as one culminating moment of the Doctrine of Concept.
61 Cf. Jameson 1990, p. 53: 'Concepts stand on the side of things, Ideas on the side of "truth"'.
62 Kosík 1976, p. 38.

realisation of the unskilled labour-power the capitalist reckons with buying, and the boring undifferentiated way the hired worker spends day after day on the job.[63] Thus, objects and relations are fetishised and the human being is alienated; the subject does not reflect on the genesis or formation of the world, nor does he take it as a processual whole. The fall of the subject in this *objectual* world to the level of an object, tool, or machine may be best expressed by the allegory of the frog, who boils to death without noticing any change in its environment. In genuine praxis, by contrast, one finds the laws behind and beneath their facticity[64] as well as a totality that has the three characteristics of being structured, evolving, and self-forming.

The approach dominated by a praxis that is not genuine praxis sees the phenomena and limits itself to them. As a result, it represents the ideological and fetishistic aspect of praxis, the result of a world in which the transparency of tools is replaced by the complexity of implements; the singular existence of the tool is to be distinguished from the plural existence of implements. The approach dominated by genuine praxis sees how those phenomena are intertwined with their essence, and how they are revealed with it. Whereas the content of an 'idea' does not 'measure up to reality',[65] the concept can 'exhaust the essence of the phenomenon, and adequately [comprehend and] explain it'.[66] The mental concretisation of reality as concrete totality is thus a movement from ideas to concepts as two apparently distinct points which are at the same time coterminous: from manipulating reality to explaining and comprehending it. According to Kosík, however, one should not assume, as Lukács does, that these two conceptions deal with two different levels of reality, one 'higher' than the other,[67] because adopting such a standpoint would lead to a dichotomy between facts and reality.

Praxis in such a relationship with reality is the inherent characteristic and the specific mode of existence of human beings. Given that such an existent always exists under some human conditions, and these conditions and human beings are related through praxis, history comes into the account.

---

63   Kosík 1976, p. 39: 'Procuring is praxis in its phenomenally alienated form', it is 'manipulation (of things and people)'. Here Kosík is manifestly drawing on these Heideggerian terms in *Being and Time*. See Heidegger 1967, esp. chaps. 3 and 4.
64   For his claim that the facticity of facts is different from their reality, see Lukács 1971a, p. 7.
65   Kosík 1976, p. 36.
66   Kosík 1976, p. 21.
67   See Lukács 1971a, p. 181: 'The developing tendencies of history constitute a higher reality than the empirical "facts"'. As will be seen later, Kosík does not see (or at least does not mention) this difference between his own reading and Lukács's.

The distinction between objectification and objectivation discussed above is also crucial in the distinction between praxis and care. In care, unlike in praxis, the social 'relations are not objectivized: they are not the subject-matter of science or objective investigation', but remain in the sphere of 'personal, individual, subjective involvement'.[68]

We have seen so far one moment of reified reality in the form of care and procuring. Two other moments are *Homo Economicus* and the Economic Factor. The activity of *Homo Economicus* is utterly dependent on the capitalist system: once the system desires this activity, the individual as a member of the system is active; once it does not so desire, the individual is not active. This is how the abstraction of *Homo Economicus* is the real abstraction:[69] it is abstraction from all individual characteristics, which turns the individual into a 'physical magnitude' imposed on him by the reality of capitalism. Only in abstraction is the individual active, only when what the system desires is carried out; thus the individual is detached from what is over and above the desire of the system. As a result, social physics turns man into an object; the subject thus becomes objectual. Man is enslaved in these moments, but praxis brings about the openness of the object of cognition toward him and his existence: 'Man surmounts [*překračuje*] (transcends) ... his condtions'.[70]

Praxis is in this sense in unity with theory, but not with *theoria* (in the sense of pure contemplation). Such a unity, the supreme postulate of materialist philosophy, is different from reducing praxis to the 'socialness of human, to a mere category, and technology'. Thus conceived, praxis is a philosophical concept and not limited to 'a category of a dialectical theory of society';[71] it reveals itself not only in theorising about society but also in transforming it. To use a classical example, Robinson Crusoe alone on his island was engaged in praxis as well, even though he did so on the basis of his previous socialisation. Highlighting the importance of praxis is indispensable in order to avoid a twofold danger: giving priority to theory leads to pure scientism, understood as the excessive belief in the power of scientific knowledge and techniques, whereas giving priority to action leads to Machiavellianism, or pragmatism, for which the truth is subordinate to usefulness.

From the point of view of materialist philosophy, however, the issue revolves around the response to a threefold question: Who is man, what is socio-human

---

68   Kosík 1976, p. 37.
69   Kosík 1976, p. 53: 'For classical economics, man exists exclusively as a part of the system, and studies even himself only by looking at himself as a part of the system'.
70   Kosík 1966, p. 167. (Translated with reference to the text in Czech.)
71   Kosík 1976, p. 135.

reality, and how is this reality formed? Man is a being whose immanent and inherent onto-formative praxis forms socio-human reality. The truth of reality, unlike its usefulness, which is what pragmatism limits itself to, cannot be simply presented – it must be *performed* and realised. In so doing, man and woman are able to grasp human and extra-human reality and leave nothing as absolutely given. This is done through and in praxis, as the mutual objectification of man and woman on the one hand and the realm of manifestation of their mastery over nature on the other. It is in this way that they realise their freedom, that is, their self-mastery.

This freedom, the possibility of the totalisation of reality, is possible in our contemporary world because revolutionary socialised praxis enables us to adopt and actualise such a process. This capacity is both a prerequisite for our era and its historical result. With the transformation of economics into science under capitalism, the individual can see his law-like existence as an element in the system: *Homo Economicus* is the constituent of this status. The multilateral interdependence of all these features within capitalism did not exist before this mode of social life; with this an unclosed horizon can be envisaged.

One important aspect of Marx's works is that 'no philosophy of labor has been developed since Marx's time'. This point is recognised by many but it should be 'coupled with the point that materialist philosophy is also the "latest" "ontology of man", in that it has not been rendered obsolete by history'.[72] The ability of humans to control time rather than being controlled, the extension or externalisation of his existence, is due to his objective* activity,[73] with the aforementioned twofold character of labour. Following Kosík's account, it seems imprecise on his part to write that the 'master-slave dialectic is *the basic model of praxis*',[74] unless praxis, as an existential moment, is reduced to labour.[75] Put differently, although labour is the manifestation *par excellence* of human praxis, praxis should not be reduced to labour.

---

72   Kosík 1976, p. 119. To the point acknowledged by Sartre that the intellectual horizon of Marxism cannot be transcended in our epoch, Kosík adds that Marxism as an *ontology of man* cannot be overcome (Kosík 1976, p. 130, emphasis added). See Sartre 1963, p. 29: 'What has made the force and richness of Marxism is the fact that it has been the most radical attempt to clarify the historical process in its totality'.

73   Kosík 1976, p. 131: 'That the problem of man's time is linked with his objective* activity is a basic point in which materialist philosophy differs from the existential conception of totality'.

74   Kosík 1976, p. 153 (emphasis added).

75   The word *práce* (C140) is translated alternatively as 'labour' or 'work' (E121). I prefer 'labour' for two reasons: first, by 'work' Kosík sometimes means the result of labour; secondly, I want to avoid a criticism of Marx's standpoint regarding the distinction between labour, work, and action developed by Arendt in *The Human Condition* (1998, chaps. 3–5).

In the same vein, the advantage of Kosík's conception becomes clearer when compared with Lukács's. As we saw in the previous chapter, Lukács hypostasises the whole against the parts, and hence hypostasises a higher reality against the reality of facts. While Kosík seems not to notice Lukács's mistake, he himself avoids it. For Kosík, reality, taken as the absolute totality of nature and history, the human and the extra-human, 'the unity of events and their subjects,'[76] both *is* and *is not* beyond the reach of the human being. It is beyond human reach because it cannot be grasped as a whole once and for all; it is not beyond human reach because what is grasped constitutes a part of the whole that in its threefold relationship with the whole – that is, structured, evolving, and self-forming – *is* the whole. To generalise the well-known Marxian aphorism from the second thesis on Feuerbach, one may say: the discussion of a whole over and above the parts, rather than of the subject-object of praxis, is a scholastic issue. While praxis permeates the whole of the human being and determines the human being's totality, it is not in opposition to theory; it is rather 'the determination of human being as the process of forming reality'.[77] This is, once more, related to the primacy of existence: Kosík of course, like Marx,[78] does not want to imply that nature, as the material substratum, is created by humans, but the material substratum in its confrontation with praxis does undergo a minimal change. The exposition of this material substratum with human praxis entails a change in this substratum: the graspable is always formed. This is the point that the exposed *Gegenstand* is already formed by the praxis of the past as well as the present, and undergoes further formation in the form of trans-formation. The role of praxis is then social-human-active *re*-formation, the *onto-formative* character of the human.

The practical-ontological recognition of the alienating character of praxis has its counterpart in the alienating character of labour. The argument may be put like this: all labour is praxis; thus, alienated labour is one sort of alienated praxis. Recognition of the fact of praxis's alienation of praxis has its counterpart in (i.e., corresponds to) praxis's actual alienation. This line of thought may be criticised on the ground that not all practice is alienated thought. To this it can be replied that under capitalism, the best example of non-revolutionary prac-

---

76 Kosík 1976, p. 84.
77 Kosík 1976, p. 137.
78 See Marx's comment in *Capital* Volume I (1976, p. 133): 'If we subtract the total amount of useful labour of different kinds which is contained in the coat, the linen, etc., a material substratum is always left. This substratum is furnished by nature without human intervention'.

tice is labour. Revolutionary praxis can lead to the revolutionising status quo, but given that the routine, 'procuring' life is the starting point of such praxis, this revolutionary praxis gains its inherence in the existing-lived life, that is, a necessity with its roots in the existing life. While we had reality as the unity of phenomenon and essence, we have here the grasp of revolutionary praxis as the product of penetration into the routine praxis. In this anti-reductionist reading, a repercussion of Marx's 'Theses on Feuerbach', *Gegenstand*, revolutionary praxis, and *gegenständlich* on the one hand are introduced; on the other hand, object, objectual, and routine praxis are also introduced. The account given here goes farther than Kosík's own account, since, following the 'Theses on Feuerbach', I see one source of such a reading in Marx's distinction between *Gegenstand* and *Objekt*.

Along the same lines, a question that may be raised is the relationship between totality and language, and the role language plays in totalisation: how language, thinking, and activity are related. In his response to this question, Kosík attributes a particular role to meaning:[79] 'The forming of a totality as a structure of meanings is thus also a process which forms the objective content and meaning of all its elements and parts as well'.[80] Through his objective* praxis, the human being has a twofold function: the formation of meanings as the sense of things, but also the access to their objective* meaning.[81]

The sursumption of the pseudo-concrete is itself accomplished through the introduction of one totality of meanings that gives way to a new totality of meanings to attain its *real* meaning. This sursumption is first realised in three ways to destroy the pseudo-concrete:

> (1) The revolutionary-critical praxis of mankind which is identical with the humanization of man, with social revolutions as its key stages; (2) by dialectical thinking which dissolves the fetishized world of appearances in order to penetrate to reality and to the *subject matter*; (3) by the realization of truth and the forming of human reality in an ontogenetic process.[82]

---

79 In so doing, Kosík improves on the standpoint introduced but left undeveloped by Lukács. See Lukács 1971, p. 163. This is the task later taken up by other Marxist thinkers; see Arthur 2004, chapter 2, p. 25.
80 Kosík 1976, p. 29.
81 Kosík 1976, p. 40.
82 Kosík 1976, p. 8.

One may argue that the key stages in humanising our species (through revolutions) *are* the ontogenetic process of the realisation of truth; accordingly, (1) and (3) can be conjoined. With this destruction, however, the sursumption is not yet complete. Although with this sursumption, the fetishistic character of the pseudo-concrete is obliterated, in order to realise the concrete totality as the dialectical-materialist standpoint of the *cognition* of reality, its intellectual reproduction of the subject matter as totality, we need to have to a particular cognition:

> [T]he cognition of the phenomenon's historical character which in a peculiar way reveals the dialectic of the unique and of the generally human; and finally, the cognition of the objective content and meaning of the phenomenon, of its objective function and its historical place within the social whole.[83]

Given that Marx sees not only thinking but also sensation as human praxis, and every discussion of truth once isolated from praxis is mere scholastic discussion, I would like to add that Marx's standpoint should be taken as representing three moments of revolutionary praxis, of ontologically-politically going from pseudo-consciousness to revolutionary consciousness. The result of such a sursumption or destruction is simultaneously the sursumption of the fetishistic surrounding environment and the liberation of the alienated subject. This is the response to the explanation of the simultaneous change in circumstances and in human beings, which also entails going further than a passive approach to truth. Thus, a materialist approach would distinguish between correctness,[84] the subject of routine life, and truth taken as the 'happening' that becomes actual as the result of revolutionary praxis; put differently, truth is to be actualised through this revolutionary human-objective praxis.

Praxis, thus generalised, is the bedrock of objectivity*, intersubjectivity, and subjectivity. That is, how social individuals in the world act on the already socially constituted objects* is interrelated with how they act in relation to other subjects and how their sensation also comes into play. Hence, this par-

---

83 Kosík 1976, p. 30.
84 Hegel puts forward such a standpoint, *inter alia*, in *Phenomenology of Spirit*. 'To such questions as, When was Caesar born?, or How many feet were there in a stadium?, etc. a clear-cut answer ought to be given, just as it is definitely true that the square on the hypotenuse is equal to the sum of the squares on the other two sides of a right-angled triangle. But the nature of a so-called truth of that kind is different from the nature of philosophical truths' (Hegel 1977, p. 23).

ticular praxis brings along with it the realisation of truth and the destruction-sursumption of the pseudo-concrete. Dialectics as *the revolutionary method of transforming reality* actualises the concretised totality or totalised concreteness through the recognition of the virtually inherent characteristic of the pseudo-concrete through its sursumption. This virtuality is due to the possibility given to man by revolutionary praxis according to which the present is chosen based on a projection into the future. This approach is different from other approaches in which the past plays the dominant role – psychoanalysis for one, or Hegel with Essence as something belonging to the past (*Wesen*)[85] for another. It is instead a standpoint in which it is not the past that plays the primordial role in the present praxis, but the future.

6   History and Totality

On the basis of what has been observed to this point we can say that, by putting praxis at the core of his thought and elaborating on its mediatory role, Kosík cannot be criticised as Lukács can for not distinguishing gnoseology and ontology.[86] Nonetheless, given the historical determination of praxis that he posits, his account will remain unsatisfactory if the notion of history and its relation to totality and praxis is not elaborated on. Demonstrating that he has done this is the task of this section.

Kosík's account of the relationship between history and totality may be best grasped by reference to Marx's third thesis on Feuerbach. There Marx underscores the point that the coincidence of change in circumstances and human activity or self-change has to be understood through the revolutionary praxis of the human.[87] This thesis is an improvement in comparison with the related passages by Marx and Engels in *The Holy Family*[88] in that it is more precise in emphasising the mutual relationship between the subject and its conditions. This will be later developed in the *German Ideology*, where Marx and Engels write: 'In revolutionary activity the changing of oneself coincides with

---

85   See Ernst Bloch's discussion in *The Principle of Hope* (Bloch 1996), in chapter 19 where Bloch sees a similarity between Hegel's *Wesen* [essence] and Aristotle's τὸ τί ἦν εἶναι in that both are dominated by the past.
86   See the previous chapter.
87   Marx 1978e, pp. 5–6.
88   Marx and Engels 1975b, p. 131: 'If man is shaped by environment, his environment must be made human. If man is social by nature, he will develop his true nature only in society, and the power of his nature must be measured not by the power of the separate individual but by the power of society'.

the changing of circumstances'.[89] Kosík draws on this passage to criticise sociologism, that is, historiography which, in reducing social reality to conditions, 'just consists in treating historical conditions independent of activity'.[90]

Kosík gives a correct reading of the standpoint proposed by Marx and Engels: history hitherto has not been class struggle, but the *history* of class struggles performed by man.[91] History as the gradual realisation of something other than man turns into history as the realisation of nothing but man! History does nothing – man does. People do enter circumstances that are independent of their consciousness and will, but once they enter them, they begin, even unwillingly, to transform those conditions. One may also add those conditions are also the process and the result of previous individuals and their praxis.

Kosík's own approach is to propose a distinction between history-historism on the one hand and historicity-historicism on the other: 'History is a history because it includes both historicity of conditions and historism of reality',[92] where 'the historism of social reality is not the historicity of conditions'.[93] He develops this by focusing on the apparent mystery of the transcendence of the work of art in history, even as it revives, totalises, or integrates itself in history. This does not mean that this durability is limited to works of art; it is also true of thought and philosophy, *inter alia*.[94] Whereas one may ascribe historicity to conditions, to a work of art one should ascribe historism. In the case of works of art, this may happen by absolutising the role that conditions play, taking the relation between conditions and the work of art as the only link between social reality and the work of art. The truth of a social practice in general and a work of art in particular should not be reduced to the conditions in which it is advanced as human objective praxis. The testimony of the work of art is twofold: it is testimony *of* its conditions, society, and era; but more importantly – and this is often neglected – it is the testimony the work of art gives us *about* its conditions, society, and era. The question is then how the limited transcends its limitedness and attains the situation of the unlimited. The work of art, though limited to its time, outlasts its conditions because it is not *only* a

---

89 See Marx and Engels 1976, p. 214.
90 Marx and Engels, *The German Ideology*, p. 60, quoted from Kosík 1976, p. 90.
91 Cf. Dardot and Laval 2012, chap. 3. (and its title: History as Class Struggle).
92 Kosík 1976, p. 83.
93 Kosík 1976, p. 79.
94 In so doing, Kosík avoids a charge that is made against Lukács's historicism. For such a criticism, see Corredor 1997, pp. 48–9. In these interviews, Lukács is criticised, by Peter Bürger, among others, both for equating methodology and historicism, and for his attempt to merge a 'Marxist philosophy of history' and a 'normative aesthetic theory'.

reflection of the conditions, but also a creative recreation of those conditions, and as a result acquires a timeless character. This is how Kosík, in an enigmatic way, advances the following complex idea: 'The timelessness of a work is in its temporality as activity'.[95] The determinism to be criticised is the determinism that takes the transient conditions to be the only reality, not just 'insofar as they are the realisation, fixing, and development of the objective* praxis of man and his history'.[96]

In this account, dialectics is distinct both from historicism, or historical relativism, and from ahistoricism. Historicism reduces history to the historicity of conditions: its temporality, transience, and irreplicability. Here the absolute and the universal are pushed aside, since the facticity of facts is equated with reality. But the facticity gives only the aspects of facts that are transient, emptied, and devalued. Ahistoricism sees in history nothing but what is insubstantial and trivial, since the essence of what is ephemeral is taken to be nothing but its natural, transhistorical, and atemporal characteristics. When reality is severed from facticity, the relative and particular are pushed aside: the transfactuality of reality is taken to be equivalent to reality. In both cases, a split between the relative and the absolute is fixed in place, or else is arrested at a particular stage of its development.[97]

According to dialectics, however, nothing is absolute or universal, or prior to and independent of history, and both absolute and relative are formed in history:

> History is history only because it includes both the historicity of conditions and the historism of reality, because it contains ephemeral historicity which recedes into the past and does not return, as well as historism, i.e., the formative of that which endures, the self-formative and the creative.[98]

As to a work of art for instance, or any work (in philosophy, history, etc.) as a socio-human activity, its historicity which is 'bad uniqueness and irreplicability' entails historism, that is, 'the capacity for concretization and survival'.[99] But historicity does not entail historism, and whereas historicity is limited to the

---

95   Kosík 1976, p. 81.
96   Kosík 1976, p. 79.
97   This is but a nuanced paraphrase of the two extremes seen in the chapter on the undialectical conceptions of totality.
98   Kosík 1976, p. 83.
99   Kosík 1976, p. 80.

ephemeral characteristics of an era, its conditions, and its testimony to those conditions, historism has for its subject the reproduction and concretisation of the era so long as they also reflect the general movement of human history of which that era is just a moment. This does not mean that such a work is not socially determined, but its social determination is not limited to social conditions. This is how the objective-historical praxis of mankind, unlike that of the individual, can transcend the historicity of its conditions.

But a question arises: How is such a conception of history related to the everyday life of the individual under capitalism and capitalism's reified totality? The approach imprisoned in care and procuring, the naïve or routine consciousness of the individual, fails to realise how history and 'the everyday' interpenetrate: it sees a cleavage between 'the everyday' and history. And in seeing one's ability to realise one's instinctive intentions, the person holding this approach is once more in a situation similar to that of a fish in a pond, or, to return to the example above, a frog in boiling water.

Let us draw an analogy between a fact and totality on the one hand, and the 'everyday' and history on the other. In this way the intrafactuality of a single fact could be understood in its interfactuality: what it inherently is can ultimately be known only in its relationship with the totality of which it is a constituent, in the same way history is what enables us to make the everyday. The everyday then both reveals and conceals history: it conceals history, since when history is taken in isolation, one cannot grasp it; but it also reveals it, since it is the partial manifestation, and the only possible manifestation, of history. The sursumption of this reified, fetishised character of the everyday and of history is accomplished through the twofold practical destruction of this reified reality, not only in its phenomenal appearance but also in its real essence. To this effect, Kosík makes fun of Hegel for treating history as the emperor on horseback. He introduces instead a dialectic between the everyday and history: divorced from history, the everyday, as the 'phenomenal "layer" of reality', becomes static; divorced from the everyday, history becomes abstract and contentless. But if this is so, it does not seem right to say, as Kosík does, that 'one grasps the *everyday* from reality, rather than vice versa'.[100] We have to admit instead that the reality of history is understood partially through the everyday, whereas the everyday is understood through the reality of history holistically. According to this alternative reading, the everyday is thus the sole phenomenal appearance of the reality of history, in a relation different from an element, or factor, within a system.

---

100   Kosík 1976, p. 45 (emphasis added). Here I am paraphrasing Kosík's argument.

7 Factor Theory, System, Structure, and Totality

That Kosík distances his standpoint from historicity and conditions and the associated misconception of totality is revealed best in the way he criticises the factor theory and the inadequate criticisms put forward by earlier Marxists. There are two contemporary views that stem from a confusion between the economic *factor* and economic *structure*: the opinion that 'class differences have been abolished in the most advanced imperialist countries',[101] and the opinion that many countries, because of their apparent lack of similarity with the so-called *normally developed* Western countries, do not have a capitalist mode of production. Both are ultimately justifications of capitalism, and stem from a confusion between the economic factor and economic structure. In such apologetic readings, 'the economy' is taken to be equal to the possession and distribution of wealth and property, along with the agency and hierarchy of power ownership. This is found, for instance, in Weber's well-known idea that social life is the triangulation among three factors that mutually influence one another: economic position, the division of political power, and the gradation of social status and prestige as independent autonomous series, as three distinct factors that influence one another. Such approaches do not see the unity of social life and its formation as a concrete totality, a totality that must also be distinguished from 'metaphysical identity', which degrades such a totality into 'abstract wholeness' or 'empty totality'.

Kosík's criticism of factor theory echoes Engels's letter to Joseph Bloch of 21 September 1890. There Engels responds to Bloch's question about whether economic relationships are the only relevant factor or whether there are other relationships that also play effective roles. Engels refines and accentuates the view of the production and reproduction of real life, which is vaster than economics as it is generally understood, as 'the *ultimately* determining' element, but also leaves room for the contingency that results from this interaction. Without mentioning the term, Engels defends a standpoint of which the cornerstone is dialectical totality. Engels's letter is even more precise in this sense: whereas Kosík says that 'the economic structure forms the unity and continuity of all spheres of social life',[102] Engels explicitly emphasises that 'the various elements of the superstructure ... also exercise their influence upon the course of the historical struggles and in many cases, *preponderate in determining their form*'. He thus highlights the interactive character of this social totality

---

101 Kosík 1976, p. 64.
102 Kosík 1976, p. 64.

through which 'the economic movement finally asserts itself as necessary'.[103] This cannot be seen by the supporters of factor theory, owing to their inability to see the real genesis of the social whole, that is, because their notion of totality is misconceived.

Kosík's criticism is not limited to factor theory but is also directed at critics that mistarget factor theory. Kosík criticises both Plekhanov and Labriola for misconceiving totality and praxis in taking 'economic factors' as the outcome of scientific investigation and suggests that they are 'of a definite historical form of development'.[104] Regarding Plekhanov's claim that 'the subjective aspect of human is precisely the psychological one',[105] Kosík says that this would explain at most 'the impact or consequences of the factors',[106] not how they originated. That said, however, it is an imprecision on Kosík's part to treat these two standpoints as equivalent, for Kosík overlooks the point that Labriola comes closer to the dialectical standpoint that he himself endorses than Plekhanov does. Kosík's similarly sweeping attack on Labriola is thus not justified, for Labriola considers Marxism an 'organic conception of history'.[107] As Labriola says explicitly: 'Separating in theory the factors of an organism, destroys them in so far as they are elements contributing to the unity of the whole'.[108] Thus, contrary to what Kosík claims, some characteristics are found in Labriola's works. They are admittedly not as coherent as in Kosík's own account though.

There are, however, some points on which Kosík's discussion of system can be criticised. For instance, he exaggerates the similarity between general system theory and dialectical standpoint, saying, 'All areas of objective reality are systems, i.e., complexes of interdependent elements'.[109] However, he is prudent enough to add: 'Only the dialectical conception of the ontological and gnoseological aspects of structure and system provides a fruitful solution and avoids the extremes of mathematical formalism, on the one hand, and of metaphys-

---

103   Engels 1980, p. 34 (emphasis added).
104   Kosík 1976, p. 61.
105   Kosík 1976, p. 76.
106   Kosík 1976, p. 61. However, Plekhanov is not entirely ignorant of this point; see, for example, Plekhanov 1980, p. 176: 'Bismarck said that we cannot make history and must wait while it is being made. But who makes history? It is made by the *social man*, who is its *sole "factor"*' (Plekhanov's emphasis). Nonetheless even his account is nuanced here: 'The character of an individual is a "factor" in social development only *where, when, and to the extent that social relations permit it to be such*' (p. 162, emphasis added).
107   Labriola 1980, p. 53.
108   Labriola 1980, p. 55.
109   Kosík 1976, p. 20.

ical ontologism, on the other'.¹¹⁰ The point he intends to make is that whereas mathematical formalism denies that mathematical formulas correspond to any substantial reality, metaphysical ontologism contends that they do, but not to any *material* reality; in other words, whereas mathematical formalism denies the content, metaphysical ontologism deprives the content of its materiality. He cannot then be criticised for reducing totality to systems.¹¹¹ In taking such a standpoint, Kosík both foresees the two types of reductionism in the Marxian approach – mathematical and metaphysical – and simultaneously distances himself from both.¹¹² This boils down to quantification of quality in the former case, and in the latter to the fixation or freezing of reality. In the former case, the critique of political economy is also turned into a positive science that remains uncritical; this can be done, and is being largely done in economics departments all over the world, but it is entirely different from a Marxian standpoint in that it deprives thinking of its critical-dialectical characteristics.

8 Criticism of Kosík¹¹³

Kosík's account of the co-constitution of the parts and the whole as a distinctive characteristic of Marxian conception of totality is sometimes imprecise and involves misconceptions. The following is an example:

> All cognition is a dialectical oscillation (dialectical as opposed to metaphysical, for which both poles would be constant magnitudes and which would regard their external, reflexive relations), oscillation between facts and *context* (*totality*), an oscillation whose immediate active center is the method of investigation.¹¹⁴

---

110 Kosík 1976, p. 21.
111 Cf. Levins 1998, p. 397: 'A dialectical approach recognizes that the "system" is an intellectual construct designed to elucidate some aspects of reality but necessarily ignoring and even distorting others', and also p. 398: 'The internal workings of the variables in a model, the dynamics of the model itself or the development of the science eventually reveals all models as inaccurate, limited, and misleading'.
112 This does not mean that similar attempts are not being made. For the former, one may mention scientism and formalism; see Paolucci (2007, p. 223) and Freeman (forthcoming).
113 It will be later seen how Kosík's account of totality may help us to develop a reading of distinctive Marxian conception of totality. In what follows in this section, I limit myself to the discussion presented in this chapter.
114 Kosík 1976, pp. 27–8 (emphasis added).

The difficulty arising from this passage lies in its equating of context and totality, thus undermining the point that this oscillation is *within* the totality.[115] The dialectic of facts and totality, or text and context, is better understood if it is made clear that the context is also *in* the totality. Moreover, with the distinction of facts in the context of reality and theory, to the clause 'the very conception of fact is determined by the overall conception of social reality',[116] I would add: 'and vice versa': the conception of social reality is equally determined by the very conception of facts.

This co-determination of the moments and the whole is also overlooked by Kosík in his political analysis. Here is an example: 'In the epoch of capitalism, capital turns into a structure of meanings that *determines* the internal content and objective sense of its elements' (emphasis in the original!).[117] What Kosík overlooks here is the co-constitution of this whole by its organic moments. This of course is not something he denies, but he does not explicitly emphasise it. Following Marx, he realises that the only means of comprehending facts is by the power of abstraction. He further demarcates a Marxian abstraction, and implicitly distinguishes it from empiricist, Aristotelian, and Hegelian versions of abstraction. He also criticises the mode of abstraction that dichotomises reality into essential and inessential, characterising it as *mere* abstraction, or triviality.

Nonetheless, a question may be raised: To what extent can this co-constitution of the parts and the whole be taken to be the only criterion for a dialectical conception of totality? An outstanding example here is undoubtedly Pascal, whose 'logic of the heart' is criticised by Kosík himself.[118] The following passage is exemplary:

> All things being caused and causing, helped and helping, mediated and mediating, and all maintained by a natural and insensitive link that joins the most remote and the most different, I hold it impossible to know the parts without knowing the whole, neither knowing the whole without particularly knowing the parts.[119]

---

115 Kosík 1976, p. 25: 'Every fact is comprehensible only in context and in a whole'.
116 Ibid.
117 Kosík 1976, p. 29.
118 Kosík 1976, p. 59.
119 Pascal 1963, p. 527. This is my translation of the following passage: 'Toutes choses étant causées et causantes, aidées et aidantes, médiates et immédiates, et toutes s'entretenant par un lien naturel et insensible qui lie les plus éloignées et les plus différentes, je tiens impossible de connaître les parties sans connaître le tout, non plus que de connaître le tout sans connaître particulièrement les parties'.

As we see here, although Pascal does recognise the criterion of co-constitution of the parts and the whole, his thinking can hardly be considered either dialectical or materialist. Nonetheless, even a materialist dialectical relationship, so long as it is restricted to the interaction of the parts and the whole, does not have to accept the revolutionary characteristic of dialectic. In a recent reading of a representative of the bourgeois approach, for instance, we read: 'Like Hayek, Marx focuses on the mutual interaction of the parts within an "organic whole"'.[120] That said, however, Marxian totality cannot be an organic totality, in the sense found in Hegel, namely, an organic whole with a soul. A change in a member of the whole does not transform the whole in an organic way, if by that one understands a process that can be interpreted teleologically. It does so only to the extent that since things exist in a closed world, as physics teaches us, each is a component of the whole, and is hence not absolutely indifferent to change in other components.

Another more important point is that Kosík does not see the limits to *social* objectivity. To help elucidate my point, I use the following example. You and I both agree that Mogadishu is the capital of Somalia, and that the combination of certain amounts of acid and base under determinate conditions inevitably results in a certain amount of salt and water. The situation is different as regards social objectivity*. Three different types of disagreement can be held regarding social phenomena. The first is the disagreement that can be reconciled through argumentation and persuasion. The second happens when you and I do not agree on something, and neither of us is convinced by the other's argumentation. For instance, before the US presidential elections in 2020, we might not have agreed on the proposition, 'If Biden is elected, there will be significant changes in the situation of the working class'. If neither of us could convince the other through argumentation, we would pass to the second type of disagreement. Now that Biden has been elected, we have the opportunity to see which of us was right. This is the level of disagreement that will be resolved by reality, unlike the first kind of disagreement, which could be reconciled by mere argumentation.

But there is still another level of disagreement; this one is an antagonistic conflict in which the two sides of the disagreement cannot be ultimately reconciled. The opposition between the 1 percent and the 99 percent is of this kind. For the 99 percent, the problem that every few seconds a child dies on this planet because of the capitalist system has a particular importance, which should be solved right at this moment. For the 1 percent it is the last problem to

---

120   Sciabarra 1995, p. 68.

be dealt with if it is one at all. Even if at the individual level an agreement may be possible, at the social level a logically possible agreement is not practically possible, given that individuals are agents of social subjectivity, namely, capital and labour. There can be no veritable dia*logue* between the two sides, for the simple reason that there is no common *logic*. Put differently, the impossibility of coming up with an agreement through dia-logue stems ultimately from each side having a different λόγος. To say, 'But they both seek power, and in this sense, they have something in common', is to miss the difference between the nature of the power of the proletariat and the power of capitalism. The impossibility of reaching an agreement at the level of happenings in reality stems from their antagonistic social statuses. Along the same lines, there is no common standpoint regarding social reality. All the attempts to tame capitalism stop here, and it remains, inter alia, a barrier to the realisation of global social justice.[121]

Since classical economics is not fundamentally different from vulgar economics, inasmuch as it too results in an objectual world, a critique of the former is as indispensable as a critique of the latter. Classical economics justifies the objectual world and its laws as if they were the real world. In this transference to unreason as the reason of capitalist society, what may be called the unreasonal realisation of reason,[122] this unrealness is transposed to the individual level as well. Only an operative individual, that is, an individual functioning in the system, is taken to be a real individual. A reified individual, defined in the sense of being a circumscribed one, is required by a reified system. The apparently independent agent of Cartesian rationalism becomes dependent and subjugated to its products. In contrast to such a reason, 'the dialectical reason not only seeks to know reality reasonably but also, and in particular, to shape it reasonably'.[123] According to this reading, the subject, an ontologically and not just theoretically conscious worker, who acts according to collective 'economic rationality', learns under capitalism to pursue his interests collectively and turns into the agent of revolution.

Rationalist reason is irrational in two senses: it cannot grasp the ultimate sense of existing reason in its totality and contradictions, which cannot abide by or be controlled by the same reason; and it forms this irrational reality as the realisation and existence of what it takes to be its rational form. Rational reason

---

121   This is a paraphrase of a text published previously on the occasion of the People's Social Forum in Ottawa in January 2013; see Boveiri 2013.
122   Cf. Marx's letter to Arnold Ruge in September 1843: 'Reason has always existed, but not always in a rational form' (Marx 1843).
123   Kosík 1976, p. 57.

thus gives the 'efficient' (*Racionelní*) instead of the 'rational' (*Racionální*).[124] This is how scientism goes hand in hand with this efficiency-oriented rationalism, which is in fact irrationalism, since mere efficiency becomes the criterion of rationality. Against this dominance of efficiency and goal-orientedness, dialectics asks whether such goals are rationally justifiable. It is a dialectical return from τέχνη to ἐπιστήμη, but this time ἐπιστήμη is oriented by revolutionary praxis. Dialectical reason implies the recognition of negativity[125] and contradiction, postulating and sursuming them, all of which is absent in such a ratiocinating reason. Here, instead of the one-sided movement of rational reason, we have a dialectical movement between the moments phenomena-essence, part-whole, and relative-absolute, where all is reversible.

As the antidote to one-sided abstraction, there is little similarity between revolutionary praxis oriented toward the destruction of the pseudo-concrete and abstraction, for the latter is at best merely critical rather than practical-critical.[126] The destruction of the pseudo-concrete is indeed the destruction of the real abstraction, which cannot be accomplished merely theoretically, since the existence of this abstraction – the pseudo-concrete – is not limited to theoretical existence.[127] It does not entail, however, that such a praxis is without a theoretical aspect. What entails the emancipation from all this is the economic structure that arises from the sursumption of the pseudo-concrete, namely, communism. This entails emphasising the role of political orientation, the importance of political praxis, class in itself, and class for itself, in contrast to pseudo-praxis in social life.

Praxis is the unifying agent between the apparently dual totalities of nature and human, the natural and the social. Such an absolute duality can be envisaged *before* praxis, but not *after*. The *given* then no longer exists as a *mere* given: the given for the contemporary human is already minimally transformed. But this praxis is different from revolutionary praxis. The mere existence of a human being is praxis-laden; its being *is* praxis. This praxis is not limited to labour, if labour is understood as the transformation of the material to make

---

124 Kosík 1976, p. 58. Cf. Von Neuman and Morgenstern 1953, p. 9: 'The individual who attempts to obtain these respective maxima is also said to act "rationally"'.

125 It will be later seen that such an approach towards negativity in relation to contradiction and totality is more fruitful than that of Raya Dunayevskaya (2002).

126 Cf. Albert Camus's observation in *La peste*: 'To fight against abstraction one has to be a little like abstraction' (Camus 2013, p. 550, my translation).

127 Kosík 1976, p. 113: 'Only the proof that economic categories are historical forms of man's objectification and that as products of historical praxis they can be transcended only by practical activity, will indicate the limits of philosophy and the point where revolutionary activity takes over'.

it usable by human beings. Such a labour has a dual function: if reduced to abstract labour it brings along real abstraction. Praxis, if limited to the existence in oneself, also leads to the change of the world and to self-change, but this change–self-change is not yet revolutionary. This is how I believe the 'revolutionary' in Marx is to be understood. This necessitates revolutionary praxis in the sense of mobilisation to put an end, inter alia, to alienating and alienated praxis. But this political mobilisation goes further than being just conjoined with revolutionary praxis. Given that 'political' here means 'having to do with the state', revolutionary praxis *is* political mobilisation. Without a political *class for itself*, what remains of praxis is just the pseudo-praxis of manipulation.

This is how the comprehension of totality, and the revelatory characteristics of concepts (in contradistinction to ideas) lead to a conscious transformation in the pseudo-totality. Unless this is done, the pseudo-totality continues to exist, but dialectically, bearing contradictions and the possibility for such transformative orientation. Unfortunately, this need for the political mobilisation of the proletariat is almost utterly absent in Kosík's scenario. The absence of this point in Marx's theses on Feuerbach is understandable, given that they were not meant for publication, but this absence cannot be justified in Kosík's otherwise exemplary account.[128]

9   Conclusion

The Kosíkian conception of totality contains distinctions and improvements that Kosík himself sometimes does not realise.[129] Nonetheless, it leaves room both for the development of a genuinely Marxian conception of totality as well as a defence of it (which is the task of the chapters to follow). By way of conclusion, here I simply sketch out the main findings of this chapter.

Kosík tells us two things at the end of his book:

> Dialectics is after the subject matter. But the 'subject matter' is no ordinary thing; actually, it is not a thing at all. The 'subject matter' that philosophy deals with is man and his place in the universe or, in different

---

128 *Philosophically* I mean. This is understandable if we remember that he was living in the Post-October era, hence both enjoying this era, and also suffering from the difficulties the Revolution faced. Compare Kosík's letter to Sartre and Sartre's response, found in 'Postface pour l'édition de 1978', in Karel Kosík, *La dialectique du concret*, trans. Roger Dangeville (Paris: F. Maspero, 1978), pp. 173–78.

129 For elaboration on this difference with respect to Lukács's own context, see Chapter 3.

words: it is the totality of the world uncovered in history by man, and man existing in the totality of the world.[130]

Regarding this passage, I would like to reiterate that the *Sache selbst* according to Hegel and in a Marxian approach are different! Hegel makes it clear that for him the *Sache selbst* is the concept.[131] However, Kosík does not mention this difference. When he says that the *Sache selbst* as the quest of dialectics, or even of philosophy, is 'man' as an ontocosmic existent, we should read this as being restricted to a particular Marxian conception of totality. Materialist dialectic and idealist dialectic have different subject matters, each with a distinctive detour [*Oklika*]. Put differently, neither Hegelian dialectical idealism nor dialectical materialism, once limited to a few characteristics of this dialectics, entails a Marxian conception of totality. In fact, as we have seen, some characteristics of totality can be adopted by plainly anti-revolutionary representatives of the bourgeoisie. As we will see in the following chapter, it is only a particular conception of totality that is a genuinely Marxian one, and only such a standpoint brings about a normative conception of totality with which the need for revolution is associated; only in this way can we witness the revolutionary comprehension-formation of reality as totality. Nonetheless, along with this comes also the increasingly nuanced grasp of totality through the different phases of development in Marx's thinking, but such a grasp is absent in the Kosíkian reading. One thing that Kosík does not say is that there is a difference between Marx's standpoint regarding totality in the 1844 *Economic and Philosophical Manuscripts* on the one hand, and the *Grundrisse* and *Capital* on the other: in the 1844 *Manuscripts*, there is a more anthropological conception of totality, whereas in his later work he develops a politico-economic conception. But this difference, *pace* Althusser, does not entail that Marx's thinking underwent a coupure. I agree rather with Kosík that there is unity through different phases of Marx's thinking, but I disagree with him in his failure to see the differences and development.[132] Rather, to repeat an oft-cited dialectical slogan, I show the similarity in difference, in the following chapters.

One further merit of Kosík's standpoint is that it sees the unity of analysis and critique in what Marx does. As Kosík puts it, 'the analysis of economic

---

130   Kosík 1976, p. 153.
131   See Hegel 1969b, p. 29: 'With the introduction of content in logical consideration, not the things but the subject matter, the concept of things, becomes the object*'' (my translation).
132   See Kosík 1976, pp. 129–30, where he expresses his infatuation with the publication of the *Grundrisse*, in which he sees Marx dealing with the themes already developed in the 1844 Manuscripts. A similar view is expressed by Schmidt 1971, p. 214.

relations is a twofold critique':[133] that is, it is a rectification of the conception implied by classical economics, accomplished by showing what the real categories are; but Marx's work also 'exhibits the real movement of economic categories as a reified form of the social movement of people'.[134] But given that Kosík highlights the function of the method of inquiry in contradistinction to the method of exposition, the question arises: At what point in Marx's work does this become possible? I will show in Chapters 5 and 6 that this is done in different phases of the methods of inquiry and exposition, and it is only in the latter that we find the categorial movement. In other words, it is not the case that 'the categories dialectically unfold the internal organization of a given society's economic structure'[135] at *every* moment of investigation. This cannot be done unless an intertwined *starting point-categorial movement* is already established, which is the case only in *Capital*, but not in the *Grundrisse*.

Likewise, when Marx says that dialectic, in its reified form, was incorporated by the Germans, this reification can apply equally to a materialist standpoint or an idealist one. To deal with this issue, the inherent revolutionariness of the dialectics claimed by Marx in the Afterword to the second German edition of *Capital* Volume I requires further clarification. A more comprehensive conception of totality, which changes in different phases of Marx's thought though it persists from his earlier phases to the later phases, is the subject of the next chapter.

---

133   Kosík 1976, p. 115.
134   Ibid.
135   Kosík 1976, p. 114.

CHAPTER 5

Marxian Totality Seen through His Works

This chapter aims to trace the development of the conception of totality in different periods of Marx's works – a development that, like the development of his position in general, is neither continuous nor smooth.[1] It is thus a response to one of the difficulties that arose from Kosík's account of totality discussed in the previous chapter: Kosík recognises a difference between the method of enquiry and the method of exposition, but he overlooks how such a difference, among others, may be traced back to Marx's works regarding totality.[2] Instead, he gives a somewhat monolithic account of Marx's conception of totality and expresses his joy at the discovery of the *Grundrisse* as the text that puts an end to the claim that there is a dichotomy between the works of the young and the mature Marx.[3]

As an alternative, this chapter, by arguing for a developmental coherence in Marx's works, proposes a nuanced reading of his conception of totality. First, it evaluates the suggestion that the later works of Marx may be considered a dialectically honed restatement and development of the claims and themes found in two of his earliest works, namely, the letter to his father and his poem *Epigrams* (hereafter, Letter and Poem respectively), both written in 1837, when Marx was only nineteen years old. In the next section, I underscore the themes found in these two texts through a close textual analysis. In each of the following sections, I will show how each of the texts from the *Economic and Philosophical Manuscripts of 1844* to *Capital* relates with these themes, what was retained, what was added, and what was surmounted or completely discarded, always in relationship with the conception of totality as my guiding thread. The result of this chapter will thus be a demonstration of the development of a Marxian conception of totality from a quasi-anthropological one in the *Economic and Philosophical Manuscripts of 1844* to a concrete onto-formative one in the *Grundrisse* and *Capital*, notwithstanding the difference between these two.

---

1 See Heinrich 2016.
2 The other difficulty arising from Kosík's account – the very distinction between the method of enquiry and the method of exposition, and the function of these two in Marx's works – will be discussed in the next chapter.
3 Kosík 1976, pp. 129–30.

This chapter then argues against the reading that believes that 'Any project of "reconstruction", in the sense of revealing a certain core of textual foundations, to be used as a main source for uncovering the coherent kernel of Marx's critique, must fail when we take into account the totality and the inner connections of the texts passed down'.[4] The conclusion recapitulates some of the characteristics of a Marxian conception of totality, which will be developed further in Chapter 6.

A Note on the Difficulty and the Strategy Adopted

But before that, a note on the difficulty of the project represented by this chapter. In a letter to Engels written on 31 July 1865,[5] the perfectionist Marx remarks that he cannot persuade himself to send what he has written for publication unless he has the whole subject in front of him. The advantage of the result would be, he claims, a text that has a dialectical structure and that forms an artistic whole. Of course, not analytical elegance but rigour, coherence and empirical confirmation were Marx's primary concerns. Nonetheless, his perfectionist attitude makes it challenging to discuss both his work in general and the subject at hand, namely, 'totality' – indeed, all the more so, given that it is estimated that we are still about a couple of decades away from the completion of the critical publication of Marx-Engels Complete Works (MEGA²) in about 120 volumes.[6]

Among all the major works concentrated on here, only the first volume of *Capital* has the characteristics endorsed by Marx – and that notwithstanding all the digressions found in it. Published after all the works discussed here, but not written after them, although placed first in the three volumes of *Capital*, it must be taken as a sort of criterion-bearer, as that which holds the criterion, for any discussion, all the more so given the general view that the latter, the more developed is always to shed light on the earlier, the less developed. But even here a challenging question arises: Which version of *Capital* is to be taken as the

---

4 Finelli 2009, p. 91.
5 Here is the full quote: 'But I cannot bring myself to send anything off until I have the whole thing in front of me. WHATEVER SHORTCOMINGS THEY MAY HAVE, the advantage of my writings is that they are an artistic whole, and this can only be achieved through my practice of never having things printed until I have them in front of me *in their entirety*. This is impossible with Jacob Grimm's method which is in general better with writings that have no dialectical structure' (Marx, letter to Engels, 31 July 1865, in Marx and Engels 1987b, p. 173).
6 Bellofiore and Fineschi 2009, p. 11.

source? Chronologically, the French translation, edited personally by Marx, was published with his introduction on 28 April 1875, three years after the second German edition; it would seem then that this version should be taken as his last word. However, the difficulty arises as to the acceptability of those modifications, generally minor as they may be. This is complicated by Marx's advice to native German-speakers to consult this French edition, even as he suggested that he has simplified the work in some parts.[7] Another difficulty is the role played by Engels, not only in editing the fourth edition of the first volume, but also because of his substantial and much debated role in the second volume and especially the third. As for the first volume, I adhere mainly to the fourth edition.[8] An alternative approach, integrating the French editions, and further exploring the points made above about these editions, would make the project unfeasible. As to the second and third volumes, I stick mainly to the texts edited by Engels, and refer to the MEGA² edition only when needed. In each case the precise references will be given.

This starting point of the finalised text as the criterion does not mean that I am ignoring the genesis of the first volume as criterion; nonetheless, this genesis is also to be understood from the perspective of this criterion.[9] The methodological implication applied is that things are to be evaluated backward, from *Capital* to the *Grundrisse* and then the so-called early writings. Given the small number of the finalised texts at hand, a large amount of speculation is in any case inevitable. All this makes the determination of a finalised text, as the criterion according to which the other works should be evaluated, impossible. This is one absolute theoretical obstacle to any Marxian study. Later, a practical absolute obstacle to such a study will be discussed.

---

7 See Marx, letter to Danielson, 15 November 1878 (Marx and Engels 1991, p. 343). See also Heinrich 2016, p. 124. I say 'this edition' (i.e., the French translation by Joseph M. Roy, revised and endorsed by Marx; available in reprint as Marx 1982), since the most well-known and most cited French translation of *Capital* is the one by Jean-Pierre Lefebvre (Marx 1993). As far as I know, the new translation into Persian (Marx 2008) is so far the only translation into any language which has integrated both the fourth German edition and the French edition by Roy. For further information, see Afary 2012.
8 That is Marx 1976 for English edition and Marx 1962a for the German edition.
9 See Bellofiore 2009, p. 179: 'The most developed is the key for the knowledge of the less developed, but we also have to understand the genesis of Marx's exposition of the concept of capital'.

1   Prelude – The Poem and the Letter to His Father:[10] Marx, a Diver in Search of the *Sache selbst* in Life in the Street

In these two texts, *The Poem and the Letter*, and in his search for the subject matter [*Sache selbst*], to use a term highlighted by Kosík, Marx introduces some themes whose development leads ultimately to a distinctive conception of totality in *Capital*. Since the themes of these two texts overlap, I discuss them thematically. I will show that while it may be rightly claimed that there is a similarity between the style of these poems and Marx's later works,[11] the continuity goes farther than this and the influence stays with Marx throughout his works.

Let us begin with a passage from his poem *Epigramme on Hegel*. In a part of this poem, we read:

> Kant and Fichte soar the ether
> Seeking for some distant land,
> I but seek to grasp profoundly
> What I found up on the street.[12]

The metaphor of the street recalls social life, where things pass both necessarily and contingently, an example of the realm of events. But what happens on the street, contingent or necessary, has laws and also evinces exceptions to those laws. Finding those laws and their exceptions necessitates analysis, and once coupled with the ought-is opposition reflected in the letter (which will be discussed later in this section), it furthermore involves action that goes beyond observation, contemplation, and the merely empirical.[13] What happens on the street and the judgement about what happens brings about both the subjective and objective aspects of the street. The response to the question, 'What, "of" that which is of the street, is of concern?' opens the door to a twofold response, objective and subjective. Moreover, this 'of' (introducing the object of discussion) will later be shown to be developed into the critique 'of' political economy: the critique of political economy is both the critique of

---

10   All the quotations from Marx's letter to his father are from McLellan 2000, pp. 9–13.
11   See Johnston 1967, p. 260: 'Yet an obvious continuity between Marx's verse and his later work lies in the style of his writing. His love of metaphor, his use of allusions, his construction of complex sentences all bear witness to his early exercises as a composer of verse'. It is noteworthy that Johnston does not deny any similarity as to content.
12   My translation. German text in Marx 1968g, p. 608: 'Kant und Fichte gern zum Äther schweifen, / Suchten dort ein fernes Land, / Doch ich such' nur tüchtig zu begreifen, / Was ich – auf der Straße fand!'
13   This diremption between 'ought' and 'is' is thought to be also the standpoint endorsed by Hegel. See 'Ausblick: Logik, Rechtsphilosophie und Marxsche Kritik' in Theunissen 1980.

the subject being discussed, and the way it is analysed by political economy. When we consider today what happened in the life of the same street yesterday, history comes in. The street is equally the reflection of the materiality of life, and its dialectic. Nonetheless, what happens on the street brings along with it not only the metabolism of the life of the street, its reason and unreason, its sociality, history-time, and the lawfulness and the contingency of what passes on the street, but also the thought about the 'tomorrow' of the street; hence, the importance of the future, a bedrock of the Marxian standpoint not only distinct from Kant and Fichte as mocked here, but also from Hegel. In taking such a standpoint, although it may not be wrong to say that Marx at this stage is not a full-fledged materialist, this may be taken *cum grano salis*, as he criticises simultaneously Kant and Fichte, as we have seen, and also finds Hegel 'to be no less fond than his predecessors of the "ether" and "the distant land"',[14] and criticises his intention by saying that even with his leadership one cannot plumb the ocean of the subject matter [*Sache selbst*].

1.1   Methodology-Logic

The relation between Marx and Hegel, especially as regards their method or logic, has been the subject of a myriad of books, dissertations, and articles. In the Letter, Marx admits that Hegel's system is distinctive: 'for it had actually to be a new logic'.[15] Explanation of this logic and the relation between his own work and Hegel's logic is something that Marx never overlooks and yet unfortunately never fully elaborates upon. That said, a becoming, a transformation for which the objects are mere abstractions is the tenet to which he remains loyal through and through.

As will be seen in the following chapter, one of the major claims to be made here is the utterly new concept of starting point, that of investigation, put forward by Marx. In this very letter, we can discern the germ of this new conception, as Marx talks about a dialogue he wrote entitled 'Cleanthes, or The Starting Point and Necessary Progress of Philosophy'. About this dialogue, he writes that art and philosophy, previously taken to be completely separate, 'regained to some extent their unity'.[16] The obsession with the starting point, as well as the unification of human knowledge referred to here, remained with Marx throughout his life. In this letter, we see the germ of the internal relation, or interconnectedness, which in the hands of some contemporary Marxist philosophers became the principal characteristic of a genuinely Marxian

---

14   Johnston 1967, p. 262.
15   Marx, Letter to his father, in McLellan 2000, p. 12.
16   Marx, Letter to his father, in McLellan 2000, p. 12.

approach.[17] The young Marx on several occasions sees this interconnectedness between 'Jurisprudence and ... philosophy' and he searches for 'an intellectual activity that finds expression on all sides – in science, art, and personal matters'.[18]

1.2 Praxis in Methodology

We know an occasion, in *The Phenomenology of Spirit*, where Hegel finds a *Zutat* from our (subjective) side to be superfluous[19] – we must merely observe. Such a standpoint is criticised in the two texts at hand. In the Poem, 'The German Public', who is personified sitting in his armchair, is mocked for merely watching and remaining ignorant while events pass by. Although the Germans will be later criticised for having accompanied freedom only at its funeral,[20] Marx's criticism here is not limited to the German public, for the same can equally be said of those who write books, that is, intellectuals. Thus, the criticism includes not only the general public but also the smart-alecks, and professorial searchers after useless minute distinctions, in adopting what Hegel would attribute to the role of philosophy: The owl of Minerva comes post factum, 'And writes a book: *The Commotion Is Over*'.[21]

Instead, what is needed is to adopt a standpoint affirming the unity of these two poles in a totality: to take all social life, including, on the one hand, the discussion of truth as a practical issue, and[22] on the other, a practical methodology competent to resolve the problems and contradictions of the status quo – a praxis to 'dissolve the shit', as Marx would put it some thirty years later.[23] With this, we see the germ of the notion of truth which will be developed and reformulated very succinctly in the *Theses on Feuerbach*. In putting forward this point here, Marx is already distancing itself from seeing the truth as the criterion of itself and of falsehood, which reminds one of Spinoza.[24] This is also

---

17 For further development of this standpoint, see Ollman 2003.
18 Marx, Letter to his father, in McLellan 2000, p. 10.
19 Hegel 1980b, p. 77.
20 This is later underscored in the opening pages of his Introduction to *A Contribution to the Critique of Hegel's Philosophy of Right*.
21 Marx 1968g, p. 607: 'der Lärm sei vorbei'.
22 See Johnston 1967, p. 265.
23 Marx, letter to Engels, 30 April 1868 (Marx and Engels 1992c, p. 25).
24 'Truth is as little modest as light, and towards whom should it be so? Towards itself? Verum index sui et falsi.* Therefore, towards falsehood?' Marx 1975c, p. 112. The complete sentence in Spinoza's *Ethics* is as follows: 'Sane sicut lux se ipsam et tenebras manifestat, sic veritas norma sui et falsi est' (As the light makes both itself and the darkness plain, so truth is the standard both of itself and of the false; Spinoza 1985, p. 479). Given the theme of the text, that is censorship, it may be said that here Marx, with his rather seemingly rhetorical

the reaction to the complete opposition between 'ought' and 'is' referred to in the letter to his father discussed in this section. This practical-methodological standpoint (a meta-methodology, so to speak), which is best reflected in an authentic standpoint with regard to totality, is, as stated by Lukács, both the result and the presupposition of the class struggle.[25] If all questions of truth ultimately find their answer in practice, this is *par excellence* true about such a Marxian thought-praxis, and also about Marx's methodology.

The relation between 'is' and 'ought' deserves further elaboration. In reference to this letter and such passages as 'Here the same opposition of "is" and "ought" which is the hallmark of idealism was the dominating and very destructive feature,'[26] David McLellan writes that Marx *soon* changed his belief 'in a romantic opposition of what is and what ought to be'.[27] In fact, it was as soon as the following page *in the same letter* that he changed his mind: '[I]f the gods before had dwelt above the earth, they had now become its centre'.[28] As will be seen, this is one of the bedrocks of *The German Ideology*.

1.3 Dialectics and Mathematics

One question regarding Marx's works is the reason for the almost complete absence of the application of mathematics in his investigation. This evaluation must be revised once it is realised that he in fact did write *Mathematical Manuscripts*,[29] and although he was admittedly not a mathematician, his knowledge was probably good enough to apply mathematical concepts in his works. But the issue runs deeper and has some similarity with Hegel's standpoint on mathematics. Hegel writes on one occasion that mathematics deals with the abstractions of number and space, the non-existent sensibles.[30] Marx, reflecting this position, writes:

> [F]rom the outset the unscientific form of mathematical dogmatism where one circles round a subject, reasoning back and forth, without letting it unfold its own rich and living content, prevented any grasp of

---

question, is being rhapsodic about truth. Cf. Milton's *Areopagitica*: 'Let her [Truth] and Falshood grapple; who ever knew Truth put to the wors, in a free and open encounter. Her confuting is the best and surest suppressing' (Milton 1918, p. 58).

25   The full quote, in which Lukács quotes a sentence by Marx to support his standpoint, can be found in Lukács 1970, pp. 89–90.
26   McLellan 2000, p. 11.
27   McLellan 2000, p. 5.
28   Marx, Letter to his father, in McLellan 2000, p. 12.
29   Marx 1983c.
30   See Hegel 1980a, p. 70.

the truth. The mathematician constructs and proves the triangle, but it remains a pure abstraction in space and does not develop any further; you have to put it beside something else and then it takes up other positions and it is the juxtaposition of these different things that gives it different relationships and truths. Whereas in the practical expression of the living world of ideas in which law, the state, nature, and the whole of philosophy consist, the object itself must be studied in its own development, arbitrary divisions must not be introduced, and it is the ratio of the object [*Vernunft des Dinges*] itself which must develop out of its inner contradictions and find unity within itself.[31]

Accordingly, an organic totality goes beyond the mathematical system and cannot be reduced to mathematical elaboration.[32]

The inability of mathematics to penetrate the *Sache selbst* and its content reminds us of the form-content relationship in dialectics. It is well known that a dialectical conception does not see this relationship as one between two segregated poles. Marx here criticises his earlier understanding of this relationship:

[Prior to this] I meant by form the necessary structure of the expressions of an idea and by matter the necessary quality of these expressions. The fault here was that I believed that the one could and must develop itself independently of the other and thus I did not obtain a true form but merely a desk into whose drawers I proceeded to pour sand.[33]

This will have very important repercussions in the future development of his work. First, as will be shown his treatment of categories is closer to Hegel than to Kant, and in it the dialectical unity of form and content leads to the categorial movement.[34] The word 'movement' here is to be understood as what Marx calls *metamorphosis*, that is, a simultaneous transformation and reproduction of form.[35] In the categorial movement, each category is transformed into the one that succeeds it and also in so doing the succeeding category reproduces

---

31 Marx, Letter to his father, in McLellan 2000, p. 11.
32 See Fahey et al. 2009, p. 263.
33 Marx, Letter to his father, in McLellan 2000, p. 11.
34 See Hegel, *The Science of Logic*, Book 2, Part 1, Chapter 3, A. Absolute Ground 2 (Hegel 1969c, pp. 80–95; Hegel 2010, pp. 389–97).
35 See Reichelt 2007, p. 36.

the prior one at a different level. The second point indicates Marx's suspicion of definition, since it is a form of 'subsumption'.[36] In the same vein, although he admits the importance of ideas, he criticises 'purely formal art which has no objects to inspire it and no exciting progress of ideas'.[37] Moreover, as is well known, Marx's methodological endeavour – which he later calls the application of the 'power of abstraction' – entails going beyond the phenomena. Here he puts it metaphorically: by 'diving off into the sea ... to bring the pure pearls up to the sunlight'.[38]

Although the themes introduced here are admittedly scattered, partly owing to the nature of the texts, and partly owing to what I am trying to demonstrate, a number of conceptions related to totality can be seen here. It remains to be seen whether these themes find repercussions in the conception of totality in Marx's subsequent works. It is to this question that we now turn.

2   Marx in the Laboratory: *Economic and Philosophical Manuscripts of 1844*

The first major point of elaboration on the conception of totality is undoubtedly the newly maturing, though still fragmentary, attempt where Marx first criticises the previous theories in political economy and philosophy and begins to develop his own – as if in a laboratory – namely the *Economic and Philosophical Manuscripts of 1844*. This elaboration can be identified in spite of the fact that the work is no more than a gathering of notes, parts of which are no longer available, written with self-clarification as their primary goal.

We witness here a critical approach towards a conception of totality, in the form of an intertwined critique of political economy and of Hegel simultaneously. As to the former, Marx first plays the game of political economy and aims at showing its shortcomings without questioning its premises. Then he does what political economy does not do: he explains the movement of the subject of political economy as it really is, this time while showing the shortcomings of the premises. A major flaw of political economy is that it does not see the alienation intrinsic to the very nature of labour, which cannot be overcome with the premises of political economy left unquestioned. As to a central point on this text related to labour, namely alienation, Marx sees all

---

36   Marx 1963a, p. 228: 'Es handelt sich nicht hier zum Definitionen, unter welchen die Dinge subsumiert werden.'
37   Marx, Letter to his father, in McLellan 2000, p. 12.
38   Marx, Letter to his father, in McLellan 2000, p. 12.

four moments of alienation as a whole. The result is the threefold alienation of the worker: from the object* and the process of his labour (objective* alienation), from himself as the subject of the labour (subjective alienation), and from others, and from his species (intersubjective alienation). This particular approach, in which no aspect is overlooked, even at this stage, provides the germ of a conception of totality that will be fleshed out only in the future, a conception that is neither objectivistic nor subjectivistic. Hence, although it may rightly be argued that Marx develops an anthropology[39] here (what leads to further study of his works as an anthropologist)[40] his attempt to distance himself from what he calls anthropology in the limited sense should not be overlooked. Through this attempt, Marx intends to adopt an ontological standpoint, which is admittedly at this stage still of rather a biological cast, encrusted with terms such as genus, species, etc.

At about the same time as these *Manuscripts*, Marx writes 'Our products would be so many mirrors in which we saw reflected our essential nature'.[41] With reference to this, some commentators have found Marx's conception of totality in the *Manuscripts* to be similar to that of Leibniz, in which 'unsursumable [*unaufhebbar*] individuality' is mirrored.[42] Nonetheless, given that individuals externalise their existence through labour, with reciprocity of their activity as its quintessential characteristic, this similarity with monads as soul-like immaterial entities may be taken *cum grano salis*. What comes right after this passage is clarificatory: 'This relationship would moreover be reciprocal; what occurs on my side has also to occur on yours'.[43]

It may be helpful in this respect to consider another passage. In a part of the *Manuscripts* we read: 'Insofar as man is human, and hence also his feeling, etc., is human, the affirmation of the object* by another is likewise his own enjoyment'.[44] The transindividuality of man is here confirmed; this is in contradistinction to the standpoint of political economy, which takes the isolated

---

39   Grumley 1989, p. 43.
40   See Patterson 2009.
41   'Comments on James Mill's Éléments d'économie politique', Marx, Engels Collected Works 3, p. 228. 'Our Productions would be just so many mirrors from which our essence reflects itself'. Marx 1968a, p. 463 (my translation).
42   Arndt 2012, p. 38. A similar point is developed in Dardot and Laval 2012, pp. 352 and 740 n. 89.
43   'Dies Verhältnis wird dabei wechselseitig, von deiner Seite geschehe, was von meiner gesch[ieht]'. Marx 1968a, p. 463.
44   Marx 1968d, p. 563: '[I]nsofern der Mensch menschlich, also auch seine Empfindung etc. menschlich ist, ist die Bejahung des Gegenstandes durch einen andren, ebenfalls sein eigner Genuß' (my translation).

individuals in their segregation as economic subjects[45] and deprives them of the totality of their social relations by reducing them to the status of an individuated worker or capitalist. Marx mocks the treatment of political economy in the following words: 'In place of the *wealth* and *poverty* of political economy come the *rich human being* and rich human need. The *rich* human being is simultaneously the human being *in need of* a totality of human life-activities – the man in whom his own realisation exists as an inner necessity, as *need*'.[46]

Although this elaboration on totality is admittedly still not even as clear as the assertion of an 'ensemble of social relations' as the essence of the human (this will be discussed in the next section of this chapter), it paves the way for this latter reformulation. To the same effect, along with underscoring internal relations, a methodological characteristic, elaborated further in *Capital* Volume I[47] (where it is claimed that the properties of an object do not stem from other objects but find their activation or affirmation by being activated in relation with others) has its background here. An excellent example of the intertwinedness of the methodological and practical questions is also found in this text: other objects are activations of the existence of one object, not of that from which their existence stems; other humans are equally the activation of each individual, and hence should not be taken to be the *means* of one another reciprocally.[48]

The not yet full-fledged materialist character of these *Manuscripts* is well-known.[49] Understanding these *Manuscripts* as a materialist text, one may ask in just what way they reveal Marx's materialist stance. The text may be taken as an attempt 'to seek the idea in the real itself'.[50] This undoubtedly has repercussions for the conception of totality. As hinted at in the previous chapter, a Marxian conception of totality is among other things a non-objectivistic materialism. If so, the idealist unity of thinking and being should be overcome[51] in order to propose such a materialist standpoint.

This is where Marx's discussion of Hegel seems to be relevant. There Marx shows not only Hegel's achievement but also the shortcomings of his two major

---

45 Halbwachs 1937, p. 10.
46 Marx and Engels 1988, p. 111.
47 Marx 1976, p. 149.
48 Marx and Engels 1988, p. 128: '[I]nsofar as each becomes a means for the other ...'
49 Cf. Marx and Engels 1988, p. 154: '[C]onsistent naturalism or humanism distinguishes itself both from idealism and materialism, constituting at the same time the unifying truth of both. We see also how only naturalism is capable of comprehending the act of world history'.
50 McLellan 2000, p. 12.
51 Marx and Engels 1988, pp. 105–6.

works, *The Science of Logic* and *The Phenomenology of Spirit*. One point in Marx's elaboration on a distinctive conception of totality is a clarification of the distinction between the status of an object* *in itself, for itself*, and *for us*. This is a distinction that is recognised in Hegel's system. To the same effect, as will be seen in Chapter 6, Marx critically adopts Hegel's term *Moment*. The point is that whereas Hegel uses this term in the sense of 'momentum' (reflected in *das Moment* and avoiding *der Moment*, which has the temporal notion of the term), at this stage Marx recognises and highlights this distinction in Hegel's system by seeing movement as the totality of moments.[52] The relationship between moments of consciousness and the object*, for instance, must be a relationship that involves the totality of the determinations of the objects* and each of those determinations must be comprehended on its own terms.[53]

To the same effect, to have a distinctive totality that is both materialist and dialectical, as a distinctive characteristic of Marxian methodology, we need a distinctive doctrine of abstraction, one that is not only distinct from Aristotelian abstraction and Lockean empiricist abstraction, but also from Hegelian abstraction. This culminates methodologically in the well-known passage in the preface to the first edition of *Capital* Volume I, in the recognition of the power of abstraction in Marx's methodological approach, as an apparatus that *replaces* a microscope and chemical agents. At this stage, Marx is critical of Hegel's abstraction. Marx gives him credit for having recognised in the *Phenomenology of Spirit* the processual characteristic of the autogenesis of the human being, its formation through labour, and its concomitant dialectical negativity,[54] and hence his highlighting the whole of human action [*Gesamtwirken der Menschen*].[55] He finds it erroneous, however, to equate the essence of human being with consciousness. Furthermore, he somewhat sardonically introduces the moments of Hegel's *Science of Logic* resulting in *Absolute Idee*, which is nothing but the totality of all the already sursumed [*aufge-*

---

52   Marx and Engels 1988, p. 152. This will be seen later in the *Grundrisse*. Nicolaus elaborates well upon this issue: 'Hegel takes "moment" from Newton, despite the general disdain for "mechanics", he derives the sense of this rather central concept from the action of the lever. ... In Marx the term carries the senses both of "period of time" and of "force of moving mass". He much improves on Hegel's use; Hegel's usage was more mechanical; and time was absent from it' (Martin Nicolaus's foreword to the *Grundrisse* in Marx 1973, p. 29; see also Gauthier 2010, pp. 69–75).
53   Marx and Engels 1988, p. 152.
54   Marx and Engels 1988, p. 149.
55   Marx and Engels 1988, pp. 149–50.

hobene] abstractions. Thus introduced, Absolute Idea is propelled to externalise itself as its exact pole of opposition, that is, nature.[56]

One important neighbouring concept of totality is undoubtedly unity. In the *Manuscripts*, Marx proposes two important points. The first is the twofold unity of nature and society on the one hand, and natural studies and social studies on the other. The second is related to the possibility of ideal reflection of a totality in a man, who in turn is a totality. Marx puts this in the following words:

> Man, much as he may therefore be a particular individual (and it is precisely his particularity which makes him an individual, and a real individual social being), is just as much the totality the ideal totality – the subjective existence of thought and experienced society present for itself; just as he exists also in the real world as the awareness and the real enjoyment of social existence, and as a totality of human life-activity.[57]

We finish this section on this exploratory writing in Marx's laboratory, by assessing Marx's standpoint regarding what makes possible the conception of totality in our era, related to the unity of society and nature on the one hand and to the study of these on the other. It has often been asserted that the concept of totality was first elaborated in modern philosophy by Spinoza.[58] A question that arises is the reason for such an elaboration in the seventeenth and eighteenth centuries. In this laboratory stage of his thought, Marx offers a reason for the possibility of the scientific conceptualisation of totality in the capitalist mode of production. In the era of developed industry, private property plays a mediating role that enables individuals to collectively grasp the existing totality and its inherent contradictions. A step forward at this stage is that, whereas political economy and Proudhon see a contradiction between private property and labour, Marx sees the contradiction within labour itself.[59] This itself is the outcome of the recognition of the practical activity of people, which equally brings about the science of humans; with this, the essential nature of the human to embrace totality is born. Thus, the tenets which put the human being outside

---

56 Marx and Engels 1988, p. 163.
57 Marx and Engels 1988, p. 105.
58 Kosík 1976, p. 17.
59 Marx and Engels 1988, p. 81: 'Political economy starts from labor as the real soul of production; yet to labor it gives nothing, and to private property everything. From this contradiction Proudhon has concluded in favor of labor and against private property. We understand, however, that this apparent contradiction is the contradiction of estranged labor with itself, and that political economy has merely formulated the laws of estranged labor'. This is further discussed in this chapter and the following.

nature and also reduce the function of the human being to mere observation utterly miss the point: their approach inevitably leads to the ascription of the status of thing-in-itself to nature.[60] Marxian totality is thus coincident with humanity: man turns into simultaneously subjective and objective* totality, in which subject and object are two moments of totality.

We will see why Marx in his later works takes it that revolutionising such a totality, which I call pseudototality, becomes possible and also necessary. The following section is one step in this direction.

3 Prototype-Genesis: Totality in the *German Ideology* and the 'Theses on Feuerbach'

In this section, I will show how the conception of totality is advanced in these two texts; and how the ascertainment of totality and neighbouring concepts by Marx and Engels in the *German Ideology* and by Marx in the 'Theses on Feuerbach' pave the way towards the maturation of those concepts in the following sections.

Marx and Engels give Hegel credit for not merely registering the objects of thought but also exposing the act of production of the objects.[61] Notwithstanding this, their book is, to a large extent, a polemical work against the tendency of the young Hegelians to simply prolong his enterprise – that is, for not being adequately critical of his views.[62] One significant component of Marx and Engels's positive alternative here is their defence of a unified science of history with its two inseparable facets, the history of nature and the history of humans, which mutually condition each other. This unified standpoint is simultaneously a criticism of Hegelian abstraction, which, with its focus on consciousness and abstract ideas, is inevitably idealistically reduc-

---

60 Cf. Sekine 1998, p. 436: 'We can only gain partial knowledge of the [behaviour of the nature] by constantly observing it from outside. ... The thing-in-itself of nature always remains beyond our reach.' On another occasion, Sekine surprisingly writes: 'Since we are ourselves not the *creator* of nature, we cannot hope to know it totally' (Sekine 1997a, p. 3, emphasis added). This may remind the reader of a famous passage in Hume's *Dialogues concerning Natural Religion* (Hume 2007, p. 25): '[I]s a part of nature a rule for another part very wide of the former? Is it a rule for the whole? Is a very small part a rule for the universe? Is nature in one situation, a certain rule for nature in another situation, vastly different from the former?' We have seen previously how a Kosíkian reading can give a satisfactory response to this dilemma: see Chapter 4, section 1 above.
61 Marx and Engels 1978, p. 14.
62 Dardot and Laval 2012, p. 137.

tionist.⁶³ Marx and Engels's alternative, underscoring the material activity of individuals through material interactions among one another, the language of the effective life as the concretisation of the subject matter [*Sache selbst*], replaces an idealist treatment of ideology with a new scientific one.⁶⁴ To the same effect, given that according to the alternative reading given by Marx and Engels, '[c]onsciousness cannot exist as anything other than a being that is conscious',⁶⁵ which in turn boils down to the being's real-life process, the cause of the upside-down character of false consciousness should be sought in real life.

This emphasis on the role of the individuals and on stripping history of its ideality should not be taken as a rejection of history as a holistic process that embraces a totality consisting of both nature and history.⁶⁶ It instead brings real individuals, the producers of material life in their life process, back onto the stage as the only history makers,⁶⁷ recognising their inherent dynamic relationship with the totality of social life.

After the criticism of Hegelian abstraction, and its idealism, putting it back on its feet, this is the second front of Marx and Engels's criticism: against a reductionist empiricism that reduces all relations to what can be experienced. Put differently, their emphasis on empirical observation in a political-social context, should be taken as a warning against mystification and speculation.⁶⁸ Hence the inference of the abstraction from the *empirical* does not entail reducing those abstractions to what can be sensibly experienced.⁶⁹ This twofold criticism, in enhanced form in later works, leads to a specifically Marxian abstraction that gives rise to a specifically Marxian version of totality.

The starting point introduced here is the activity of people's material life – not what they say, think, or imagine, but the actual life process in its materiality.⁷⁰ Ideology, thought, morality, religion, and imagination are taken to be

---

63 This is also criticised by Marx and Engels in *The Holy Family*, particularly the chapter 'Das Geheimnis der spekulativen Konstruktion' (Marx and Engels 1962, pp. 59–63).
64 Marx and Engels 1978, p. 18.
65 The subtlety and beauty of the phrase cannot be adequately translated into English: 'Das Bewußtsein kann nie etwas Andres sein als das bewußte Sein' (Marx and Engels 1978, p. 26).
66 Grumley 1989, p. 48. 'The totality of history has no immanent meaning aside from that created and ascribed to it by the practices of living, concrete individuals'.
67 Marx and Engels 1978, p. 25. This will be developed by Marx into the guiding thread of his subsequent works; see Marx 1961c, p. 8.
68 Marx and Engels 1978, p. 25.
69 Arndt 2012, p. 59: 'It derives its abstractions from the empirical experience [*das Empirie*], without reducing them to what is sensually experienceable' (my translation).
70 As will be seen later, the starting point becomes more nuanced and complex in later works but the materiality introduced here is kept through and through.

rather like the epiphenomena of this life, which are often nothing more than illusion [*Schein*], and have illusory independence. An ascending movement from the concrete to the abstract, here in the form of the movement from earth to heaven, will take the place of the descent from the abstract to the concrete, from heaven to earth, reminiscent of what was seen in the previous section with its focus on street life. This is an anti-metaphysical methodological movement: going from the material life of individuals as the producers of consciousness to consciousness, instead of from the consciousness of individuals to them as individuals. While the former movement concentrates on history and its development, the latter focuses on the epiphenomena of the former. That is how the *German Ideology* comes up with the well-known slogan that it is not consciousness – with the clarification seen here – that determines the life, but life that determines consciousness.[71]

Here a series of presuppositions are introduced for such a standpoint. In introducing them, the *German Ideology* distances itself from a Hegelian standpoint, as found in the beginning of the *Science of Logic*, where being presuppositionless and having presuppositions are both shown to be wrong starting points, and the beginning is a presupposed-presuppositionlessness. That said, it seems to be difficult to introduce an objection against the presuppositions proposed by Marx and Engels here. These presuppositions are, put briefly, the existence of individuals and their relations to nature to meet their needs; these relations bring up newer needs; with that comes the need to produce progeny; this entails a twofold natural-social relationship. These are what the later works take as already established points. This is the earthly basis that should, as a whole, be taken into consideration in any historical treatment of a society.[72]

As seen in Chapter 4, a distinction is made here between history as the real historical subject of study, and history as the sum of dead facts. What turns the real history into the sum of dead facts is the active living process of the individuals. This is the precise twofold criticism seen previously: neither the abstract individual proposed by Feuerbach, nor the haughty Subject of the idealists can do the job of displaying the real historical process.[73] Nonetheless, mere criticism is insufficient, and this is one of the dictums of the *German Ideology*: the impetus, the driving force of the history of religion, of philosophy or any other theory is the revolution not the critique.[74]

---

71   Marx and Engels 1978, p. 27.
72   Marx and Engels 1978, p. 28.
73   Marx and Engels 1978, p. 27.
74   Marx and Engels 1978, p. 38.

As to the relationship between the role of revolution and communism, compared with the *Manuscripts of 1844* a more nuanced account is being developed here. Whereas communism, 'the position that is the negation of negation', was introduced in the *Manuscripts of 1844* as the mystery and solution to the status quo,[75] a mediating step needed towards socialism, communism is here introduced not as a state of affairs to be realised, nor as a teleologically envisaged ideal, but as the daily effective real movement whose conditions stem from the current situation. Interestingly, whereas in the *Manuscripts* communism was taken to be closer to sursumed [*aufgehobene*] totality, here it is closer to the sursuming totality [*aufhebende*], on account of the moving character attributed to communism.[76] In the search for the subject matter [*Sache selbst*] in its totality, underscoring of the process of the genesis [*Entstehungsprozeß*][77] of history is intertwined with the highlighting of the social praxis of individuals as the only makers of that totality. This is in contradistinction to the mere criticism that is said to be necessary but inadequate. It is the clarification of ideas according to social and material praxis and also the amplification of praxis according to ideas, while priority is given to social-material life.

Two points are being simultaneously accentuated here to reinforce this conception of a materialist totality: a totality of social life instead of their ideal repercussions and the reciprocal relationship between the individuals and circumstances in this totality. The sum total of the forces of production and social forms of intercourse [*Verkehrsformen*], replaces substance and essence. This new dispersed or, so to speak, decentralised essence, is to be sought in the social totality. This has two intertwined consequences: first, an immanent historical criterion [*Maßstab*] must be adopted for any genuine analysis; and second, a total radical change [*totale Umwälzung*] of such a totality, its metabolism, and its contradictions is needed. This view, which incorporates the relationship of man with nature in history, will provide us with the reality of each historical period and history in its totality instead of an illusion. The ability to have such a conception of totality – the forces and the relations of production – is the result of the independence of these forces and their development. One can see the capitalist system of production and its inherent contradictions in their totality; one sees how the forces of production – individual producers and means of production – come into an insurmountable contradiction with social relations. These individuals are no longer just abstract constituents of the totality,

---

75   Marx 1968d, p. 546; Marx 1968d, p. 536.
76   Marx and Engels 1978, p. 37.
77   Marx and Engels 1978, p. 38.

as found in the individualism of Feuerbach, but have effective living content [*wirklichen Lebensinhalt*].⁷⁸

The appropriation of the totality of the means of production by individual producers is not only to activate themselves, but also to affirm their existence. This appropriation is principally conditioned by appropriation of the object* – the productive forces which are developed into a totality and exist only within an existing universal interaction.⁷⁹ The universal relationship of this appropriation gives it a universal character. This appropriation in turn is nothing but the result of the development of the capacity of the corresponding means of production. The appropriation of the means of production is therefore already an expression of the development of a totality of the capacity of the very individuals,⁸⁰ which will in turn be conditioned by the appropriating individuals (anticipating a distinctive Marxian totality that will be developed later).

The individuals capable of appropriating this totality and of playing the role of the revolutionary agents of the radical change of this status quo are simply the proletarians, no longer restricted like other suppressed classes in the past. This absence of previous restrictions makes it possible for the first time for these new individuals to subdue the minority under the new rising majority, of which they are the constituents. As conscious beings, who find the contradictions of the existing totality to be inherent to its nature, proletarians, as the collective agent, are the bearers of the new totality – and this with a revolutionary approach, given that communism as a movement would have to erupt in a revolution [*in einer Revolution eklatieren*].⁸¹ They do not replace just one characteristic of this totality in its global relations [*Weltverhältnisse*], nor each characteristic in its abstraction and isolation from others, but the totality of its characteristics engenders this new totality. This is realised in practical, social, and political life, and not merely in contemplation on the will of individuals, or in conceptual hairsplitting.⁸² This genesis of the new totality arising from *contemplations* is impossible, since contradictions in reality have to be dealt with in reality and cannot be simply theorised away.⁸³

---

78   Marx and Engels 1978, p. 67.
79   Marx and Engels 1978, pp. 67–8.
80   Marx and Engels 1978, pp. 67–8: 'Die Aneignung einer Totalität von Produktionsinstrumenten ist schon deshalb die Entwicklung einer Totalität von Fähigkeiten in den Individuen selbst'.
81   Marx and Engels 1978, p. 74.
82   Marx and Engels 1978, p. 245.
83   See Bourdieu 2007, p. 598.

Marx and Engels here draw an essential distinction between two types of totality in order to elaborate on the relationship between theory and social life. The contentful totality of a theory is saturated with the positive content of the developed social life and its struggles, as found in England and in the works of Bentham and Mill. What may be called the contentless totality of a theory, on the other hand, comes with an undeveloped struggle of the bourgeoisie, as found in pre-revolutionary France, and leads to a mere philosophising of social life, as found in the works of Helvetius and Holbach.[84] To the same effect, although an organic totality in thought is what will be advocated, particularly in the works that are discussed in the next section, in the *German Ideology* Marx and Engels mockingly criticise any mystification, as in their criticism of Karl Grün, as attaining such totalities in appearance only, and they denounce any erroneous ascription of organic relation among and between irrelevant elements.[85]

Along the same lines, in their criticism of True Socialism, they find it unrealistic to say that the future communism connects atoms in an organic whole and say instead that the connection of atoms to the organic whole is as impossible as that of a square to a circle.[86] What they seem to imply is the substitution of molecules for atoms. This analogy, which is accurate in chemistry – since it is not the atom of a substance but the molecule that is the smallest representative of its existence – is another example of a wrong generalisation of individuals and society as a whole.[87] The criterion for the distinction between a personal individual who plays a role in a given society as a totality, on the one hand, and an incidental individual, on the other, is not a conceptual difference but a historical fact.[88]

This is the place that the discussion of totality in the *German Ideology* may be related to the 'Theses on Feuerbach', which unlike the former was not intended for publication. The absence of the word 'totality' in the 'Theses on Feuerbach' is a textual fact. This has led to what I consider to be two imprecise interpretations. On the one hand, Lucien Goldmann[89] takes this absence to be a by no means negligible lacuna in a project that aims at the construction of dia-

---

84 Marx and Engels 1978, p. 397.
85 Marx and Engels 1978, p. 501.
86 Marx and Engels 1978, p. 446. As will be seen, particularly in the section on *Capital, cellule* is used instead of atom to draw a more precise analogy.
87 Cf. Marx and Engels 1978, p. 469.
88 Marx and Engels 1978, p. 71. This is a difference that will be discussed in the following pages.
89 This is the full quote in original: 'Il manque seulement pour la formulation globale du matérialisme dialectique le concept de Totalité, ce qui est évidemment une lacune non négligeable' (Goldmann 1968, p. 43).

lectical materialism. In making this argument, Goldmann does not fully recognise the role the appearance of the word *ensemble* in thesis 6[90] may play as a term that is very close to 'totality', particularly when the interactive relationship between subject and the environment or conditions is already straightforwardly advanced in the third thesis,[91] in contrast with other doctrines that overlook this mutual relationship between subject and environment and treat their relationship one-sidedly.

In another interpretation of the third thesis, Pierre Macherey[92] takes the usage of the word *ensemble* as *das ensemble* in its French usage, with lower-case *e*, instead of *das Ensemble*, as an indication of the absence from the German language of a word that expresses the grouping, collection or association of the elements which are simply collected or reunited, and hence put in an *ensemble*, without having to constitute a totality in itself. The word *ensemble*, according to this reading, implies a multiplicity that is indefinitely open and avoids a form closed on itself. For Macherey, the term *das Komplex* may be used as a synonym for *ensemble* here to reflect a sum of elements that exist without being unified in a totality. This is, according to this reading, the reason why Marx avoids the terms *das Ganze, die Ganzheit*, and *die Totalität* and the closure they imply.

I would suggest, instead, that the term *ensemble* introduced here, in a dictum that is valid in a transhistorical manner, is the prototype of a particular open totality; the particular analysis of this totality and the criticism showing its contradictoriness are left to be elaborated on in the later works. At stake is the ensemble of the social relations of a given society at a given time. What connects these social relations is that they are all existing social relations in their dynamicity. If so, one may read the tenth of the theses on Feuerbach[93] as a suggestion of one open totality, namely, humanised society or socialised humanity as an alternative to bourgeois society. The contradictory characteristic of this society is inseparably intertwined with it as a totality, which both makes its transformation inevitable and a particular revolutionary sursumption possible. By using the word *ensemble*, in saying that the essence of the human is in effect the ensemble of its social relations, with its real-material world, Marx iterates also the dispersed-decentralised totality seen above. Thus, Marx's usage of the

---

90 Marx 1978e, p. 6.
91 Marx 1978e, p. 6.
92 Macherey 2008, pp. 150–1. See also Harvey 2010, p. 196.
93 Marx 1978e, p. 7 'Der Standpunkt des alten Materialismus ist die bürgerliche Gesellschaft, der Standpunkt des neuen die menschliche Gesellschaft oder die gesellschaftliche Menschheit'.

term *ensemble* here is not because he wanted to avoid 'totality' or similar terms, but because he was still unable to present his own totality or incorporate it into his account.[94]

As mentioned in the first section of this chapter, one important aspect of the discussion of totality is its relationship with truth put forward in the second thesis. Here Marx introduces three aspects of the truth of human thought: this-sidedness, power, and reality. Undeveloped as it is, this is a step beyond a correspondence theory of truth. An expanded discussion and detailed elaboration of this open totality will be presented in the following sections on totality in the *Grundrisse* and *Capital*. It will be shown that such a totality is something quite different to a simple juxtaposition of the elements that make it up.

4   Totality in Oscillation: The *Grundrisse*

By the end of *The German Ideology*, unpublished as it was, the break with Hegel and his incongruous disciples is achieved, although methodologically it will continue to be further honed. A critique directed against political economists actualises another break. In this section, I am going to untangle the way the conception of totality is discussed in the texts known as the *Introduction* and the *Grundrisse of the Critique of Political Economy*, or, what Marx once thought to be an appropriate title for this work, *Critique of Economic Categories*.[95] To do this, I first elaborate on the methodological findings in the *Introduction* that relate to totality, then move to see how the same conception is dealt with in the notebooks under the titles of the 'Chapter on Money' and 'Chapter on Capital'. In the treatment presented here, although I cannot go so far as to say that these two chapters along with the *Introduction* form an 'organic whole',[96] I would say that, as the 'core' of the book, these texts can be discussed together as essentially a single more or less coherent text.

---

94   This opens a new horizon of the discussion. In Chapter 2, I argued for the distinction to be drawn between the whole and the totality; ensemble is added here. The members of the ensemble do not have to have any relation (like the mechanical-chemical-organic) to one another apart from their membership of that ensemble; put differently, they do not necessarily form a whole. Cf. Hall 2003, p. 136: 'The relations of production of a mode of production are articulated *as an ensemble*'.

95   Marx, letter to Ferdinand Lassalle, 22 February 1858 (Marx 1978c, p. 550). Perhaps because of this alternative title, there has been a somewhat reductionist view of Marx's works in general. See, e.g., Hall 2003, p. 145: 'The whole of Marx's mature effort is, indeed, the critique of *the categories of Political Economy*' (emphasis added).

96   Marx 1973, p. 13.

4.1   Introduction to the *Grundrisse*

Written between 23 August and mid-September 1858, what is known as the *Introduction* to the *Grundrisse* is a very rich and extremely complex text. Its importance lies also in the fact that this is the longest text on method that Marx ever wrote. However, more than answers and clarification, it provides us with material for further thought and paths to take. Marx builds up on what he has already developed. Sometimes some passages are very similar to works written some ten years earlier. In his discussion on method, for instance, his thematic repetition of the themes developed in the *Poverty of Philosophy* is remarkable.[97] Here, I attempt merely to follow the features of the text, elaboration upon which can help us see Marx's treatment of the conception of totality.

The text is in a sense an attack on abstraction and hence on what we may call non-concrete, a response to the question: What is concrete? With reference to Chapter 4, we may say that Marx evades whatever method leads to a false totality, abstract totality, bad totality, empty totality, or the pseudo-concrete instead of a real concrete.[98] So while it is right to say that an abstraction that leads to 'fixation of the unity against multiplicity' and also 'fixation of the differences in relation to the unity'[99] is an erroneous abstraction, this is equally true of other modes of abstraction. Instead, Marxian abstraction must lead to nothing but concrete totality, 'a rich totality of many determinations and relations',[100] a concrete totality [*konkrete Totalität*], a thought totality [*Gedankentotalität*]. This is why Marx says: '[T]he rise of the method of abstract to concrete, is just the way of the thought, to appropriate the concrete, to reproduce mentally the concrete'.[101] Later, in the Afterword to the second edition of *Capital*, he gives a nuanced version of this: appropriation of the world does not stop at merely collecting the data, but also brings about the accommodation of the social subject, that is modern bourgeois society. This is the movement from the chaotic given totality, as the realm of the intuition, to the thought totality as the concretisation, reproduction of that totality by that subject. This is how one may understand the point that the *Introduction* actualises the duty of the recommended method of political economy and links it to totality.[102]

The revolutionary nature of the *Introduction* is twofold. On the one hand, it goes against the idealisation of social life found in Hegel; and on the other hand,

---

97   The following passage is just one example: Marx 1977, p. 126.
98   See Chapter 4, section 1 above.
99   Arndt 2012, p. 133, my translation.
100 Marx 1973, p. 100.
101 Marx 1973, p. 101.
102 See Arndt 2012, p. 129.

it goes against taking social laws in general, and the laws of material production in particular, as 'inviolable natural laws' as political economists preceding him mainly did. The structure of the elements of political economy is discussed physiologically, so to speak: A physiological critical analysis that unlike the one suggested by Ricardo proposes in later works a different starting point: 'Marx showed that Ricardo's starting point of his physiology of bourgeois system was problematic'.[103]

This is why the term *Moment* is brought up here. The social praxis initiated by the thinking head is distinguished from the self-generating action of the concept, which Marx finds in Hegel. It is demonstrated in the *Introduction* that the totality of the moments of the capitalist mode (production, reproduction, distribution, exchange, consumption of commodities, service *and* information) are neither essential to social life in *general* nor *natural* nor *eternal*. They are particular to this mode, and they have a historical genesis, a development which entails their inevitable disappearance at some point in the future. The moments of this mode do not merely form coherent organic moments but more than that, they are dialectical, contradictory moments in incessant tension.[104]

To avoid treating dialectics as the counterbalancing of concepts, to grasp the real relation, the path recommended is to go from reality to textbooks instead of the other way around. This entails prioritising the social-material over the ideal and purely theoretical. But this move from the status quo, from reality to theory, which reminds us of Marx and Engels's dictum in the *German Ideology*, is further developed here.

The move from the abstract to the concrete, which presupposes the empirical appropriation of the concrete and its reproduction in the mind,[105] is not a move from the universal, analysing the riches of the concrete, decomposing it into its elements, and arriving at particulars. On the contrary: the move has to be from the simplest and the uncomposed to the most composed; from the initial product of the Marxian abstraction to the enriched concrete; from the more or less fixed and simple single moments such as labour, division of labour, need, and exchange value, rising to the state, exchange among nations, and the

---

103   Arndt 2012, p. 140, my translation.
104   The distinction between the organic and the dialectical is underscored by Lukács in his response to Luxemburg. Particularly in the chapters 'The Marxism of Rosa Luxemburg' and 'Critical Observations on Rosa Luxemburg's "Critique of the Russian Revolution"'. I elaborate on this in Boveiri 2018.
105   Marx 1983a, p. 35.

world market;[106] *from the dumbness of the lived concrete* – another way of putting Marx's chaotic whole – to the enriched whole. The result of the Marxian abstraction, the enriched whole arrived at, will not be well-defined, because of its tension-laden characteristic; but it will be rich, unlike an abstractionist universal that is well-defined but poor.[107]

To search for a clear-cut, ideal definition of *capital*, or of any of the categories discussed by Marx, is doomed to result either in a ridiculous schematisation or in stripping reality of its dialectical character. Like graphic illustrations, such efforts can only camouflage the abstractness of the abstraction.[108] This precision through definitions is the procedure adopted by the metaphysician, unable to face and understand the contradictoriness of the subject of study.[109] The attempt should be instead to grasp the complexity of each category, as a totality that is simultaneously *das-der Moment* of the contradictory Totality, namely, the capitalist mode of social life: that is simultaneously the dynamic, with *das Moment*, but also the temporal entity, with *der Moment*, in each totality. I say in each totality of the Totality because the capitalist mode of social life as a Totality is composed of constituents, each of which is itself a totality. An analogy between the whole body and the organs of the body and the cells constituting each is clarificatory.[110] In the same way that there is nothing over and above *concreta*, there is no production over and above concrete productions. Instead, any considered production can be taken as either a particular branch of production or the totality of particular productions. The generalisation of those particular productions, agriculture, manufacture, etc., that is, the generalisation of those *concreta*, constitutes universal production.

What appears to the single individual in everyday life to be the determinant realm of social-economic law is not production but distribution. To see the reality of distribution as an aspect of capitalist society in its totality and as a moment in the totality of production, the individual must go beyond what appears as it does, *to destroy the pseudoconcrete*, to repeat a Kosíkian phrase. In so doing, the individual no longer sees the moments as quasi-independent moments, dictated by the dominant ideology of this mode of social life, but as internally related, as in any other organic totality. As for this

---

106   Marx 1983a, p. 35. It is notable that the starting category of *Capital*, namely the commodity, is not in this list.
107   Lobkowicz 1968, p. 484.
108   This is further illustrated in Ilyenkov 1982, p. 101. Cf. a passage from *Capital* Volume II referred to earlier, Marx 1963a, p. 228.
109   Ilyenkov 1982, p. 262.
110   See 1. 2 above.

quasi-independence of the particular moments of distribution, the scientifically enlightened individual sees this as the threefold complex of the distribution of the products of production, the distribution of the means of production, and the subsumption of the individuals in the society (including that individual too) within the relations of production of social life in its entirety.[111] This interdependence of the moments, which is simultaneously distinct from taking them as identical moments (something ascribed by some to a Hegelian totality),[112] also counters a quasi-independence of the moments, and leads to the introduction of their unity as differentiated but interrelated moments which are the constituents of an organic Totality. The analogy between the organic totality on the one hand, and the members of the whole and their mutual co-constitution on the other, is emphasised in the *Introduction*. Nonetheless, more than being merely organic, this mode, namely, the capitalist mode of social life, is *also* contradictory, a characteristic left unelaborated in the *Introduction* but further developed by Marx on numerous occasions.

In this totality, production and consumption, traditonally seen as separate moments, are here shown to be in an organic relationship. This is against a reading influenced by the dominant ideology of the capitalist mode of production, in which they are thought of as opposing poles, the endpoint and the starting points of a study. Instead, they mediate each other: production mediates consumption since it provides consumption with what-is-to-be-consumed; consumption mediates production, because it is only consumption that creates the subject who will use the products produced by production. Far from being the endpoint of a discussion of capitalist society, consumption gives rise to the object of production in a subjective form; it creates the impetus for production, and actualises production; the reality of production is thus accomplished in consumption. This is how a social product, a commodity for instance, is distinguished as an object* from a natural object.

The complexity of production, and production during the process of exchange, as far as it can be so called, is to be left for *Capital*; nonetheless, the point that the prioritisation of any of these mediating but also mediated moments (production, distribution, exchange, consumption) over others in the totality, what is necessary for the existence of all moments, is a methodological error, and the result of an 'empty abstraction' [*leere Abstraktion*][113] with clear political implication, is accentuated in the *Introduction*. One economist who

---

111   Marx 1983a, p. 31.
112   See Althusser 2005, p. 206.
113   Marx 1983a, 31.

took a standpoint akin to the one outlined here is Ricardo. Known as an economist who stressed the importance of production, he was unable to find the proper mechanism of production as a moment in totality in organic relation with other moments (distribution, exchange, and consumption); he was thus led to introduce distribution as the exclusive subject matter of economics. In the contemporary world, a counterpart political alternative is the view holding that the problem of capitalist society does not lie in its totality but in the organisation of distribution.[114]

This is true about all other moments of the capitalist social mode[115] besides production, namely, distribution, exchange, and consumption, which are all moments in movement and moments of an overall movement.[116] Socialisation of the moments then means their totalisation as moments of an organic whole. In all this totality of processes, the subject (the capitalist, the worker) always plays an active role. This is notwithstanding the fact that some passages taken in isolation may convey the issue differently. Take for instance the point that 'the articulation [*Gliederung*] of distribution is entirely determined by the articulation of production'.[117] Another example is where Marx compares production with ether,[118] which was thought to be a particular determining gravity for all other moments. This has led some to attribute over-determinacy to production.[119] As an alternative reading, I propose that such sentences must be read along with the passages which accentuate equally the determining roles of all the moments of totality, which is the case in any living organ. Take the claim that production showcases [*darbietet*] the object* of consumption externally, whereas consumption posits the object* of production ideally, as the inner image, need, impetus, and goal.[120] The examples given by Marx to illustrate this point are numerous: houses, railroads, and clothes left unused and unconsumed are not houses, railroads, or clothes; they remain only unactualised

---

114 This emphasis on distribution has been criticised in Postone 2003.
115 I avoid using the term 'mode of production' to incorporate the idea that the mode comprises all moments (production, distribution, exchange, and consumption). The more common word 'system' is perhaps more accurate, since it may be argued that it adds 'superstructure' to 'forces and relations' already implied by 'mode'. But I avoid using it following the criticism of system theory in Chapter 4.
116 Hall 2003, p. 119.
117 Marx 1983a, p. 30; or as another one, take Marx's assertion that the question of the relationship between the distribution that determines the production and the production itself lies obviously within the production (Marx 1983a, p. 32).
118 Marx 1973, p. 107.
119 For one such reading, apart from Althusser, see Hall 2003, p. 128.
120 Marx 1983a, p. 27.

entities, as potentialities. Similarly, the metaphor of ether used here should not be taken to mean that it can actualise its function without the needed milieu. Hence one may talk of codetermination instead.

This does not, then, involve an absolute totality that determines all its constituents, with a function for each of the members. *That* would be an idealist-religious totality. This is true about all totalities, as in orchestras, and even the biological totalities.[121] Following this, the claims similar to the following need to be nuanced: '*Each* of the aspects and elements of the structure of the capitalist organism found therefore its concrete theoretical expression, and was reflected in a concrete historical abstraction'.[122] If this is taken seriously, the result will be a Hegelian, closed totality.

In the same vein, it should be clear that, just as the concrete appeared in two types, we also have two types of totality: a real totality and the mental reproduction of a real totality: the real movement and the exposition or representation thereof in the movement of categories.[123] These two, and the search for them, should not be conflated. A similar search for a totality in the former just as in the latter is an example of this conflation.[124]

An explication on the *Introduction* in general, and with regard to totality in particular, cannot leave out an elaboration on a well-known Marxian aphorism: 'The anatomy of man is a key to the anatomy of ape'.[125] First, it should be noted that the introduction was written just a few weeks before the publication of Darwin's *On the Origins of Species* (published 24 November 1859). One can speculate as to how Marx would have reformulated this sentence after reading Darwin's book. That said, the corollary of this dictum is to take the present as the starting point of an analysis of the past.[126] Nonetheless, this can be taken a bit misleadingly as well. An anatomist studying the anatomy of apes does not refer to human beings to affirm his knowledge of apes, unless a diachronic evolutionary knowledge of the anatomy of ape becomes requisite.

---

121 See Lewontin 2000, p. 81: 'It is by no means true that every part serves a function. Many features of organisms are the epiphenomenal consequences of developmental changes or functionless leftovers from remote ancestors. Only a quasi-religious commitment to the belief that everything in the world has a purpose would lead us to provide a functional explanation for fingerprint ridges or the patches of hair on men's chests'.
122 Ilyenkov, 1982, p. 220 (emphasis added).
123 This will be further elaborated in 5.
124 For a search of totality in literary works, see Jameson 2016.
125 Marx 1983a, p. 39: 'Die Anatomie des Menschen ist ein Schlüssel zur Anatomie des Affen'.
126 Cf. Deleuze and Guattari, 2005 p. 168: 'We do not write with the memories of childhood but through the blocs of childhood that are the becoming-child of the present' (my translation).

This is, however, true about social sciences: social development necessitates taking a more advanced phase as the point of departure for a non-advanced phase. Put differently, except in a unique set of circumstances, the ape does not necessarily evolve into a human being, but feudalism does necessarily pass over to some more developed stages of the development of means and relations of production and distribution. That is, while capital is needed for the understanding of rental revenue, for instance, the anatomy of the human being does not need to be considered in order to understand the anatomy of the ape. Otherwise, taken literally, this aphorism makes the role the ape plays here similar to Hegel's owl of Minerva. As is well known, with this analogy in the introduction to *The Philosophy of Right*,[127] Hegel declares that the function of philosophy is *post factum*, that is, it comes after the complete accomplishment of the social development. Nonetheless, the similarity between these two passages is deceptive. Notwithstanding the limits to knowing the subject at hand, for Marx, a conscious change of the world comes first, whereas for Hegel, the only function philosophy can play is confined to the time after the new status quo has established itself. It is a contemplation, a reflection of the past. The philosopher is always a belated teacher, whose role in the change of the status quo is nil.[128]

That said, the Marxian aphorism introduces intrinsic and absolutely unsurmountable theoretical and practical barriers to knowing the phenomena at hand. Since we are not living in the aftermath of capitalist society,[129] our ability to grasp these phenomena is limited, and to grasp them fully an orientation to further conscious changes, based on the contradictions we recognise in the subject matter, is inevitable. The desire to fully grasp the capitalist mode of social life entails the desire to transform it, whereas the desire to transform it should be actualised without the possibility of full comprehension of this mode. Of course, this is possible only if a particular relationship between totality and history is adopted in defence of historism against historicism, namely, the iteration of concrete historicism in contradistinction to abstract historicism, as Ilyenkov puts it,[130] or even better put, the defence of historism against historicism as elaborated by Kosík. The only methodological point I would like to put across is the dialectical relationship between diachrony and synchrony within totality as the differentiated unity of all the moments: whereas historism

---

127 Hegel 1989, p. 28.
128 Hegel 1989, pp. 27–8.
129 This is the practical aspect of the absolute barrier in any Marxian study.
130 See Ilyenkov 1982, pp. 212–22. A similar distinction is introduced by Stuart Hall (2003, p. 133), in distinguishing *the historical* and historicism.

enables us to see the totality and its inherent contradictions, and hence offers an objective* vantage point for viewing its transformation, historicism, by giving the dominant role to conditions, fails to do so.[131] This is also the response to the mistakenly posed dichotomous question of whether capitalism should be studied logically or historically, a point that will be elaborated upon in the following chapter.

4.2   The Chapter on Money in the Grundrisse

We turn now to the notebooks that constitute the principal text of the *Grundrisse*. The first notebook of the *Grundrisse*, written in October 1857, is entitled 'The Chapter on Money', and continues into the second notebook, written in November of the same year. The starting point in money follows from the proposition that since capital 'comes initially from circulation … [I]ts point of departure is money'.[132] Even in the most extensive elaborations on the relationship between totality and money, this relationship is not adequately discussed. In Fred Moseley's brilliant book *Money and Totality*, for instance, there are two insufficiencies related to our discussion: first, it supplies hardly any independent discussion of totality; second, on the two occasions where Moseley discusses money with some textual reference to the *Grundrisse*, one sees hardly any reference to totality,[133] and the other is too short and contents itself with several references without elaboration.[134] Moseley's extensive discussion in the book on money and all the interpretations of the transformation problem does not meet this requirement of discussing money in relation to totality. This may be owing to the fact, rightly stated, that '[t]he *Grundrisse* is almost entirely at the level of abstraction of capital in general',[135] but this should not obstruct an elaboration on money and totality and their relationship as found in the *Grundrisse*'s 'Chapter on Money'.

The same shortcoming can be seen in the most recent collective work published on the *Grundrisse*, entitled *In Marx's Laboratory*.[136] There is no chapter devoted to the relationship between money and totality, and in Part II of the book, dedicated to 'Abstract Labour, Value and Money', this relation is barely

---

131   See Chapter 4, section 6.
132   Marx 1973, p. 253. The beginning of the *Grundrisse* carries ambiguities resulting from indefiniteness of this moment of investigation. On one occasion, the socially determined individuals as producers in society are said to be the *natural* starting point of material production (Marx 1983a, p. 19).
133   Moseley 2015, pp. 47–55.
134   Moseley 2015, pp. 121–3.
135   Moseley 2015, p. 47.
136   Bellofiore, Starosta et al. 2013.

discussed. All this necessitates a textual analysis on the relation between the category of money and totality as presented in this chapter of the *Grundrisse*. The present section aims at filling this lacuna.

The question is: How can the totality under discussion in this chapter, namely, money, which is generally thought of as something fixed and solidified, be grasped in its processual determination, rather than as a simple thing? Generally counterposing totality against purity but also against abstraction, Marx's response comes with his discussion of the three functions ascribed to money in the text. Money can be the measure of value; it can be the medium of circulation; and it can represent all commodities, and hence it can be the material representative of wealth, or simply put, it can be money as money.[137]

As a criterion, or measure of value, money represents the exchange value of any singular commodity. Money itself does not have any use value per se: you cannot eat it or dress yourself in it, nor is any other function related to its substance, for the characteristic of money, as representing the exchange value of every other commodity, obstructs such use. What remains then is money's exchange value – the only value it can have. The complexity here lies in the fact that the exchange value of money itself, unlike that of other commodities, cannot be calculated according to the well-known criterion introduced by Marx, namely, the number of abstract socially necessary labour hours put into it, a concept that is elaborated on in *Capital*. The characteristic of money as the criterion of value lies in admitting these peculiarities.

In its role as the medium of exchange, an undetermined exchange value, once determined – that is, once its price is found – can be compared with money or expressed in money terms. The social consequences of this function are better seen when money is counterposed to the value-producing cause, that is, labour. The corresponding opposite of money, labour, the creator of values, is, unlike money, merely a movement; hence the natural measure for it is time.[138] Money as the general equivalent makes the outright division of labour possible. It can do this because of its independence from the specific product it exchanges for, from the immediate use value of its product for it. Along with this division comes a worker, who is the producer of the exchange value represented by this general equivalent, with ever more and more particular products, though this worker possesses an ever-smaller role in production.

---

137 The two first functions are also discussed later in the Notebooks (Notebook VII, Marx 1973, pp. 789–819). This is itself a support for the suggestion of the oscillation of categories in the *Grundrisse* and the categorial movement in *Capital*.

138 Cf. Aristotle 1993, 219b1 (p. 44): 'Time is the number of change in respect of before and after'.

The whole social movement is reflected in circulation as a process, or rather as the totality of all economic processes. Circulation is thus the first form in which something appears not only in its money or exchange value forms, but also in its totality. The only medium through which the circulation of all particular exchange values can be accomplished is money, but exchange value as what forms the substance of money is itself wealth. It is the totality of these particularities which each commodity finds in the opposing pole of money in exchange; the totality of these particular substances form the substance of money as the general representative of wealth. Thus, the third function comes onto the scene.

Like every other issue, in order to be expressed relationally, money has to be put into relation, and it cannot have a universal relation unless put into relation with a universal. Once production in its totality is taken into consideration, the money relationship is itself related to the production relation. With the function of money as the abstract representation of wealth, it turns into the god of commodities; the totality that exists as the epitome [*Inbegriff*] of all commodities. It is hence the material representation of the totality of wealth as well as the universal form of the totality of wealth. This twofold representation, once taken individually, is happenstance, but it gains significance only if taken universally; for instance, there is nothing inherent in a twenty-dollar bill which makes it a representative of this unit of wealth. Nevertheless, in its totality as the universal, wealth gains a significance that it lacks in a singular case of value: a billionaire gains power and social status according to the accumulation of these individually random components of the totality of wealth. The relation money has to all other commodities, or to the whole world of wealth, constitutes wealth as such. In money, universal wealth not only finds a form but also a content. To the claim that 'money ... stands in a logical, rather than material relation to commodities'[139] the chapter reacts as follows: in money the price is realised, and the substance is wealth in abstraction from its particular modes of existence, and also in its totality. The realisation of the price in exchange and the criterion of wealth, however, do not overlap. Regarding price, commodities are exchanged according to the labels they bear; regarding value, they demonstrate the number of hours put into their production as exchange values. These two barely coincide.

This is the complexity that is overlooked quite often by the representatives of political economy. Such misconceptions of totality criticised by Marx, the overlooking of money in all its moments, with regard to the function of social

---

139   Arthur 2004, p. 9.

exchange in general and the usage of the means of this exchange, money, in particular, can probably be best understood in his criticism of Adam Smith. It shows how the relationship between the individual and the society as a whole, once mispresented, can justify the status quo. Such a standpoint implies the following abstract axiom: in the pursuit of his individual interest in social exchange, the individual unintentionally and unconsciously promotes the universal interest of society in its totality. Marx, however, argues that from such an abstract axiom, one can equally argue that this conflict of interest can lead to universal negation in the form of a war of all against all. Such a standpoint ignores the fact that the form and the content of the pursuit of individual interest are given by social conditions that are independent of the individual.

If such a concrete totality were brought into the discussion, it would be clear that, since individuals are the producers of the general equivalent, best found in money, they have a reciprocal indifference towards each other in society as a whole. This generalised indifference has its roots in the constant need for exchange that is based on the production of commodities, with the primary motive being their exchange values.

In the same vein, as was seen above, the means of the social bond and the social power of the individual in the pocket, the incarnation of exchange value as an 'all-sided mediator' [*Tauschwert als allseitigem Vermittler*],[140] that is, money, does not constitute any use value for any individuals in the society; it is, however, the result of what each individual does as a producer of exchange value. Nonetheless, the power of the medium of exchange is in inverse relation to the social bond that relates the individuals to each other in the totality of the society. The relation between individuals is metamorphosed into a relation between things. Since the capacity for the activity of each individual is measured by other individuals as that individual's capacity to produce money, the individual's personal capacities, their personal intersubjective dependence, turns into, but also is subordinated to, an interdependence among things.

Methodologically, common-sense bourgeois apologists are not able to see the dual contradictory relationship between money and other commodities. To them, they are either essentially different or else there is no distinction at all between money and other commodities. This goes along with the inability of such apologetics to understand how, for money, its entering into circulation must itself be a moment of its remaining with itself and its remaining with itself a moment of entering into circulation. That is, money, as realised exchange value, must simultaneously posit itself as a process in which the

---

140   Marx 1983a, p. 90.

exchange value is already realised. Politically, they do not want to affirm that within this lies the potential crisis of this contradictory totality, namely, capitalism. Money, as the actualised exchange value, must simultaneously posit itself as price, in which the exchange value is already actualised. Thus, money is simultaneously the negation of itself as a purely thing-like form.[141] They are not ready to admit that this contradictory unity, which is merely generalised by the no longer slave-like function of money, as a 'necessarily displaced social form',[142] turns into the *cause* of the subordination of the individuals under the autonomous relation of the products of their labour, and their alienation; this turns the relations between them into a relation among things, and this contradiction can be externally manifested only through violent explosion. This violent explosion cannot be *ultimately avoided* through reforms or any amelioration in circulation, ignoring the relationship between the threefold role that money plays in its organic relationship with production, and the totality of the capitalist social mode of life; this is why totality under this mode of social life is simultaneous totalisation and detotalisation. In noting this, Marx here shows, at least schematically, that the three functions of money represent the three moments of singularity, particularity, and universality, each a totality, and shows how the last one will lead the reader to the discussion of capital as the Totality. The last point reflects Marx's always political attitude in his analysis-criticism, even in a highly abstract discussion.

That said, his discussion of money presented here suffers from two shortcomings. Although he names metallic money, paper money, credit money, and labour money, there is no account of coin and paper money; but more importantly, the circuit of commodity-money-commodity, mediated by money, that is, C-M-C, remains undeveloped. The transition from the third function of money – namely, money as the representative of wealth – to capital is not developed here.[143] Starting from this point, the discussion of money in 'The Chapter on Capital' at the end of the second notebook (titled by Marx 'Money as Capital') is introduced. This is the way 'the all-dominating economic power of bourgeois society', that is, capital, is introduced. This is what we come to now.

---

141 Marx 1983a, p. 161; or that modern credit systems are both cause and effect of the concentration of capital. Marx 1983a, p. 58.
142 Murray 2005.
143 For further development of this along these lines see Rosdolsky 1977, p. 149; Moseley 2015, pp. 121–22.

4.3 The Chapter on Capital in the Grundrisse

'The Chapter on Capital' consists of what Marx wrote between November 1857 and June of 1858. It begins a few pages into Notebook II, where 'The Chapter on Money' (or what Marx entitled 'The Chapter on Money as Capital') ends; this chapter finishes with Notebook VII.[144] Although money is 'the first form in which capital as such appears',[145] capital cannot immediately follow from money as such.[146] A mediating step is needed: capital must first posit itself as 'money as capital'. In positing itself as capital relying on the third function of money, seen in the previous section, money goes beyond its simple character as money.[147] This is the reason behind introducing 'The Chapter on Money as Capital' between 'The Chapter on Money' and 'The Chapter on Capital'.

Historically as well as conceptually, money as a category takes precedence over capital. Historically, there are societies with money but without capital. Nonetheless, if capital exists in a society, so does money. Conceptually, where both synchronically exist, the understanding of capital makes the thorough understanding of money possible.

'The Chapter on Capital' is divided into three sections: i. 'The production process of capital'; ii. 'The circulation process of capital'; and iii. 'Capital as the fructifier or fruit-bringer [*Frucht-bringend*]. Interest, profit (production costs, etc.)'.[148] Marx aims not to deny the contradictions within each moment, but to demonstrate and develop the contradictions in each of these three moments of totality, each in turn shown to be a totality.[149] This demonstration must be done in order to go beyond an 'empty negation', since in that case the negation would remain barren.

---

[144] I am not discussing the few pages entitled Batistat and Carey.

[145] Marx 1973, p. 253.

[146] This is the miscomprehension that follows from the translation of the sentence 'Innerhalb des Systems der bürgerlichen Gesellschaft daher folgt auf den Wert unmittelbar das Kapital' (Marx 1983a, p. 177) as 'Within the system of bourgeois society, capital follows immediately after money' (Marx 1973, p. 252).

[147] Marx 1973, p. 250: 'Money as Capital is an aspect of money which goes beyond its simple character as money'.

[148] In Marx 1983a, this goes from page 165 to page 670, after which Marx introduces supplements to the chapters on money and capital.

[149] Marx 1973, p. 351: 'We are the last to deny that capital contains contradictions. Our purpose, rather, is to develop them fully'. Cf. Engels, *Outlines of a Critique of Political Economy* (Engels 1975, p. 421): 'In the critique of political economy, therefore, we shall examine the basic categories, uncover the contradiction introduced by the free-trade system, and bring out the consequences of both sides of the contradiction'.

4.3.1 The Production Process of Capital

Along with the general emphasis on the point that the subject matter [*Sache selbst*] must be taken as a process not as a thing, the totality of capital is posited here as the moment of the production process of capital. However, that totality – that is, the totality of capital – presupposes production, circulation, and the unity of these two; any other standpoint according to Marx is merely 'empty chatter'.[150] The discussion of this first moment will then be possible only if one makes this complex presupposition of the totality of the totalities – namely, capital, or more precisely the capitalist mode of social life.

In capital, exchange value posits itself for the first time as exchange value. It does not become deprived of substance; rather, it actualises itself as the totality of all substances. Nor does it lose its form determination; rather, it preserves its identity in all the various substances. It is then not any particular commodity but the totality of commodities or totality of the particularities. For each commodity, its 'Exchange value posited as the unity of commodity and money is capital, and this positing itself appears as the circulation of capital', which does not form a circle, but a 'spiral, an expanding curve'.[151] Through the process of differentiation of capital from labour, with its role as the yeast which causes the fermentation of the process, capital becomes a process. Labour as well as capital bears totality and abstraction: the totality of all labour stands potentially against capital and it is circumstantial against which capital in particular it stands.[152] In its confrontation with capital, labour as the living source of value – which, given that it is an activity, experiences inactivity as death – bears a contradiction: it is the absolute poverty once turned into an object, but also 'the general possibility of wealth'. Marx here continues what he saw as early as his dissertation regarding the relationship between totality and contradiction.[153] This is a two-step exchange: the worker sells his only commodity, labour (introduced later as labour power) with a use value and a price, and receives a specific sum of money; then the capitalist obtains labour, which, as an activity, posits value, which is the productive labour that not only maintains capital but multiplies it. While the first exchange is ordinary exchange and falls within familiar circulation, the second one is a formally and qualitatively different one that belongs to an essentially different category; it is named exchange only 'by

---

150 Marx 1973, p. 266.
151 Marx 1973, p. 266. See also Gauthier 2010, p. 98, where Hegel's *System der Wissenschaft* is depicted as a circle of circles.
152 Marx 1983a, p. 218: '[D]ie Totalität aller Arbeiten steht ihm δυνάμει gegenüber, und es ist zufällig, welche ihm gerade gegenübersteht'.
153 Marx 1973, p. 296. The significance of this dual aspect is neglected by some commentators (Postone 2003) in quoting Marx that being a worker is a miserable thing.

misuse'.[154] With this, the capital which was considered until this step only in its material form, in terms of the simple production process, is from the side of its form determination the process of self-valorisation.

We have seen in the *Introduction* that the co-constitution of all the moments of capital (production, distribution, exchange, and consumption) is, like all organic totalities, not a causal one. The liver does not create the kidney, nor does the kidney create the liver.[155] Rather, the moments co-constitute each other as different totalities within another totality; they constitute the totality, but are also constituted by that totality – in this case capital.[156] It should be seen now how production is related to another moment, namely, circulation.

4.3.2 The Circulation Process of Capital

In the second section, the totality of capital is posited as the circulation process of capital itself as totality. The reciprocal relation between production and circulation is noteworthy here. Whereas originally capital-based production starts off from circulation, we witness how production has circulation as its own condition, and the production process in its immediacy is a moment of the circulation process; just as much, the circulation process is a moment of the production process in its totality. In this way 'The totality of the moments of its circulation are themselves moments of its production – its reproduction as well as its new production'.[157]

The circulation process of capital is the moment of realisation of the surplus value already created in the moment of the process of the production of capital. Capital – taken as the production that relies entirely on wage labour as the subjective condition of production unified with the objective [*objektiven*] conditions of production, material and instruments aiming at having the surplus product in its totality – objectifies [*objektivierend*] the surplus labour in its totality[158] and posits circulation as the necessary moment of the whole movement.[159] This is an externalisation of labour power, of which every particular moment stands as the totality.[160] 'The totality of the free worker's

---

154 Marx 1973, p. 275.
155 Of course, I mean synchronically; diachronically, the bud does create the blossom and the latter the fruit, to use a classic example from Hegel (1980, p. 12).
156 Marx 1973, p. 278. See Kosík 1976, p. 29: 'totality *concretises* itself *in the process of forming its whole as well as its content*'.
157 Marx 1973, p. 516.
158 Marx 1973, p. 451.
159 Marx 1983a, p. 328.
160 Marx 1983a, p. 377: '[Ü]ber jeder besondren Äußerung steht das Arbeitsvermögen als Totalität'. In Marx 1973, p. 464, oddly enough, this sentence is translated as follows: 'labour capacity as a totality is greater than every particular expenditure'.

labour capacity appears to him as his property, as one of his moments, over which he, as subject exercises domination, and which he maintains by expending it'.[161] Throughout this process, while the individual worker is alien to the combination of different types of labours as their totality, the entirety, as the totality of workers, find themselves equally alien to this totality of labours and, along with that, alien to the product of their labour.[162] The result of this totality of the development [*diese Totalität der Entwicklung*] of this power, is its universal objectification, which appears as the total emptiness of human innerness.[163] Through this totalisation of capital as totality, in contradistinction to the previous moment, a step farther in the discussion is taken. A step that equally tends to help along the impartial objective [*objektiven*] contradictions.[164]

Regarding the relationship between the totality of this moment, that is, circulation and the totality of capital, a clarificatory point is needed. It is related to the following passage by Marx: '[W]hen we take circulation as a totality, as a *self-enclosed process*, C-M-M-C [commodity-money-money-commodity], then the matter stands differently'.[165] Here, as elsewhere when Marx talks about closed, or self-enclosed totality, this is notwithstanding the fact that ontologically such a totality does not exist. This is just an assumption, in the same way that in studying the fall of an apple, the physicist ignores the existing influence of Jupiter on this fall. That is, in this case the totality is taken to be close so that an elaboration of the process may be possible.

The constituents of constant capital need clarification. The part of constant capital continually used and replenished is circulating or floating capital; this consists of raw materials, etc. Another part of constant capital is more fixed and its use involves a change of form of the material but it is not used *up*; this is the fixed capital. The production of capital appears as the production in definite portions of circulating capital and fixed capital, so that capital itself produces its double way of circulating as fixed capital and circulating capital.[166] In this circulation, however, unlike the Hegelian circulation of concepts, so to speak,[167] capital as *value in process*, does not stop at merely sustaining itself

---

161 Marx 1973, p. 465.
162 Marx 1983a, p. 382.
163 Marx 1983a, p. 396. With regard to alienation, a comparison with the *Manuscripts of 1844* is interesting; see section 2 above. As can be seen, Marx does not ignore it here. For a critical evaluation of this standpoint see the discussion below in section 4.3.3.
164 Marx 1983a, p. 319.
165 Marx 1973, p. 201, emphasis added.
166 Marx 1973, p. 722.
167 Cf. Hegel 1980a, § 161, p. 309.

formally, but realises itself as value, reproduces the value, and adds new value to the already existing value.[168]

4.3.3 Capital as the Fruit-Bearer: Transformation of Surplus Value into Profit

In the third section, the totality of capital is posited as the unity of the process of production and circulation of capital, as a social relation the *individual* production of which – like the individual production of language – is an absurdity or 'non-thing' [*Unding*].[169] In the first step, the first section here in the production process of capital (where this totality was simply presupposed), surplus value is created through labour, which plays the role of the fermenter. This does not mean that it is realised; that realisation was accomplished in the previous section. In the third step, capital as the unity of these previous steps, in its totality, both reproduces itself as value, and also as value which generates value.[170]

The way capital posits itself is put in a nuanced way. Although in its totality, capital is posited in the money market, while forming a syllogism with other sources of the other classes of society, namely, the workers with wages and landowners with rent, capital must always hold the position of the active middle term.[171] This centrality of the antithesis (so to speak) is an important methodological difference between Marxian and Hegelian dialectics overlooked by some commentators.[172]

The result of the alternative reading is the recognition of an organic interconnection between natural life and social life. Marx makes the point in the following passage:

> Nature builds no machines, no locomotives, railways, electric telegraphs, self-acting mules etc. These are products of human industry; natural material transformed into organs of the human will over nature, or of human participation in nature. They are organs of the human brain, created by the human hand; the power of knowledge, objectified. The development of fixed capital indicates to what degree general social knowledge has become a direct force of production, and to what degree, hence, the

---

168 Marx 1973, p. 536.
169 Marx 1983a, p. 398 'Sprache als das Produkt eines einzelnen ist ein Unding'. Nicolaus translates *Unding* as 'impossibility' (Marx 1973, p. 490).
170 Marx 1973, p. 745.
171 Marx 1983a, p. 201.
172 See Smith 1993a, pp. 13–22. The criticism of this standpoint will be given further in a forthcoming book. For a discussion of Hegel's syllogism and the floating character of the middle term, see Gauthier 2010, pp. 73–5.

conditions of the process of social life itself have come under the control of the general intellect and been transformed in accordance with it. To what degree the powers of social production have been produced, not only in the form of knowledge, but also as immediate organs of social practice, of the real life process.[173]

This is how, through the assimilation-accommodation of the external world by the subject, the external world is internalised whereas the internal world is externalised. However, the priority of the world of thoughts over the world of external reality in their joint totality should not be taken mechanically. The idea of an as-yet-non-existent house yields place to the house once it exists.[174] Nevertheless, the idea of a house is not possible without the existence of the external world in its entirety; hence, the general materialist dictum of the primacy of matter, or objectivity over consciousness is recognised.

In this process, however, one distinctive characteristic of the Marxian totality, in contradistinction to the Hegelian totality, should always be borne in mind. The 'dominance', and not the absolute dominance, of a category suffices for a Marxian analysis. Notwithstanding the fact that Marx does on one occasion introduce capital as 'the all-dominating economic power of bourgeois society',[175] this should not be taken in the Hegelian sense developed in his system, outside of whose realm nothing exists.[176] Overlooking this can lead to misinterpretations, and all the more so once it is recalled that the processual unity of the production and realisation of capital is linked to external conditions as well.[177] For instance, although it is true that the study of wage labour is possible after the study of capital, the absolute dominance of wage labour, the transformation of *all the producers* into wage labourers, is not necessary for capital to posit itself.[178]

---

173 Marx 1973, p. 706.
174 Ilyenkov 1982, p. 252.
175 Marx 1973, p. 107.
176 Cf. Finelli, 2009, p. 106: 'In the whole of the *Grundrisse* manuscript, Marx identifies the essence of capital, following Hegel, in terms of what I suggest a definition of as "the circle of presupposition and posit" (Bellofiore and Finelli, 1998, pp. 48–51). That is, in the sense that the nature of capital is *totalitarian, tending to not leave anything that has autonomous logic outside of itself. Capital tends to translate all external "presuppositions" into products (to "posit") within its own logical course*' (emphasis after 'totalitarian' added).
177 Marx 1973, p. 407.
178 This is elaborated in Rosdolsky 1977, p. 39: 'However wage-labour, although it represents both conceptually and historically the fundamental condition for capital and the capitalist mode of production, requires for its full development the precondition that this mode of production has taken hold of the totality of social relations and transformed

The 'totality of production' now incorporates the objective* incompatibility between the productive development of society and its existing relations inherent in the totality of capital, in which contradiction the growth of 'scientific power' also plays a role. At a certain point, this objective* contradiction turns into an insurmountable barrier [*Schranke*], makes the self-preservation of capital no longer possible, leads to explosions, and necessitates 'a higher state of social production'.[179] That the principal barrier to the existence and expansion of capital as the totality is capital itself, stems from the production of surplus value;[180] and although it seems that it can overcome the barriers posed by capital itself ideally (i.e., according to the picture presented by bourgeois political economy), it does not do so in reality.[181] This totality, capital, or rather the capitalist mode of social life, is thus a contradictory totality, and the world market is where production is posited as a totality together with all its moments and also all its contradictions.[182]

This contradiction, as a fundamental contradiction between the foundation of bourgeois production (value as measure) and its development, and between its relation to the totality of forces of production and social relations, is elaborated on by Marx as follows:

> Capital is itself the processing contradiction [*prozessierende Widerspruch*], [in] that it strives to reduce labour time to a minimum, while it posits labour time, on the other side, as sole measure and source of wealth. Hence it diminishes labour time in the necessary form so as to increase it in the superfluous form; hence posits the superfluous in growing measure as a condition – question de vie et de mort [question of life and death] – for the necessary. On the one side, then, it calls to life all the powers of science and of nature, as of social combination and of social intercourse, in order to make the creation of wealth independent (relat-

---

even the rural producers into wage-labourers. Consequently, we can only study this category exhaustively after we have studied capital and landed property'. Notwithstanding some sweeping negative evaluations of this book (e.g., Dunayeskaya 1978), Rosdolsky's book remains, in my judgement, a powerful forerunner of the existing interpretations of the *Grundrisse*. For a more nuanced judgement see Martin Nicolaus in Marx 1973, p. 23 n. 16. According to Callinicos, Rosdolsky's book is one of the few commentaries to 'have passed the test of time, setting standards for their successors to match up to' (Callinicos 2014, p. 19).

179 Marx 1973, pp. 749–50.
180 Marx 1973, p. 408.
181 Marx 1973, p. 410.
182 Marx 1973, pp. 227–8.

ively) of the labour time employed on it. On the other side, it wants to use labour time as the measuring rod for the giant social forces thereby created, and to confine them within the limits required to maintain the already created value as value. Forces of production and social relations – two different sides of the development of the social individual – appear to capital as mere means, and are merely means for it to produce on its limited foundation. In fact, however, they are *the material conditions to blast this foundation*.[183]

As can be seen here, in the *Grundrisse* Marx reiterates, though in a manner different from his previous works, the contradiction paradigm; hence the idea that there is a shift in the *Grundrisse* from ignoring the paradigm of contradiction in works preceding the *Grundrisse* to the paradigm of abstraction in the *Grundrisse* does not bear scrutiny.[184] The paradigm of contradiction, the inherent contradiction of capital, further elaborated on in *Capital*, is understandable solely through the Marxian abstraction presented here. Along the same lines, the claim that there is a shift of negative connotation from contradiction to abstraction, as from 'alienated labour' to 'abstract labour',[185] is equally inaccurate. What is added to the alienatedness of labour in *The Economic and Philosophical Manuscripts of 1844* is its being abstract. The reading

---

183 Marx 1983a, pp. 601–2: 'Das Kapital ist selbst der prozessierende Widerspruch [dadurch], daß es die Arbeitszeit auf ein Minimum zu reduzieren strebt, während es andrerseits die Arbeitszeit als einziges Maß und Quelle des Reichtums setzt. Es vermindert die Arbeitszeit daher in der Form der notwendigen, um sie zu vermehren in der Form der überflüssigen; setzt daher die überflüssige in wachsendem Maß als Bedingung – question de vie et de mort – für die notwendige. Nach der einen Seite hin ruft es also alle Mächte der Wissenschaft und der Natur wie der gesellschaftlichen Kombination und des gesellschaftlichen Verkehrs ins Leben, um die Schöpfung des Reichtums unabhängig (relativ) zu machen von der auf sie angewandten Arbeitszeit. Nach der andren Seite wie es diese so geschaffnen riesigen Gesellschaftskräfte messen an der Arbeitszeit und sie einbannen in die Grenzen, die erheischt sind, um den schon geschaffnen Wert als Wert zu erhalten. Die Produktivkräfte und gesellschaftlichen Beziehungen – beides verschiedne Seiten der Entwicklung des gesellschaftlichen Individuums – erscheinen dem Kapital nur als Mittel und sind für es nur Mittel, um von seiner bornierten Grundlage aus zu produzieren. In fact aber sind sie die materiellen Bedingungen, um sie in die Luft zu sprengen'. Marx 1973, p. 706, modified translation, emphasis added. Cf. 'Thus, growing wealthy is an end in itself. The goal-determining activity of capital can only be that of growing wealthier, i.e. of magnification, of increasing itself'. Marx 1973, p. 270.
184 Finelli 2009, p. 107.
185 Cf. Finelli 2009, p. 105: 'In short, in my opinion, the negative connotation of labour changes from *Economic and Philosophical Manuscripts* to *Grundrisse*, from a definition of "alienated labour" to that of "abstract labour"'.

presented here in these two cases is more dialectical-integrative, as it shows how these two moments of Marx's thought may be put in relation to one another.

It needs to be emphasised that capital as a totality should be understood as *more* than a concept; hence in its analysis and criticism both a twofold systematic and a historical exposition is necessary.[186] It is of course a concept. However, this concept is the concept of an objective* entity bearing objectively* all its inherent contradictions.[187] Capital, as that entity, is according to Marx the foundation of bourgeois society, and its concept the fundamental concept of modern economics, with the concept as merely the counter-image [*Gegenbild*] of the entity. This of course merely repeats what is found in the *Grundrisse*,[188] where Marx also criticises Sismondi for the misconception of taking capital as a commercial concept.[189] This would leave the reader puzzled as to how a concept 'presses to reduce labour time', as we see in this passage. This is also a repercussion of the claim I advanced in Chapter 4, that for a Marxian dialectics, the subject matter [*Sache selbst*], unlike in the Hegelian dialectic, is not a *Begriff*. In this reading the contradictions of the totality under study as well as the very totality itself are both objective* and social.[190]

Another noteworthy point that should be highlighted in the *Grundrisse* with reference to the terms used in this passage is related to what is really at stake, namely, determinations [*Bestimmungen*] and relations [*Beziehungen*]. Unlike the translation given by Nicolaus, who translates *Bestimmungen und Beziehungen* correctly as 'determinations and relations', in the translation of the same passage in Rosdolsky's seminal *Making of Capital*, we read 'definitions and relations'.[191] Stressing this point is important not only because of the difference between these two terms in Marx and Hegel, but also because some readings of Marx's works discuss them as if the whole project can basically be summed up as an effort to provide the reader with definitions.[192] Whereas determination is

---

186 Bellofiore, 2009, p. 179: 'As a totality, *capital has to be known as a concept, and hence through a systematic exposition*' (emphasis added). Cf. Marx 1973, p. 310:
      'This dialectical process of its becoming is only the ideal expression of the real movement through which capital comes into being'.
187 We will return to the objectiveness of the contradictoriness in the following section on *Capital*.
188 Marx 1973, p. 331.
189 Marx 1983a, p. 230, as he quotes Sismondi saying: 'Das Kapital ist ein kaufmännischer Begriff'.
190 Cf. Weston 2012. This subject will be later discussed.
191 Rosdolsky 1977, p. 27.
192 For one example of this kind, see Finelli 2009.

to be taken, along with totalisation and concretisation, as a metacategory that is practically quasi-omnipresent in any genuinely dialectical work, this is not true of definition.[193]

4.4 Conclusion

While it is correct to say that the *Grundrisse* is of inestimable value in that it allows us to see the method of inquiry being implemented,[194] the drawback of the book would be the impossibility of an exposition; the exposition that cannot be performed without the inquiry being performed here.[195] What we witnessed here, after the *Introduction*, was *not* the exposition of totality as a metacategory, nor the exposition of the categorial movement of categories, but an oscillation between two major categories, namely, 'money' and 'capital' (with a return to the discussion of money near to the end of the Notebooks), to each of which a chapter was allotted. Among the instances of the absence of categorial movement in the *Grundrisse*, the following are perhaps noteworthy. Whereas in Section Two of the *Grundrisse*, 'The Circulation Process of Capital', the discussion of both constant and variable capital appear, these are presented in different moments of the discussion, constant capital and variable capital in Volume I, fixed capital and circulating capital in Volume II.

Exposition of the *Sache selbst* is then left for *Capital*. Hence, it is right to say that the key elements of Marxian development and overthrow of the Hegelian philosophy (although 'overthrow' is a bit too strong) are found here. A philosophical conception of the bourgeois totality is taken up,[196] but the language remains to a large extent within the frame of the Hegelian dialectic, so much so that it is not wrong to say that '[a]lmost every sentence in the *Grundrisse* (Rough Draft) is reminiscent of this prototype [i.e., Hegel's philosophy] in the choice of words'.[197] With all that said, for a dialectical exposition of totality, one

---

193 This is the case not only in Marx's works, but also in Hegel, best seen, I think, in the *Science of Logic*. For further elaboration on this, see Boveiri 2016b.
194 Marx 1973, p. 7.
195 The development of this relationship is the subject of the following chapter.
196 Schmidt 1971, p. 214: 'A study of this work [i.e., the *Grundrisse*] can contribute in particular to the demolition of the legend, which still presses heavily on discussions of Marx, that only the thought of the 'young Marx' is of philosophical interest, and that the later, factually economic, problematic buried all the original impulse of real humanism'. As we have seen in Chapter 4, this is admitted also by Kosík.
197 Reichelt 2001a, p. 3: 'Fast jeder Satz in den *Grundrissen* (Rohentwurf) erinnert in der Wortwahl an dieses Vorbild' (my translation).

must refer to *Capital*. What is seen in the *Grundrisse* at the surface is built into the exposition in *Capital*.[198] Nevertheless, we must disambiguate a point first. In a letter to Lassalle of 22 February 1858, in which he calls the work *Critique of Economic Categories*, Marx says that it is simultaneously an exposition of the capitalist system, and through this exposition, a critique of it.[199] I suggest that the term 'exposition' [*Darstellung*] should be taken in a non-technical sense to mean simply exposition of research. For the exposition of the *exposition*, so to speak – that is, for the method that must be formally distinguished from the method of inquiry – one has to wait for *Capital*. As Marx himself puts it on another occasion, what is at hand in the *Grundrisse* is the 'method of elaboration'.[200]

In this section, up to this point, we have depicted the material introduced in the *Introduction* and in the *Grundrisse*, but only with reference to the brief guidelines on method in these works; no attempt could be fully realised to elaborate on method without a reference to other equally succinct points presented in the Afterword to the second edition of the first volume of *Capital*. It what follows, it will be more clearly shown that the threefold function of the method of inquiry, as elaborated by Marx in the Afterword, is also found in the *Grundrisse*, and is retained in his manuscripts as long as they are not intended for publication: the material is incorporated in detail, the forms of the development of the material are analysed, and some unity is implied in these forms. That said, the movement from the abstract to the concrete involves some exigencies that the structure of the *Grundrisse*, notwithstanding the common dialectical terms found therein – and insofar as a structure may be ascribed to it – necessarily *fails* to meet. Politically, once the discussion has been enriched by the concretisation-totalisation discourse which is the result of the exposition [*Darstellung*] of the totality of capital, the utopian optimism of the *Grundrisse* should also be overcome. Furthermore, whereas the 'historical and dialectical [exposition] are still treated as parallel in the *Grundrisse*',[201] we will see that Marx recognises their difference, notwithstanding their interrelatedness, in the three volumes of *Capital*. Hence in *Capital*, historical exposition follows theoretical exposition. The interrelatedness of the two moments lies in the fact that the systematic theoretical exposition has the historical premise behind it and vice versa.[202]

---

198 Marx 1973, p. 60.
199 Marx 1978c, p. 550.
200 Marx 1978b, p. 260.
201 Reichelt 2007, p. 37 n. 119.
202 C.f. Stuart 2003, 139.

In the last one and a half pages before the text of the manuscript breaks off, at the very end of Notebook VII, titled 'Value', Marx writes, 'Dieser Abschnitt nachzunehmen'.[203] Nicolaus translates this as: 'This section to be brought forward'. It can also mean: 'This section to be taken [into consideration] further'. Marx does both: he brings it forward and elaborates on it. He follows this phrase with a disclosure: 'The first category with which the wealth of the bourgeoisie exposes itself is that of a commodity'.[204] This may be identified as the fruit of the Odyssey of the *Grundrisse*, the result of the method of inquiry in the *Grundrisse*. It is still to be seen how this starting point, this object* [*Gegenstand*], carries along the categorial movement with itself. For that, one must wait for *Capital*[205] – the subject of the following section.

5   Totality in Categorial Movement: *Capital*

This section argues for a process of totalisation-concretisation of the categories in Marx's *Capital*, where this process of totalisation-concretisation is shown to be at the same time the process of socialisation of the categories.[206] This entails a movement from one totality – namely, 'commodity', the cellular bearer of the Totality – to another totality, namely, 'classes', or a movement from what is primarily a thing to history. We witness the socialisation, totalisation, and concretisation of the commodity. This is the movement through which the synthesis that begins from the moment of the Process of Production in Volume I, passes through the moment of the Process of Circulation (distribution and exchange) in Volume II, and culminates in Configurations of the Total Production [*Gestalltungen des Gesamtprozeßes*] in Volume III. All this development has a peculiar characteristic: in contrast to what was seen in the *Grundrisse*, the three volumes of *Capital* barely discuss totality *per se*. This does not, however, entail that this is not dealt with. Quite to the contrary! In the same way, the

---

203   Marx 1983a, pp. 767–8.
204   Marx 1983a, p. 767: 'Die erste Kategorie, worin sich der bürgerliche Reichtum darstellt, ist die der Ware'.
205   There are still further intermediary passages between the *Grundrisse* and *Capital*. Take the following widely quoted passage from *Zur Kritik der politischen Ökonomie* as an example: 'Die *Gesamtheit* dieser Produktionsverhältnisse bildet die ökonomische Struktur der Gesellschaft, die reale Basis, worauf sich ein juristischer und politischer Überbau erhebt, und welcher bestimmte gesellschaftliche Bewußtseinsformen entsprechen' (Marx 1961c, p. 8, emphasis added).
206   The term 'socialisation' is what I prefer to 'externalisation' to characterise Marxian categorial movement, as suggested by Callinicos 2014, p. 124.

word 'biology' might not appear in a book on biology, but it would certainly appear in a book that explains what biology is.[207] The relationship between the former and the latter is somewhat analogical to the relationship between *Capital* and the *Grundrisse*. Whereas the totalities in the *Grundrisse* are far from a haphazard potpourri, they are equally far from a categorial movement involving socialisation-concretisation-totalisation.

By demarcating the differences between these two works, this section of the book paves the way for what will be argued in the next chapter, which I venture to propose is its contribution to contemporary Marxian studies. To do this, I begin with an analysis of the first paragraph of the first volume of *Capital*. From this analysis, drawing on an explanation regarding the role each of the three volumes plays in Marx's total exposition as found at the beginning of the third volume of *Capital*, I accentuate the points where Marx's explanation gives support to the strategy I adopt, in arguing for the view that there is in *Capital* a threefold categorial movement of totalities. By linking this with the last category in Marx's *Capital* at the end of Volume III, namely, 'Classes', I show how the moments between these two beginning and ending moments support my view regarding the totality in categorial movement. In this way we will see how the first totality, namely, commodity, is concretised, totalised, and socialised.

That said, this section does not aim at depicting all the categories or determinations found in the three volumes of *Capital*. This would be neither helpful nor necessary. It would not be helpful, because similar efforts, aiming at different problems, already exist in the literature.[208] It is not necessary, since my goal here is different, namely, to reveal the quasi-omnipresence of the metacategory of totality and its major characteristics in these three books. One of the theses proposed in this chapter is that *Capital*, unlike all of Marx's other works, has a definite starting point that is necessary, absolute, and mediated, and which constitutes a categorial movement and is in turn constituted by this movement. The following pages are devoted to arguing for this claim.

5.1   Categorial Movement in Capital *Volume I*

5.1.1   The Opening Passage of *Capital* Volume I

The beginning of Volume III of *Capital* elaborates on the role attributed to each of the three volumes as a whole. The elaboration on this passage functions as the 'leading thread' of the account which follows here.

---

207   Cf. Althusser's (2005, p. 205) claim that the Hegelian terms appear rarely in *Capital*, and hence this book is not a philosophical but a scientific work.

208   Sekine 1997a, 1997b; Smith 1990.

Regarding the first volume, we read:

> Volume 1 of *Capital* investigated the appearances [*Erscheinungen*] exhibited by the capitalist *production process*, taken for itself [*für sich*], i.e. the immediate production process, in which connection all secondary influences external to this process were left out of account.[209]

This is then an incomplete moment of a larger account towards recreation of the reality at hand, namely, the capitalist social mode. This analysis is done by taking the production process

> both as an isolated event and as a process of reproduction: the production of surplus-value, and the production of capital itself. The formal and material changes undergone by capital in the circulation sphere were assumed, and no attempt was made to consider their details. It was, therefore, assumed both that the capitalist sells the product at its value and that he finds in the circulation sphere the material means of production that he needs to begin the process anew or to continue it without a break. The only act within the circulation sphere which we had to dwell on in that volume was the purchase and sale of labour-power as the basic condition of capitalist production.[210]

As noted before, however, at the very end of the seventh notebook, after writing that this section has to be brought forward, Marx writes: 'The first category with which the bourgeois wealth exposes itself is commodity.'[211] Interestingly, this is said to be how this wealth [*Reichtum*] is exposed. This needs apparently little modification to suit the wording of *Capital*. Let us quote the first paragraph in full:

> Der **Reichtum** der **Gesellschaften**, in welchen kapitalistische **Produktionsweise herrscht**, **erscheint** als eine 'ungeheure Warensammlung', die ein-

---

209 Marx 1991a, p. 117 (translation modified). 'Im ersten Buch wurden die Erscheinungen untersucht, die der kapitalistische *Produktionsprozeß*, für sich genommen, darbietet, als unmittelbarer Produktionsprozeß, bei dem noch von allen sekundären Einwirkungen ihm fremder Umstände abgesehn wurde. Aber dieser unmittelbare Produktionsprozeß erschöpft nicht den Lebenslauf des Kapitals'. Marx 1964, p. 33.
210 Marx 1992a, pp. 428–9.
211 Marx 1983a, p. 767: 'Die erste Kategorie, worin sich der bürgerliche Reichtum darstellt, ist die der Ware'.

zelne Ware als seine *Elementarform*. Unsere *Untersuchung* beginnt *daher* mit der *Analyse* der *Ware*.²¹²

In this paragraph, which is left unchanged from the first edition,²¹³ we witness several important methodological points. The first important word of the paragraph, 'wealth' [*Reichtum*], reminds the reader of Adam Smith's *The Wealth of Nations*; however, Marx's subject is not the wealth of nations, but the wealth of societies. The reason is clear: several nations can be constituents of the capitalist mode of social life; the nations composing societies are then to be discussed according to the similarities prevailing throughout a society, which can be common among various nations. The concept of society (in this respect, like nation) carries within it the notion of contingency different from that found in natural objects, a consequence of the distinction between object and object* we discussed earlier.²¹⁴ To confirm this interpretation, the paragraph following this uses the word object* [*Gegenstand*].

The next noteworthy phrase is 'the capitalist mode of production'. As I suggested before, I think we may ignore 'production', and say instead 'the capitalist mode of social life' to be able to stop focusing just on production. In so doing, we will be able to incorporate all the moments of a capitalist society, and not just production, distribution, exchange, and consumption, as was suggested in the *Introduction* of the *Grundrisse* and discussed in the previous section, but also the superstructural as well as the technological features (forces of production) of capitalist society. The word 'dominates' [*herrscht*] also implies an important distinctive point in the Marxian approach. One is related to the consequences of this domination. The domination (or generalisation) of this form of production brings about the contradictory characteristics in the totality of social life which stem from the basic contradiction within this cellular form. The social totality is constituted by the determination of the commodity by this 'smallest social form in which the labour product is exposed in the current society'.²¹⁵ The logic of the necessity of this generalisation imposes itself on all aspects of the totality. There are limits to this analysis: only those societies which share those characteristics can be discussed here, and some societies

---

212 Marx 1962a, p. 49 (emphasis added).
213 Marx 1983b, p. 17: 'Der Reichthum der Gesellschaften, in welchen kapitalistische Produktionsweise herrscht, erscheint als eine "ungeheure Waarensammlung", die einzelne Waare als seine Elementarform. Unsere Untersuchung beginnt daher mit der Analyse der Waare'.
214 See Chapter 4 and section 1 above.
215 Marx 1987b, p. 369: 'einfachste gesellschaftliche Form, worin sich das Arbeitsprodukt in der jetzigen Gesellschaft darstellt'.

therefore remain outside the scope of the discussion. Empirically, the life of the natives *per se* (in their own societies) cannot be discussed in this analysis, nor can societies where what is dominant is not the capitalist mode of social life. Take Occupied Palestine for instance: the relationship among people in that territory cannot be analysed with reference to the Marxian approach presented here, because the characteristics of such relationships are themselves overshadowed by the relations of the occupation. These relationships among people can, of course, be analysed in their relation to the totality of this mode, insofar as it influences or even creates them, as is arguably the case in Occupied Palestine. What is at hand, then, is an *open totality* that incorporates the externality[216] as well.[217]

All this wealth, the text goes on, 'appears' [*erscheint*] as an amalgam of commodities. From a methodological point of view, the word 'appears' is more *precise* than the word 'exposes' that we saw at the end of Notebook VII of the *Grundrisse*. It 'appears' so only to those who have already finished their inquiry, and equally to those familiarised with this exposition. The idea is that this tremendous mass of commodities will be shown to be far from a haphazard potpourri. Not only because, as can be instantly known, these are not natural but man-made objects*, but also because each, as a thing, is a false abstraction which detaches whoever focuses on it from the processual life of the society dominated by the capitalist mode. This is a reminder that a commodity is a totality 'of capitalism's abstract and undeveloped determinations'[218] in capitalism as the Totality. The question that arises immediately is whether it *is* also as it *appears*. This duality of *appears-is*, or let us say *appearance-essence*, remains a crucial point through the three volumes of *Capital*. Given that equating appearance and essence is, to say the least, not always correct, an effort is necessary. This reminds us of the detour or bypass [*Oklika*] underscored in Chapter 4. The equivalent of this [*Oklika*] here is the [*Untersuchung*], or investigation, which begins with the analysis of the commodity. The analysis [*Analyse*] itself is what the investigation begins with. The commodity, introduced as an element, is later known to be the product of this mode, the particular existence of which constitutes the capitalist mode in its totality, as its element. Being a

---

216   The term 'externality' is an alternative proposed by Enrique Dussel (2001) in preference to 'totality'.
217   Then, those claims miss the point that go so far as to say '*there can be absolutely no aspect of human existence that does not become determined as an instance of this metabolic interaction inverted as an attribute of capital. However, inverted in its form, this is the mode in which the materiality of human life exists. As a consequence, there can be no exteriority to its movement*' (Starosta 2016, p. 202, emphasis added).
218   Kosík 1976, p. 109.

totality, it also has the germ of all the contradictions inherent in wealth, but also of the whole capitalist mode; this is why, therefore [*daher*], the analysis must begin with that.[219] Being an elementary form [*Elementarform*] is for a commodity true in two senses: it is the starting point, and it is also the smallest cellular form of this mode or this apparent wealth. It also appears as only an elementary *form*. Since this form is not an empty form, it has a content; moreover, given that form, according to Marx, is the mode of material existence, in this case the cellular form is simultaneously the cellular mode of material existence of that totality, namely, the capitalist mode.

However, the goal is not mere analysis of this mode, but as the title of the book implies, its *critique*. Hence, showing the contradictions of this mode within this cellular form is what Marx's masterpiece begins with: contradictions within this cellular form of totality represent the contradictions of this mode of social life in its totality once they have passed through subsequent steps shown to be also inherently related to all other moments-totalities. What we witness in this paragraph is then the movement from totality to Totality, where totality is the commodity and Totality the capitalist mode of social life, the contradictions of which will be revealed through the movement between the commodity and how commodity appears as wealth. Each moment of this Totality, then, is at the same time a totality.

The question that remains to be answered is: If the starting point of investigation is supposed to be the commodity, why does such a precise starting point appear in this book, and not in the *Grundrisse*? While an adequate response to this question cannot be given here – for that the reader must wait until the following chapter – it may be accepted for the time being that perhaps in the *Grundrisse* Marx was dealing with a somewhat different problem, namely, the method of inquiry. Last but not least, one further word that does not appear in this text, and that is of utmost importance, is the word 'process', a word repeated in the subtitle of all three volumes of *Capital*: the categories discussed are not things but the processes of which their thing-likeness is just an abstraction.

However, the introduction of the very starting point, the first category, namely, the commodity, comes as the introduction of the horizon to which the moment of this category leads, namely, the capitalist mode of social life; it can even be said that this starting point is the result of envisaging such a horizon. This very starting point, however, is the result of the recognition of a contradiction lying in this very category, namely, its dual existence, made up of realities

---

219 This will be further elaborated in Chapter 6.

which repel each other but also cohere.[220] According to this reading, all other categories, including abstract labour, which produces the exchange value of each commodity, are categories and determinations that will be derived from the commodity as the starting point.[221]

The claim presented here regarding the existence of systematic dialectical method in the form of categorial movement in *Capital* does not entail that this movement is smooth. More precisely, the fact that there are moments of discordant or out-of-tune analysis[222] in Marx's account in *Capital* in general and in the first volume in particular, does not entail the absence of such a movement.

5.1.2 Categorial Movement in *Capital* Volume I

It has been argued previously that a truly genuine dialectical conception of totality gives weight equally to the whole and to the parts in an organic relationship. In *Capital* Volume I, Marx elaborates on the topic of heterogeneous and organic manufactures: discontinuous processes involving workers with many different skills as in manufacturing locomotives, and 'organic' continuous manufacturing. Whereas in the former the cooperation is scattered and loosely connected, this is not the case in the latter: direct cooperation of all the workers is absolutely necessary. He emphasises a totality in the latter type of manufacturing, in which each worker keeps the other workers busy, and the relationship is such that the whole crumbles when one member or group that is constituent of the totality, as an 'organ of a single organism', functions improperly: 'the whole body is paralysed if only one of its members is missing'.[223] 'The collective worker, from the combination of the many specialised workers',[224] turns the homogeneous abstract labour (as that which produces exchange value) and the heterogeneous concrete labour (as that which produces use value) into a totality in the action of the individuals working together as a whole. The result is the objective* world of commodities, possessing the dual characteristics of use value and exchange value.

---

220 Cf. Hegel 1969c, p. 556: 'Die konkrete Totalität, welche den Anfang macht, hat als solche in ihr selbst den Anfang des Fortgehens und der Entwicklung'.

221 Cf. Smith 1990, p. 59: 'Abstract labour … is the starting point in the reconstruction of the capitalist mode of production proposed by Marx'.

222 The examples abound in the literature. Paul Mattick, Jr. argues that in *Capital* the necessity of money as 'the necessary form of the appearance' of abstract labour is not derived through a logical argument but practical requirements; see Mattick 1993, pp. 115–34. In the same volume where Mattick's paper appears, Geert Reuten (1993) argues that the derivation of labour is not a dialectical but rather an analytical or reductive abstraction.

223 Marx 1976, p. 466.

224 Marx 1976, p. 464.

In further elaborating on the objectivity of this totality, in his discussion in the third section of the first chapter, on the Value Form or Exchange Value, Marx introduces an objectivity* [*Gegenständlichkeit*] to contradistinguish this from the objectivity found in physical objects. In the former, there is not even one atom found in the commodities as physical objects, when considered with respect to their 'value objectivity'* [*Wertgegenständlichkeit*].[225] Its immateriality, however, should not be taken to entail the absence of objectivity, nor should it be taken as evidence against Marx's being a materialist; rather, it indicates not only that Marx's materialism 'centers on material practices in the social world',[226] but also attributes this materiality to the material world, as seen in his discussion regarding contradictions in nature. Given that value is a social relation, the fact that you cannot 'see, touch or feel' it[227] does not entail that it is not objective*.

Notwithstanding the difference in objectivity or materiality that Marx introduces here in the context of the distinction between use value and exchange value, or social objectivity* versus natural objectivity, this difference should not be taken to interrupt objectivity, let alone to express any sweeping denial of objectivity,[228] or, following from that, the objectivity of the contradictions themselves. If one recalls the sociality of the commodity, it is not surprising that such a standpoint leads to claims like that of the non-existence of society,[229] found also in the mouths of the founders of the current neoliberal era.[230] Marx's approach is quite different. According to him, the same law of the transformation of quantitative changes into qualitative changes at a particular point, the law that is true of natural phenomena, holds equally true in society and social history.[231] These contradictions constitute an objectively* contra-

---

225   Marx 1976, p. 138: 'Not an atom of matter enters into the objectivity* of commodities as values; in this it is the direct opposite of the coarsely sensuous objectivity* of commodities as physical objects'. In this, Marx iterates the standpoint already put forward in the *Grundrisse*: 'Das Kapital ist seinem Wesen nach immer immateriell' (Marx 1983a. p. 230).
226   Smith 1993b, p. 17.
227   Harvey 2010, p. 33.
228   Cf. Žižek 2002, p. 181: '"There is no world" means: there is no "true objective reality", since reality as such *emerges from* a distorted perspective, from a disturbance of the equilibrium of the primordial Void-Nothingness' (emphasis added).
229   Žižek 2002, p. 182.
230   Cf. Thatcher 1987: 'They are casting their problems at society. And, you know, there's no such thing as society. There are individual men and women and there are families. And no government can do anything except through people, and people must look after themselves first'.
231   Marx 1962a, p. 327: 'Hier, wie in der Naturwissenschaft, bewährt sich die Richtigkeit des von Hegel in seiner *Logik* entdeckten Gesetzes, daß bloß quantitative Veränderungen auf

dictory totality, and they can only be transformed objectively*. The expression of contradiction found in prices, for instance, is the reflection of the real objective* immanent contradiction in this mode of production.[232] In Chapter 3 of *Capital*, in the discussion of the metamorphosis of commodities and inherent contradictions, Marx refers to a specific natural phenomenon, that of planetary motion. The realisation of contradictions and their resolution in the exchange process of commodities is claimed to be similar to the realisation and resolution of the contradiction between momentum and gravitation in elliptical motion.[233]

As to the elementary form of this totality with 'its sensuous characteristics extinguished',[234] since no matter how and how many times a commodity is turned and twisted around, its value-possessing character cannot be sensuously grasped at all, it is particularly this objectivity* which deprives the commodities of qualitative difference;[235] thus their exchange value (the only characteristic left to them) necessitates the application of the power of abstraction as the only available means for their analysis. To call this activity a 'method' of solving contradictions, as Marx does, is what permits me to say that the Marxian method is in a sense a metamethod, in that it admits the impossibility of solving contradictions simply in theory, and instead searches for a resolution of the contradictions in the only remaining manner: praxis in the objective* sphere of the contradictions. This is the repercussion of the second thesis of Feuerbach, in which the role of praxis in truth is highlighted.

The totality thus taken has different representations. 'The totality of heterogeneous use-values or physical commodities reflects a totality of similarly heterogeneous forms of useful labour, which differ in order, genus, species, and variety: in short, a social division of labour'.[236] The individual labourer owns a constituent part of the totality of the labour power, and comes into

---

einem gewissen Punkt in qualitative Unterschiede umschlagen'. Cf. p. 623: '[D]er Hegelsche Widerspruch [ist] die Springquelle aller Dialektik'.

232 Marx 1976, pp. 322–3: 'If, therefore, such expressions as "£90 variable capital" or "such and such a quantity of self-valorizing value" appear to contain contradictions, this is only because they express a contradiction immanent in capitalist production'.
233 Marx 1976, p. 198.
234 Marx 1976, p. 128.
235 Marx 1976, p. 128: 'As use-values, commodities differ above all in quality, while as exchange-values they can only differ in quantity, and therefore do not contain an atom of use-value'.
236 Marx 1976, p. 132. This twofold totality overlooked by some commentators leads to drastic consequences. For an example see Postone 2003.

relation with other labourers; this has a social form only once they exchange their labour power for money or for means of subsistence.[237] Their relationship with each other turns into a relationship with things, which entails spectre-like objectivity* [*gespenstige Gegenständlichkeit*].[238] Furthermore, in the perpetual need for self-alienation, they lose their identity in its totality.[239]

In Marx's treatment of the cause of the distinction between labour and labour power, the elaboration on this category takes us beyond the point that had been reached in *The Economic and Philosophical Manuscripts of 1844*. Here in *Capital*, he repeats the interconnection between the earth and work, as a twofold source of wealth. Whereas 'labour-power itself is, above all else, the material of nature transposed into a human organism',[240] what is provided by nature is the material substratum that remains once all the useful labour is subtracted from any commodity.[241] This twofold source of use values is the finding to which Marx remains loyal in his later works.[242] After having 'illustrated the movement of surplus-value sufficiently in Volume I'[243] of *Capital*, this discussion must find its place in relation to circulation – which it does in Volume II.

---

237 Marx 1976, pp. 165–6: 'Objects of utility become commodities only because they are the products of the labour of private individuals who work independently of each other. The sum total of the labour of all these private individuals forms the aggregate labour of society. Since the producers do not come into social contact until they exchange the products of their labour, the specific social characteristics of their private labours appear only within this exchange. In other words, the labour of the private individual manifests itself as an element of the total labour of society only through the relations which the act of exchange establishes between the products, and, through their mediation, between the producers. To the producers, therefore, the social relations between their private labours appear as what they are, i.e. they do not appear as direct social relations between persons in their work, but rather as [thing-like] [*dinglich*] relations between persons and social relations between things'.
238 Marx 1962a, p. 52.
239 Hegel 1989, § 67, pp. 144–5: Quoted in Marx 19762a, p. 272.
240 Marx 1976, p. 323.
241 Marx 1976, p. 133: 'If we subtract the total amount of useful labour of different kinds which is contained in the coat, the linen, etc., a material substratum is always left. This substratum is furnished by nature without human intervention'.
242 See Marx 1987b, p. 15: 'Die Arbeit ist nicht die Quelle alles Reichtums. Die Natur ist ebensosehr die Quelle der Gebrauchswerte (und aus solchen besteht doch wohl der sachliche Reichtum!) als die Arbeit, die selbst nur die Äußerung einer Naturkraft ist, der menschlichen Arbeitskraft'.
243 Marx 2016, p. 83.

5.2   Categorial Movement in Capital Volume II

Regarding the second volume, we read:

> But this immediate production process [discussed in the first volume] does not exhaust the life cycle of capital. In the actual world, it is supplemented by the *circulation process*, and this formed our object* of investigations [*Gegenstand der Untersuchungen*] in the second volume. Here we showed, particularly in Part Three, where we considered the circulation process as it mediates the process of social reproduction, that the capitalist production process, taken as a whole, is a unity of the production and circulation processes.[244]

The categories introduced here therefore are to be set free from the immediacy found in the first volume. What was 'left out of account' is brought back in it. The general movement in this volume aims at depicting how the circulation process totalises itself in unity with the production process: from the metamorphoses of capital in the first part to the turnover of capital in the second part, culminating in the reproduction and circulation of the totality of social capital.

Loyal to the distinction introduced in the 'Theses on Feuerbach', Marx avoids the word *Objekt* and introduces *Gegenstand*, which I have been indicating up to here as object*.[245] Considering this object* by setting aside the assumptions necessary just for the 'formal manner of exposition' [*nur formelle Manier der Darstellung*][246] of the totality found in the first volume, the real movement of the subject matter [*Sache selbst*] can be laid out. This new moment of exposition brings with it the openness of totality that is characteristic of the Marxian totality introduced before in this book, one of the principal theses argued for here,[247] which is elaborated on in *Capital* Volume II, and could only find its place in that volume. The point is that, although the capitalist mode has this tendency to 'transform all possible production into commodity production', it is equally conditioned by 'modes of production lying outside its own stage of development'.[248] Whereas Parts I and II of this volume focus on the individual capitalist, part III examines circulation and reproduction,

---

244 Marx 1991a, p. 117, translation modified. Marx 1964, p. 33.
245 See Chapter 4, section 3 above.
246 Marx 1963a, p. 393; Marx 1992a, p. 470.
247 Cf. Starosta 2016, p. 202 where he denies the exteriority.
248 Marx 1992a, p. 190.

this time no longer from an individual but from a social perspective, with the final chapter (Chapter 21) discussing reproduction on a large scale.[249] The constituents of capital introduced in the first volume as constant and variable capital are developed further in this volume by introducing departments of production, as well as by elaborating on constant and variable capitals, and the account is also enriched with the addition of fixed and circulating capital in Chapter 20.

Regarding these two latter terms, one point is noteworthy. In the 'Theses on Feuerbach', we saw that the essence of the human is asserted to be the ensemble of the social relations constituted. This characteristic is not limited to human beings. The same object* found in different relations with its milieu goes from one category to another. Whereas fixed and circulating capital are at first glance mutually exclusive, the same entity – an ox, for instance – as a means of labour is fixed capital, but once it is slaughtered, it becomes circulating capital. Likewise, the change in the relation of the constituents of a totality to the Totality changes not only those constituents, but also the Totality at hand. A house can be a place of work, and therefore a constituent [*Bestandteil*] of productive capital, but once it turns into a dwelling place it loses this function.[250]

Regarding the constellation of categories presented here, further discussion is necessary. The same category, namely, simple reproduction, discussed in Chapter 21 of the first volume, is taken up here under the circulation of surplus value (Chapter 17), and its role in reproduction and circulation is elaborated (Chapter 20), this time incorporating it into extended reproduction (Chapter 21), thus giving a more comprehensive account of total capital. Whereas up to here in the discussion of *Capital* (both Volumes I and II), capitalists have been considered mainly in their role as non-consumers, here (Chapter 20) they are considered as consumers. Marx does this by introducing two departments of social production. Department I of social production produces new means of production – those produced to be put into the production of commodities. Department II of social production produces other commodities to be consumed by capitalists and workers. This latter department is divided into two subdivisions: necessary means of living, and luxury goods. Once the scene is set, Marx moves from constant capital in Department I, to variable capital and surplus value in both departments, and then constant capital in both departments. Without the discussion presented in Chapter 20, Marx could

---

249   Cf. Fox 1985.
250   Marx 1992a, pp. 280–1. The twofold essence of the *Sache selbst* is emphasised here.

not move to accumulation in both departments and extended reproduction in Chapter 21. With this, Marx has brought circulation into unity with production in the totality of the capitalist mode.

We saw in a previous section the contradictions found in relation to money in the 'Chapter on Money' in the *Grundrisse*. Now an elaboration on the way money is treated in this volume can be useful – this time, in contrast to the first volume, in money's role in circulation. Turned into money-capital, money demonstrates characteristics that were not shown in the first volume.[251] In the fourth chapter, money is considered together with the natural and the credit economy and their intertwined character in the totality of capital is emphasised.

We saw previously[252] that one characteristic of a genuinely dialectical totality is the reciprocal determination of parts and the whole, which is also stressed in the Introduction to the *Grundrisse*.[253] This is more concretely discussed in the second Volume of *Capital*. In Chapter 4, Marx first introduces the three figures of the circuit process [*die drei Figuren des Kreislaufprozesses*]:

(I) M–C ... P ... C'–M'
(II) P ... Tc ... P
(III) Tc ... P (C').

where M and C stand for money and commodity, M' and C' for newer money and commodity, P for production or the valorisation process, and Tc for the total circulation, or valorised value. All these three circuits have the valorisation of value as their goal and impetus or driving motif [*treibendes Motiv*]. In this account in which the third circuit is the unity of the first two, thus introducing the process in its totality, Marx goes further than the similar discussion in Volume I; here he aims at a dialectical sursumption [*Aufhebung*] of the inevitably formal discussion presented there,[254] further incorporating the complexity of the real. Only when this is done can he write: 'The total circuit presents itself for each functional form of capital as its own specific circuit, and indeed each of these circuits conditions the continuity of the overall process; the circular course of one functional form determines that of the others'[255] – 'and is determined by others', one may add.

---

251 Marx 1992a, p. 429.
252 See Chapter 1.
253 See the previous section.
254 Volume I, Chapters 2 and 3.
255 Marx 1992a, p. 184.

The constant presence of the different moments of capital (commodity capital transformed into money; money capital transformed into productive capital; and productive capital transformed into commodity capital) is mediated by the circuit of the total capital. Taken as a processual whole instead of a static thing,[256] the totality of capital is thus constituted by the presence of all these fluid moments and the codetermination of these among themselves, and this also determines the total capital.[257] This is how two processes, the production process and the circulation process, which are mutually exclusive in time,[258] form a unity in the last chapter.

The purchase and repurchase of labour power is the subject matter [*Sache selbst*] of the circulation process discussion, with labour acting as the 'work of combustion' being 'a necessary moment of the totality' of capitalist production. It is only now that Marx can write: 'This labour ... is a necessary moment of the capitalist production process in its totality, and also includes circulation, or is included by it'.[259] We have seen previously how Marx speaks of this as the fermenting agent; here he uses as an analogy the combustion that sets some material alight.[260]

The clearest account of totality is probably given in Chapter 18. Each singular commodity constitutes an organic member or limb of the total social capital, and each is likewise a singular capital:

> The movement of social capital consists of the totality of independent fragments, the turnover of the individual capitals. In the same way that the metamorphosis of a singular commodity is a member of the series of the metamorphoses of the commodities in their totality, so the metamorphosis of each singular capital, its turnover, is a member of movement circle of the social capital.[261]

---

256 Marx 1992a, p. 185.
257 Marx 1992a, p. 184.
258 Marx 1992a, p. 203: 'Circulation time and production time are mutually exclusive. During its circulation time, capital does not function as productive capital, and therefore produces neither commodities nor surplus-value'.
259 Marx 1992a, p. 208.
260 Marx 1992a, p. 208.
261 Marx 1963a, p. 352: 'Die Bewegung des gesellschaftlichen Kapitals besteht aus der Totalität der Bewegungen seiner verselbständigten Bruchstücke, der Umschläge der individuellen Kapitale. Wie die Metamorphose der einzelnen Ware ein Glied der Metamorphosenreihe der Warenwelt – der Warenzirkulation – ist, so die Metamorphose des individuellen Kapitals, sein Umschlag, ein Glied im Kreislauf des gesellschaftlichen Kapitals'. Marx 1992a, pp. 427–8 (translation modified). Cf. 1963a, pp. 353–4; 1992a, pp. 429–30.

This total process embraces consumption at both the individual and the social level; the individual seller of labour power constitutes a class at the social level, dealing with the buyer of this labour power.[262] This circulation, which prior to this was the circulation of the commodity capitals, turns into circulation of surplus value. As Marx puts it: 'Thus, the circuit of the individual capitals, therefore, drawn into the social capital, i.e. considered in their totality, do not embrace just the circulation of capital, but also the general commodity circulation in general'.[263]

This is quite a novel treatment of the totality of social production in unity with circulation. It is radically different from a standpoint, like that of Proudhon, who in taking the production *en bloc* fails to see the distinction of the moments of that totality, with their historical and economic characteristics.[264] This particular treatment paves the way for a still more comprehensive account in Volume III. This is what we turn to now.

5.3 *Categorial Movement in Capital Volume III*

Following some commentators,[265] in my discussion I prefer the title originally given by Marx, namely, *Gestaltungen des Gesamtprozeßes*, or the *Configurations of Total Production*, rather than the modified version chosen by Engels, *Der Gesamtprozeß der kapitalistischen Produktion*, or *The Total Process of the Capitalist Production*. For whereas the former title leaves some room for the less definite elaboration presented in the work and also permits the openness of the account, the latter misses this in suggesting the completion of the project.[266] This is misleading not only in relation to what are generally agreed to be very sketchy passages, such as the one dealing with classes, but also with respect to some others in which the issues are discussed in more detail, such as the discussion of competition.[267] That said, I refer to the MEW edition and the translation of Marx's manuscripts for *Capital* Volume III. Given the debates on the negative influence of Engels on the overall text intended by Marx, I provide in Appendix II other versions of some of the passages discussed here.[268] Non-

---

262 Marx 1963a, p. 353.
263 Marx 1992a, p. 428.
264 Marx 1992a, p. 509.
265 Callinicos 2014, p. 41; Heinrich 1996–7, pp. 452–66. For a detailed account regarding the differences between the published text as Volume III of *Capital* and the *Manuscripts*, see Fred Moseley's Introduction in Marx, 2016, pp. 1–44.
266 Heinrich 1996–7, p. 457.
267 On the incompleteness of the third volume of *Capital* concerning competition, see Moseley 2014, p. 116.
268 That is: what is known as *Capital* Volume III (Marx 1991a); the original text in German in

etheless, to facilitate the discussion, I will continue to refer to the text discussed here as *Capital* Volume III. Throughout the discussion, I completely avoid what Engels added as the 'Supplement and Addendum' at the end of the book,[269] since this is widely thought to offer an interpretation different from Marx's own.[270]

Regarding the third volume, the text says that after having already shown that the process of production is the unity of both the production process and the circulation process:

> It cannot be the purpose of the present book to make general reflections on this 'unity'. What is necessary is rather to discover and present the concrete forms [*Formen*] which grow out of the process of capital, considered as a whole. (In their actual movement, capitals confront each other in certain concrete forms, for which both the shape of capital in the direct production process and its shape in the process of circulation appear merely as particular aspects of their movement. The forms [*Gestaltungen*] of capital, as we develop them in this book, thus come closer, step by step, to the form [*Form*] in which they appear at the surface of society, in the everyday consciousness of the agents of production themselves and finally in the action of the different capitals upon each other, namely competition.)[271]

We see then a movement from abstract to concrete as the promising path advised in the Introduction to the *Grundrisse*, a movement from essence to its apparent form. This means arriving at the phenomenal forms after this long exposition of the categories, which can be realised only at this stage. In adopting a movement from essence to the apparent forms of social totality, the Marxian standpoint is radically different from that taken by the vulgar economists who take the phenomenal forms as their starting points. This is why it is only at this point that Marx can write: '*At last* we have arrived at *the forms of manifestation* which serve as the *starting point* in the vulgar'.[272]

Das Kapital III, in *MEW* 25 (Marx 1964); the translation of the manuscripts of 1861–3 (Marx 2016) on the basis of which Engels prepared *Capital* Volume III; and the original text of these manuscripts in *MEGA*² II. 4.2, Teil 2 (Marx 1992b).

269 Marx 1964, pp. 895–922; 1991a, pp. 1027–47.
270 For one example, see Callinicos 2014, pp. 38–43.
271 Marx 2016, p. 49; Marx 1992b, p. 7.
272 'Endlich sind wir angelangt bei den Erscheinungsformen, die dem Vulgär als Ausgang-

The totality so far shown in more theoretically abstract forms is here demonstrated to function at the concrete level. For instance, after having discussed the totality of value and the rate of surplus value, it will be shown here how these are transformed into profit and rate of profit. More concretely, whereas up to here we have discussed the relationship among values in totality, what is at stake here is to show how prices reciprocally interact in a totality, along with production and circulation, and with industrial capital and commercial capital among the other forms which capital takes.[273] The individual production price of a commodity is not the same as its value, but once the prices are taken in their totality, and attention is turned to the total value of commodities in a branch of production, the price is determined relatively by the value.[274] Whereas the relationship between different single values and single prices is generally contingent and depends on myriads of coincidences, this is not the case when a whole branch of production is taken into account. In that case, the sum of prices coincides with the sum of values.[275]

An excellent example of the concrete form of presenting the unity of different moments of the capitalist mode can be seen in Marx's discussion in Chapter 10 of the role of competition. Competition, which belongs to a different moment of totality from production, plays the role of the distributor of the total capital. In this process, 'equal amounts of capital' ultimately 'receive equal shares of the totality of surplus value that is produced by the total social capital'.[276] In the same vein, once the transformation of the surplus value into

---

spunkt dienen ...' Marx and Engels 1974, p. 74. The *Collected Works* adds 'conception' to the text. Marx, letter to Engels, 30 April 1868, in Marx 1992c, p. 74 (first emphasis added). See Postone 2003, p. 137.

[273] See, Luxemburg 2013, p. 246: 'For the totality of all branches of production the rise in prices in one case and the fall in prices in another compensate for one another, and as a whole *the outcome will be what theory has shown us*' (emphasis added).

[274] Marx 1992b, p. 700; Marx 1964, p. 766.

[275] Marx 1992b, p. 236. Marx 2016, p. 271.

[276] Here is the full quote: '*Competition* distributes the social capital between the various spheres of production in such a way that the *prices of production* in each of those spheres > (disregarding the question of how large a portion of the fixed capital goes into these prices for wear-and-tear) < are equal to the prices in the spheres of mean composition, i.e., k + p, > where k is the cost price, but a *variable* magnitude, and p is a constant magnitude, namely is equivalent to the magnitude of the < percentage profit in that sphere (which in the sphere of mean composition coincides with the surplus-value). The rate of profit is thus the same in all spheres of production, because it is adjusted to that in those branches of production where the average composition of capital prevails. The sum of the profits for all the different spheres of production would then be equal to the sum of surplus-values, and the sum of the prices of production for the total social product would then be equal to the sum of its values. It is evident, however, that the equalisa-

profit and the rate of surplus value into rate of profit is established, a change happens that goes further than the formal difference.[277] The final configuration of the economic relation concealed in its essential form, the kernel form of the commodity, comes to the surface in a quite different and even reversed form.[278]

The stepwise incorporation of social contingency in the totality of this mode, 'the underlying unity of seemingly diverse and incoherent movements'[279] and moments, is also quite remarkable at this stage. On one occasion Marx presents a law as the cause of crises (the law of the tendential fall of rate of profit). He puts this law, the discovery of which he takes to be his own contribution,[280] in very simple terms: '[T]aking any particular quantity of average social capital, e.g., a capital of 100, an ever greater portion of this is represented by means of labour and an ever lesser portion by living labour'.[281] Thus, 'the worker finds him or herself in a vicious circle in which the increases in productivity turn against him or her in creating unemployment that functions as a lever to the intensification of labour'.[282] Following its exposition, the dis-

---

tion between spheres of production of different composition > (whether these differences are based simply on differences in the ratio between constant and variable capital, or also arise from variations in circulation time) < must always seek to adjust these to the spheres of mean composition, whether these correspond exactly to the social average or just approximately. Between those spheres that approximate more or less to the social average there is again a tendency to equalisation, which seeks a possibly ideal mean position, i.e., a mean position which does not exist in reality. In other words, it tends to shape itself around this ideal as a norm. In this way there prevails, and necessarily so, a tendency to make production prices into mere transformed forms of value, or to transform profits into mere portions of surplus-value that are distributed, not in proportion to the surplus-value that is created in each particular sphere of production, but rather in proportion to the amount of capital applied in each of these spheres, so that equal amounts of capital, no matter how they are composed, receive equal shares (aliquot parts) of the totality of surplus-value produced by the total social capital >' (Marx 2016 p. 284; Marx 1992b, p. 249).

277 Marx, letter to Engels, 30 April 1868, in Marx 1992c, p. 22: '[W]hile profit is at first only formally different from surplus value, the rate of profit is, by contrast, at once really different from the rate of surplus value, for in one case we have m/v and in the other m/(c + v), from which it follows from the outset, since m/v > m/(c + v), that the rate of profit < than the rate of surplus value, unless c = 0'.
278 Marx 1992b, p. 279; Marx 1964, p. 219.
279 Harvey 1999, p. 405.
280 Marx 2016, p. 322.
281 Marx 2016, p. 324.
282 My rather free translation from Dardot and Laval 2012, p. 274: 'Le travailleur est pris dans un cercle vicieux dans lequel les hausses de productivité se retournent vers lui en créant un chômage qui sert de levier a l'intensification du travail'.

cussion of the law is immediately followed[283] by a whole number of counteracting influences which check, delay, and condition that law.[284] Although 'the law in its generality [*Allgemeinheit*] is independent of that division [of profits] and of the mutual relationships of the categories of profit deriving from it',[285] when it comes to the level of particularity it faces these counter-influences.

A more illustrative example of the discussion of totality is in the famous trinity formula.[286] Here, we are reminded that the totality of dual relationship of subjects or members of society with nature and with each other forms the society.[287] We see in that chapter how the sources of income – capital in the form of interest-profit, land in the form of ground rent, and labour in the form of wages – once shown in organic relation to each other, and with the whole process displayed in its totality with labour together with nature as the ultimate source of wealth, make possible a concrete analysis of the process of production in its most general form.[288]

To remain a revolutionary account, with an echo of the 'expropriation of the expropriators' in Volume I, the discussion of book three must end with a discussion of classes[289] to reflect the fact that contradictions, seen from the very beginning, cannot be simply theorised away.[290] Marx does not search for a formal and logical consistency in something which is essentially inconsistent, which is also the theme in those passages where he criticises James Mill.[291] In his discussion of crises, Marx deals with the way the limits and barriers inherent in a capitalist society lead to crises. Crises, always inherent in the capitalist mode, become apparent to the eyes of the non-dialectical researcher, who must either take the crisis as an exception to a law or a cognitive mistake – not a

---

283 This is found in the Manuscripts under the title ⟨CHAPTER THREE *The Law of the Tendential Fall in the General Rate of Profit*⟩ *with the Advance of Capitalist Production* Marx 2016, p. 320. In Marx 1991a, Chapters 13 and 14.

284 The most general counteracting causes include: 1. More Intense Exploitation of Labour; 2. Reduction of Wages below their Value; 3. Cheapening of the Elements of Constant Capital; 4. The Relative Surplus Population; 5. Foreign Trade; 6. The Increase in Share Capital, Marx 2016, p. 337. See also pages 375 in Marx 2016 and *Capital* III, p. 375, where he introduces other aspects that condition the falling rate of profit.

285 Marx 2016, p. 322.

286 Chapter 48 in Marx 1991a, Marx 2016, p. 528 and p. 445.

287 Marx 2016, p. 528, Marx 1991a, p. 957.

288 Marx 2016, p. 898. Marx 1991a, Chapter 49.

289 Marx 2016, p. 949 ff. Marx 1991a, Chapter 51.

290 Cf. Hall 2003, p. 121.

291 Marx 1968e, p. 29.

real crisis but a merely apparent one. According to Marx, on the other hand, being a contradictory totality objectively makes theorising away this contradiction ridiculous.[292] For him, these contradictions inhere in objective* reality, and the only way to do away with them is through revolutionary praxis, echoing the 'Theses on Feuerbach'.[293] Now that it has not only been stated but also demonstrated that the true barrier holding back the capitalist mode as a transitory and historical and not a natural eternal mode is capital itself,[294] a mode the development of which comes into contradiction with its own development, it may be said that there is an objective* need to revolutionise this contradictory totality. As Marx writes to Engels seven months after the publication of the first volume of *Capital*, now that the movement in its totality in its apparent form is depicted,

> [S]ince those 3 items (wages, rent, profit (interest)) constitute the sources of income of the 3 classes of landowners, capitalists and wage labourers, we have the *class struggle*, as the conclusion in which the movement and disintegration of the whole shit resolves itself.[295]

5.4 Conclusion

One may say that what we witnessed in the three volumes of *Capital* is a particular movement: a movement from one aspect of reality, concretely abstracted totality, abstracted reality in its kernel, germinal form, namely, commodity, to the level of the totality that is concretised-socialised-totalised; a movement from a rather monocular perspective of reality to an increasingly panoptic perspective of reality. Through this movement, the more formal differences (e.g., between profit and interest) turn into real social differences in the form of the antagonistic conflict between the two sides of the class struggle. This is equally a movement from a level where several points were neglected or assumed because of their off-topic insignificance, or because they could not be discussed at that particular moment, notwithstanding their effects on what was discussed, to this particular moment in the third volume, where those influences are reincorporated and their influence, and the contingency that they carry along with them, can be dealt with.[296] The fact that this categorial move-

---

292 Cf. Ilyenkov 1982, p. 239.
293 This will be discussed further in the following pages.
294 Marx 1992b, 324; Marx 2016, p. 359.
295 Marx, letter to Engels, 30 April 1868 (in Marx 1992c, p. 25).
296 For a discussion of the movement of the assumptions and their role in economic methodology, see Musgrave 1981.

ment does not embrace a teleological movement is one distinctive aspect of the Marxian standpoint.[297]

One technical point before presenting the conclusion of our discussion: my collation of the passages in MEGA² and MEW on the one hand, and the translation of the Manuscripts and Fernbach's translation on the other, leads me to the conclusion that the difference between the passages does not harm the argument developed here.[298] Hence similar results could be inferred from either of these two sources or their translations.

6 Conclusion

In discussing the developments, a general idea holds: 'No straight, unbroken path exists from simple to more complex development, either in thought or history'.[299] Thus, in the development of the conception of totality discussed here, it is natural to witness a porous and unsmooth path. At the end of this journey, the reader can see how the conception of totality and its neighbouring concepts found their way into Marx's works, from the letter of the nineteen-year-old Carel to the notes of what is often known as the third volume of *Capital*.

That said, it may be legitimately asked why many works in which totality is developed in one way or another are here left undiscussed.[300] One reason is space: integrating all these texts into the discussion would make this already long chapter even longer. More importantly, however, is the belief that the works discussed here represent the evolution of this conception adequately enough to give an accurate account of its genesis and evolution. That said, the developmental, dialectical coherence argued for here should not be equated with completeness. Hence many aspects need further development.[301]

We have seen previously that, according to Kosík, '[t]he method of explication is no evolutionist unravelling, but rather the unfolding, exposing, "complicating" of contradictions, the unfolding of the thing by way of contradictions'.[302] Kosík is right; however, the proposition that the method of exposition

---

297 Cf. Arndt 2012, p. 135: 'The criticism of Hegel builds up the construction of a teleological model of history' (my translation).
298 The reader can verify this by referring to Appendix II, where *some* of the discussed passages in different versions are given.
299 Hall 2003, p. 133.
300 One interesting example is Marx's doctoral thesis, particularly Notebook 1.
301 See Lebowitz 1998.
302 Kosík 1976, p. 16.

is no evolutionary unravelling does not entail that Marx's conception of totality cannot be evolutionary. The latter claim has been elaborated upon and argued for in this chapter.

That said, the relation between the way this movement is distinct and what the *Grundrisse* and *Capital* achieve is left undiscussed. This second problem, raised at the end of Chapter 4 as one of the shortcomings of Kosík's account of Marx's standpoint on Totality, is the topic of the next chapter.

CHAPTER 6

The Relationship between the *Grundrisse* and *Capital* and between the Method of Enquiry and the Method of Exposition

*The fact that Marx never wrote a text on the 'laws of dialectic' that would show how to 'strip' it of the 'mystical form'[1] in Hegel's method is undoubtedly a cause of the misconceptions and long-standing disagreements on the distinctive nature of his own method. In 1955, in the foreword to his groundbreaking *The Making of Marx's Capital*, Roman Rosdolsky wrote: 'Of all the problems in Marx's economic theory the most neglected has been that of his method, both in general and, specifically, in its relation to Hegel. Recent works contain for the most part platitudes which, to echo Marx's own words, betray the authors' own "crude obsession with the material" and total indifference to Marx's method'.[2] The literature on Marx's method has developed enormously since Rosdolsky wrote these lines. In a work written some thirty years later, we read: 'Surely no ground within the terrain of historical materialism has been trodden more often than method'.[3] But as the literature has grown, so too have the disagreements, and so have the accounts that attribute a rupture to Marx's works. This chapter elaborates on one of them.

The idea that there is an epistemological rupture in Marx's works is not limited to Althusser's thesis that there is such a rupture between the works of the young Marx and those of the mature Marx who was the author of *Capital*. Jacques Bidet believes that the rupture is actually lies between the *Grundrisse* and *Capital*.[4] Thus, unlike what is found even in some most recent works on

---

* An earlier version of this chapter was presented at the conference Materialistische Dialektik Marx-Lektüren im Dialog in Berlin in 2015, and published in German in Breda, Boveiri et al. 2017.
1 Marx, letter to Joseph Dietzgen, 9 May 1868: 'When I have shaken off the burden of my economic labours, I shall write a dialectic. The correct laws of the dialectic are already included in Hegel, albeit in a mystical form. It is necessary to strip it of this form' (Marx, 1992d, p. 31).
2 Rosdolsky 1977, p. xii.
3 Horvath and Gibson 1984, p. 12.
4 Bidet 1984. See also Callinicos 1978; 2014.

Marx's method,[5] the claim of the inner unity and coherence as to Marx's methodology needs seriously to be argued for.

In light of the discussion of the conception of totality in *Capital* and the *Grundrisse* in the two last sections of the previous chapter, this chapter will argue against the view that there is a rupture in Marx's works, and proposes instead that the relationship between the *Grundrisse* and *Capital* is that between the method of enquiry and the method of exposition.[6] On this view, the *Grundrisse* accomplishes the threefold task that Marx introduces as the function of the method of enquiry – namely, 'to appropriate the material in detail, to analyse its different forms of development and to track down their inner connection'[7] – and thus makes the method of exposition in *Capital* possible. In proposing this view, I will suggest a solution to the long-standing problem of the relationship between the method of enquiry and the method of exposition.[8] To do this, I describe in the first section the roots of the thesis of a rupture between the *Grundrisse* and *Capital*; in the second section, I state and criticise the passages in the contemporary literature which argue for a rupture between the *Grundrisse* and *Capital*; finally, I put forward an alternative reading of this relationship.

1   The Roots of the Thesis of a Rupture in Marx's Works

It may be correctly argued that the idea of such a dichotomy principally stems from the apparent incoherence between what Marx writes in two texts. In his Introduction of 1857, which was later published at the beginning of the *Grundrisse*,[9] he writes:

---

5   See, e.g., Starosta 2016, p. 17: 'The existence of an inner unity underlying the different phases of Marx's intellectual project is now part of the "ABC of Marxism"'. For a critical review of this book, see Boveiri 2020.

6   Here, as in Marx's German text, the words *Methode* and *Weise* are used interchangeably (Marx 1962a, pp. 25 and 27). They are both translated as 'method' in the Penguin translation (Marx 1976, pp. 100 and 102), and as *méthode* in the French translation edited by Lefebvre (Marx 1993, pp. 15 and 17). In the French edition of Joseph Roy, however, the only one supervised and modified by Marx, *Methode* is translated as *méthode* and *Weise* as *procédé*; see Marx 1982, p. 350.

7   Marx 1962a, p. 27; 1976, p. 102.

8   Hoff, Petrioli et al. 2006, p. 29.

9   I discussed elements of this passage in Chapter 5, section 4.1 above. Here I link the discussion to the methodological question of this chapter, about the relation between the method of enquiry and the method of exposition.

> The concrete is concrete because it is the concentration of many determinations, hence unity of the diverse. It appears in the process of thinking, therefore, as a process of concentration, as a result, not as a point of departure, even though it is the point of departure in reality and hence also the point of departure for observation [*Anschauung*] and conception. Along the first path the full conception was evaporated to yield an abstract determination; along the second, the abstract determinations lead towards a reproduction of the concrete by way of thought ... whereas the method of rising from the abstract to the concrete is only the way in which thought appropriates the concrete, reproduces it as the concrete in the mind. But this is by no means the process by which the concrete itself comes into being.[10]

What is emphasised here is the so-called logical movement that seems to be independent of phenomena and their temporal and historical succession. The achievement of concrete determinations does not bear any sign of the temporality of the object* (*Gegenstand*).[11] With such an elaboration, what we witness is akin to what is found in Hegel's *Science of Logic*.[12] Later in the text Marx says explicitly: 'It would therefore be unfeasible and wrong to let the economic categories follow one another in the same sequence as that in which they were historically decisive. Their sequence is determined, rather, by their relation to one another in modern bourgeois society, which is precisely the opposite of that which seems to be their natural order or which corresponds to historical development'.[13]

This account sounds problematic if read together with what Marx writes later. In the Afterword to the second edition of *Capital*, on 24 January 1873, Marx quotes an article by I.I. Kaufmann – a text that includes quotations from Marx himself – that appeared in the *Europäischer Bote* in Saint Petersburg. The article is written in support of the thesis that the method used in *Capital* really is dialectical (though Marx argues that Kaufmann does not understand this). In this article, from which Marx quotes, Marx first admits that the method of *Capital* has been the subject of 'conceptions that contradict each other'.[14] Fol-

---

10   Marx 1973, p. 101.
11   The reader may refer to Chapter 4, section 4 and above where the distinction is elaborated upon.
12   See Hegel 1969c, p. 511: 'Das synthetische Erkenntnis geht auf das Begreifen dessen, was ist, d.h., [darauf], die Mannigfaltigkeit, von Bestimmungen in ihrer Einheit zu fassen'.
13   Marx 1973, p. 103.
14   Marx 1976, p. 99. In German: 'einander widersprechenden Auffassungen' (Marx 1962a, p. 25).

lowing this comes a passage that is particularly important for our discussion, since Marx affirms that it describes what he takes to be a dialectical method:

> The one thing which is important for Marx is to find *the law of the phenomena* with whose investigation [*Untersuchung*] he is concerned; and it is not only *the law which governs these phenomena*, in so far as they have a definite form and mutual connection within a given historical period, that is important to him. Of still greater importance to him is *the law of their variation, of their development, i.e. of their transition from one form into another, from one series of connections into a different one*. Once he has discovered this law, he investigates in detail the effects with which it manifests itself in social life ... Consequently, Marx only concerns himself with one thing: to show, by an exact scientific investigation [*wissenschaftliche Untersuchung*], *the necessity of successive determinate orders of social relations, and to establish*, as impeccably as possible, the facts from which he starts out and on which he depends ... *A critique of this kind will confine itself to the confrontation and comparison of a fact, not with ideas, but with another fact*. The only things of importance for this enquiry are that the facts be investigated as accurately as possible, and that they actually form different aspects of development *vis-a-vis* each other. But *most important of all is the precise analysis of the series of successions, of the sequences and links within which the different stages of development present themselves*.[15]

After this passage, Marx writes that what the author of the article calls his real method is nothing else but the dialectical method, and that Kaufmann's depiction of it is 'striking [*treffend*]' and 'generous [*wohlwollend*]'.[16]

As we see here, the significance of the phenomena is underlined, and by attending to the succession of phenomena the laws of this succession are discovered. The phenomena that are the objects* of the critique of political economy – commodity, production, money, etc. – both exist in time and have a history. It may be said that their time-bound historical aspect turns out to be the subject of the study, and any logical succession to follow the succession of the phenomena results, so to speak, from their sequence.

Different readings have been given regarding the relation between these two passages. Rosdolsky, for instance, does not seem to see a significant difference between the *Grundrisse* and *Capital*. In reference to this passage in the

---

15   Marx 1976, pp. 100–1, emphasis added.
16   Marx 1962a, p. 26.

Grundrisse he writes: '[O]utline (as did *Capital* later) follows the path from abstract definitions to the concrete'.¹⁷ Tony Smith, on the other hand, does recognise this difference. Like Rosdolsky, Smith supplies only meagre commentary, but unlike Rosdolsky, he does suggest a sort of solution, or rather some reasons to prioritise a systemic view.¹⁸ But before proposing an alternative reading, let us first review the idea in the contemporary literature that there is a rupture between these two books.

2 The Idea of a Rupture between the *Grundrisse* and *Capital*

Here I discuss the two major texts which see a rupture between the *Grundrisse* and *Capital*. I begin with a passage by Bidet where he formulates the last version of his thought:

> The 'epistemological rupture' to be considered is not so much the one which distinguishes the mature Marx from the young Marx, it is rather the one that separates the *Grundrisse* from *Capital*. In his first draft, Marx systematically works with the help of Hegelian logic. In his published work, he gradually gets rid of its formal support, [comes up with] the theoretical exposition that imposes its particular logic, which is based on a new conception, one for which some dialectical tools show themselves unsuitable. The 'dialectical superiority' of the *Grundrisse* to *Capital* does not give it any theoretical superiority. This superiority does not warrant the usage of the 'logic' of the first presentation for the interpretation of the second. It is more convenient to resist fascination, and take all the theoretical progress into consideration, from the very first draft up to the very last version, namely, the French edition of *Capital*. Progress that does not arise from points of detail but from principle.¹⁹

---

17 Rosdolsky 1977, p. 27.
18 See Smith 1993, Chapter III.
19 Bidet 2005, p. 1, my translation. The original reads: '[L]a "rupture épistémologique" à considérer n'était pas tant celle qui distingue le Marx de la maturité du jeune Marx, que celle qui sépare les *Grundrisse* du *Capital*. Dans sa première esquisse, Marx travaille systématiquement à l'aide de la logique hégélienne. Dans son œuvre publiée, il s'affranchit progressivement de son support formel, l'exposé théorique imposant sa logique propre, fondée sur une nouvelle conceptualité, à laquelle certains instruments dialectiques s'avèrent inadéquats. La "supériorité dialectique" des *Grundrisse* sur *Le Capital* ne lui confère donc aucune supériorité théorique. Elle n'autorise pas à recourir à la "logique" du premier exposé pour l'interprétation du second. Il convient plutôt de résister à sa fascination, et de

Regardless of the duality between the theoretical and the dialectical found in this passage, Bidet does not tell us what is meant by dialectical superiority. He talks about the theoretical superiority of *Capital* but is silent regarding what, if anything, *Grundrisse* passes on to *Capital*. Following the chapter on totality in the *Grundrisse*, I think it is plausible to claim that what is seen in the *Grundrisse* is in fact *not* the reflected dialectic – and this notwithstanding the dialectical terminology.

In another passage Bidet writes: 'In Capital, Marx, under a decisive theoretical constraint, frees himself from the dialectical presentation that was his in the *Grundrisse*, but without being in a position to draw all the conclusions imposed by this'.[20] I think it is wrong to read this line as Bidet's negation of what is thought to be 'the "soul" of Marx's method of political economy – his dialectic!'[21] That said, in this regard, I think that what is missing in *Capital* is *not* the dialectical representation or rather *exposition* but dialectical *enquiry*, which is achieved, as far as it can be, in the form of the manuscripts not intended for publication, which are found in the *Grundrisse*. This is one major thesis of this chapter.

In his elaboration on the difference between *Capital* and the *Grundrisse* Callinicos writes: 'Marx follows "the method of rising from the abstract to concrete" in *Capital*. In other words, he starts from highly abstract determinations ... and from them develops ... more complex determinations'.[22] Indeed, Marx asserts in the *Grundrisse* that the ascent from the abstract to the concrete is the 'scientifically correct method'[23] of political economy. Once it is agreed that this is not what we find in the *Grundrisse*, the question then arises regarding the function of the *Grundrisse*, if any, in making this ascent in *Capital* possible.

With regard to the scientific character of *Capital*, Callinicos writes: 'By the time that Marx writes the manuscripts that have come down to us as *Capital*, he has rejected the idea, common to both Hegel and the classical conception of science, that the content of science is implicit in the starting point'.[24] As

---

      prendre toute la mesure des progrès théoriques qui se manifestent d'une version à l'autre, de la toute première esquisse jusqu'à la toute dernière version, française, du *Capital*. Progrès qui ne relèvent pas du détail, mais du principe'.

20   Bidet 2005, p. 2, my translation. The original reads: 'Marx, dans *Le Capital*, sous une contrainte théorique décisive, se détache de la présentation dialectique qui était la sienne dans les *Grundrisse*, sans être cependant en mesure d'en tirer toutes les conclusions qui s'imposent'. Bidet 2005, p. 2 (my translation).
21   Rosdolsky 1977, p. 562.
22   Callinicos 2014, p. 72.
23   Marx 1983, p. 35.
24   Callinicos 2014, p. 133.

we saw in our discussion of the categorial movement in the three volumes of *Capital*, this is acceptable with regard to the method of enquiry but incorrect regarding the method of exposition.[25] Since Callinicos does not take note of this difference, he poses the following question: 'If the movement from abstract to concrete is something that unfolds within thought, how does Marx's theoretical discourse acquire factual content?'[26] Regarding this question, I would like to note, first, that Marx needs the factual (*sachlich*) content to distance himself from Hegelian Idealism. Apart from that, there is a confusion regarding the fact that for Marx *the concrete* is of two types: the real concrete and the thought concrete (*Gedankenkonkrete*). This will be elaborated on in the following section.

Callinicos writes in another comment on *Capital*, this time in his critique of Althusser's dichotomy claim, that '[t]he difficulty that [Althusser's] approach has is the presence of the Hegelian terminology in the work that Althusser identifies as the pinnacle of Marx's scientific achievement, namely, *Capital* itself'.[27] Regarding this, it is noteworthy that Althusser is generally right when he says that Hegelian terminology is not as prominent in *Capital* as it is in the *Grundrisse*: indeed, it abounds in the latter, but not in the former.[28] The problem just lies elsewhere. As seen from the preceding chapter, what is missing in the *Grundrisse* is the categorial movement. In *Capital* we do see the categorial movement of the categories – which is both similar to and different from a Hegelian categorial movement. What is not found in *Capital* is the conspicuous recourse to such terminology that is apparent in the *Grundrisse*.

More specifically, as regards the relationship between the method of enquiry and the method of exposition, Callinicos criticises the idea, put forward by Ernest Mandel (*inter alios*), that a difference can be seen between these methods, such that the one exhibits the movement from concrete to abstract, and the other the movement from abstract to concrete.[29] Firstly, it should be noted that this does not represent precisely what Mandel says, as he also insists that these two have to be seen as related methods.[30] Moreover, the reading presented in this chapter is partly in agreement with what Callinicos writes, as I think these two moments of abstract and concrete are jointly coherent but also distinct.

---

25 See Chapter 5, section 5.
26 Callinicos 2014, p. 132.
27 Callinicos 2014, p. 71.
28 See Althusser 2005, p. 205. It should be said, however, that Althusser exaggerates the absence of Hegel in *Capital*.
29 See Callinicos 2014, p. 73; Mandel 1975, p. 14.
30 Mandel 1975, p. 14.

Thus, my reading adheres to the well-known dialectical principle, put forward by Hegel, against arguing a case one-sidedly[31] – a practice typical of reasoning based on understanding instead of reason (*Vernunft*).

Following this criticism, Callinicos puts forward his own view by quoting Ilyenkov in agreement: '[T]he method of presentation [i.e., exposition] of material in *Capital* is nothing but the "corrected" method of its investigation'.[32] The principal thesis advanced by Callinicos, following Ilyenkov, is what may be called the *correction standpoint*, or the postulation of a correction relationship between the method of exposition and the method of enquiry. In the next section, I criticise this interpretation, and show how a different understanding of the relationship can begin to help us answer a long-standing question in the Marxist literature, especially in the debates on Marxist methodology and epistemology referred to previously.

3 The Alternative Reading

What is at stake seems to be, at least in part, resolving the problem of the apparent incongruence of the synchronicity of political-economic categories on the one hand and the diachronicity of the historical development of political-economic entities on the other. My main critique of the idea of a rupture in Marx's thinking is that it overlooks the formal distinction between the method of exposition and method of enquiry – a distinction that is already emphasised by Marx.[33] Not only is emphasising this distinction an attempt to respond to a difficult and crucial problem in the history of philosophy, it also suggests a solution to the problem of the relationship between the method of enquiry and the method of exposition.

Up to this point, I have said a great deal about the important passage in the Afterword to the second edition of *Capital* Volume I, but without quoting it. Let us now read it in Marx's own words:

> Of course, the method of exposition must differ in form [*formell*] from that of enquiry. The latter has to appropriate the material in detail, to analyse its different forms of development and to track down their inner connection. Only after this work has been done can the real movement

---

31 Ilyenkov 1982, p. 138.
32 Ilyenkov 1982, p. 144.
33 This difference is correctly thought to be 'of central importance for Marx's own methodical understanding' (Heinrich 1996–7, p. 457).

be appropriately presented. If this is done successfully, if the life of the subject-matter is now reflected back in the ideas, then it may appear as if we have before us an *a priori* construction.[34]

The threefold function of the exposition is formulated still more clearly by Kosík: 'Appropriating the material in detail, mastering it to the last historically accessible detail; Analysing its different forms of development; Tracing out their internal connections, that is, determining the unity of different forms in the development of the material'.[35]

The exposition will be possible once this threefold function of enquiry is accomplished. In calling this a threefold function of the moment of the enquiry, the reading presented here is distinct from that of Kosík, in that while he speaks of three *levels* of enquiry and therefore enumerates these functions and implies a tripartite procedure, this alternative reading, which sees them as a whole, is explicitly more in harmony with Marx and Engels in the *German Ideology*, where the partition of the whole is opposed.[36] There are then not three levels or stages, but three moments of the integrated method of enquiry. Another, still more important, distinctive point of the reading presented here compared with Kosík's is that he does not see the *Grundrisse* as specifically exhibiting the method of enquiry.[37]

---

34 Marx 1976, p. 102 (emphasis added in the second sentence). The German text reads: 'Allerdings muß sich die Darstellungsweise formell von der Forschungsweise unterscheiden. Die Forschung hat den Stoff sich im Detail anzueignen, seine verschiednen Entwicklungsformen zu analysieren und deren innres Band aufzuspüren' (Marx 1962a, p. 27).
35 Kosík 1976, p. 15. (In quoting Kosík, I deliberately do not enumerate these steps.)
36 See Marx and Engels 1978, p. 29: 'Übrigens sind diese drei Seiten der sozialen Tätigkeit nicht als drei verschiedene Stufen zu fassen, sondern eben nur als drei Seiten, oder um für die Deutschen klar zu schreiben, drei "Momente", die vom Anbeginn der Geschichte an und seit den ersten Menschen zugleich existiert haben und sich noch heute in der Geschichte geltend machen'. English translation: 'These three aspects of social activity are not of course to be taken as three different stages, but just as three aspects or, to make it clear to the Germans, three "moments", which have existed simultaneously since the dawn of history and the first men, and which still assert themselves in history today' (Marx and Engels 1975, p. 43). One may go farther and claim that such an approach – taking different moments of enquiry that are unified and distinct but not separate – will be always accepted for all different researches. For the application of such a standpoint in the human sciences see Lemieux 2010, particularly the section 'Mettre en énigme ce qui paraît normal'. This is not apparently the case in Gramsci's discussion, and he seems to have overlooked this characteristic; see Gramsci 1971, p. 137. This is equally true in Dieter Wolf's discussion regarding the *Grundrisse* (Wolf 2016, p. 45).
37 See Nicolaus's introduction to the *Grundrisse* in Marx 1973, pp. 8 and 25. Although Nic-

After the above quotation, Marx goes on to say that once the function of the method of enquiry is completely realised, and only then, the real movement of the *Stoff* can be ideally mirrored.[38] The simultaneous threefold function makes possible rather a mediated starting point as well as a categorial movement. This starting point is given only at the end of the last Notebook,[39] where the method of enquiry is most fully developed. As the previous chapter made clear, in the *Grundrisse* itself there is no categorial movement, but rather oscillation between the categories, principally between the main chapters on Money and Capital.[40] Oscillation is undoubtedly a movement but not a logically necessary movement that leads each category inevitably to the next, as seen in *Capital*. The absence of a mediated starting point goes hand in hand with the absence of categorial movement: there is no categorial movement in the *Grundrisse*, such as is found in *Capital*; nonetheless, the oscillation between the categories of money and capital in the *Grundrisse* is a sign that Marx is in search of a categorial movement. This is an alternative to the readings that say the categories in the *Grundrisse* are not developed[41] or, metaphorically, that they are not 'flattened out'.[42]

It may be asked where in this account the moment of critique can be found. Marx thinks that critique is intertwined with exposition, or that an exposition cannot avoid being critical in the same way that critique cannot be expositional.[43] This should not, however, be taken to mean that there is no critique during the realisation of the threefold function of the method of enquiry. This is just to say that, as can be seen in, so to speak, the submoments of the method of investigation, the moment of enquiry tends to be more descriptive, explanat-

---

olaus recognises that the *Grundrisse* is the work where method of enquiry is developed, he does not recognise the threefold function presented here.

38 See Marx 1962a, p. 27: 'Erst nachdem diese Arbeit vollbracht, kann die wirkliche Bewegung entsprechend dargestellt werden. Gelingt dies und spiegelt sich nun das Leben des Stoffs ideell wider, so mag es aussehn, als habe man es mit einer Konstruktion a priori zu tun'. Cf. Marx 1961, p. 398, where Marx stresses a unity between the exposition and reality.

39 Cf. Marx 1983, p. 127, where circulation is introduced as the first totality under the economic categories. As we saw in Chapter 5, section 4, other starting points are introduced on other occasions.

40 Cf. Smith 1993b, p. 16: 'I believe that in *Capital and elsewhere* Marx did indeed make use of systematic dialectical method similar to that found in Hegel' (emphasis added).

41 Fineschi 2013, p. 72.

42 Negri 1991, p. 12.

43 See for example, Marx's letter to Lassalle on 22 February 1858: 'The work at hand is the *critique of economic categories* or if you like, the system of bourgeois economy critically exposed. It is simultaneously exposition of the system and through the exposition its critique' (Marx 1978c, p. 550, my translation).

ory, and analytic. Moreover, it has been rightly pointed out that the *Grundrisse* 'neither offers a more detailed explanation of what is meant by economic categories, nor are these discussed in connection with the "exchange abstraction"'.[44]

In this way, the reading presented here is different from that of the authors of the *neue Lektüre*[45] who argue that 'one can find a proper dialectical exposition of categories only in that text [i.e., the *Grundrisse*], while the logical consistency was weakened in subsequent writings'.[46] What is proposed here is also in harmony with the interpretation of Roberto Fineschi to the extent that he criticises that viewpoint, but it diverges from his view that the dialectical exposition is also found in the *Grundrisse*.[47] What Fineschi overlooks here is the result of the confusion between exposition *tout court* and exposition as a method that is formally distinct from the method of enquiry. The shortcomings of his reading are not limited to this however. Fineschi does not recognise the importance of the method of enquiry. Moreover, he asserts, without elaboration, that Marx's method of exposition is similar to Hegel's:

> 'Mode of research' [*Forschungsweise*] and 'mode of exposition' [*Darstellungsweise*] are the expressions used by Marx to define his own method in the afterword to the second German edition of Capital Volume I (in Fowkes's translation: 'method of enquiry' and 'method of presentation') (Marx 1993, p. 102). The category 'exposition' (or 'presentation') is a crucial one; in fact, the German term 'darstellen' does not simply regard the way given results are presented, but the way the theory itself develops through its different levels of abstraction toward totality. It is in fact explicit that Marx is referring to Hegel's Darstellung when he uses this word. The process of exposition posits results.[48]

Fineschi seems to ignore the fact that Marx explicitly draws a particular distinction between the method of enquiry and the method of exposition which is absent in Hegel. Thus, there are important differences between Marx's and Hegel's views.

The alternative thesis is the considered result of the different interpretations of the relationship between the method of enquiry and the method of

---

44 Reichelt 2007, p. 8.
45 See Reichelt 2001 and Backhaus 1997.
46 Fineschi 2013, p. 72.
47 Fineschi 2013, pp. 71–2.
48 Fineschi 2013, p. 71 (emphasis added).

exposition of the capitalist mode of production, distribution, exchange, consumption of commodities, service, information, *and* capital. The unambiguous realisation of the method of exposition is found in *Capital*,[49] but between the *Grundrisse* and *Capital* a step is taken in the direction of the realisation of this exposition. The *Contribution to the Critique of Political Economy* (1859) also begins with the commodity, and hence is a partial realisation of the method of exposition – partial because the developed categorial movement of *Capital* is not seen there. It is only the co-constitution of a mediated, absolute, and necessary starting point[50] and the categorial movement found in *Capital* that exhibits the coherent realisation of the method of exposition.

A comparison of the starting point of *Capital* with Hegel's *Science of Logic* is noteworthy here. Whereas Hegel argues at the beginning of that book that a proper starting point is neither mediated nor immediate and must be both mediated and immediate,[51] *Capital* begins with a definite starting point that is mediated, absolute, and necessary, namely, the commodity. This starting point is mediated through the capitalist mode of social life as a totality; it is absolute since there is no smaller divisible moment-category than the commodity, and it is necessary because no other category can play this particular role. As the starting point of the exposition of the critique of political economy, the commodity is the integral processual moment of the social reality under study, and plays a role similar to that of a morpheme, or word meaning as the smallest indivisible meaning-bearer,[52] in contradistinction to a phoneme, or that of a molecule as opposed to an atom. The analogy is meant to imply that while such smallest units bear a similarity in nature to the Totality of which they are component totalities, this is not true of the other units. That which stems from the commodity as starting point (the subject at hand) goes further and affects not only every other category, but also the Totality of the categories and the categorial movement as a whole.

This is the horizon that such a particular present-time starting point opens.[53] As was explained in section 4 in discussing the totality in the *Grundrisse* in the previous chapter, such a starting point does not and cannot exist in the

---

49 Callinicos 2014, p. 64.
50 See Chapter 5, section 5.1.1 above.
51 See Hegel 2010, p. 46: '[T]here is nothing in heaven or nature or spirit or anywhere else that does not contain just as much immediacy as mediation'.
52 For the development of 'word meaning' as the unity of thought and speech see Vygotsky 1986.
53 Harootunian 2015, p. 31: '[S]tarting from the commodity rather than its concept meant also that one must start from the present rather than the past'. For a critical review of this book, see Boveiri 2016c.

method of enquiry. But such a starting point, as the first totality and bearer of the contradictions of the Totality, determines the categorial movement and is also determined by the categorial movement. This is why there is not only no starting point in the *Grundrisse*, but no categorial movement either. Without the categorial movement of the Totality that entails and is entailed by a definite starting point (after doubt and examination), namely, commodity as a totality, and without the realisation of the method of enquiry (*Grundrisse*), a concrete critique (*Capital*) integrating the empirical data cannot be undertaken. This is also embodied by the introduction in *Capital* of the category of 'socially necessary labour time', which is absent in the *Grundrisse*. This is seen from the use of the verb 'to appropriate' (*aneignen*) in both texts: in the *Grundrisse*, Marx speaks of the appropriation of the concrete, and in the afterword to *Capital* he discusses in detail the appropriation of the material. The goal is to form a concrete totality in thought by the application of the force of abstraction. The method of enquiry anticipated the method of exposition, whereas the method of exposition fulfils the plan set by the method of enquiry. Regarding this, in one of the comments on the relation between the *Grundrisse* and *Capital*, we read: 'The question of logic of presentation [i.e., exposition] is resolved differently in the *Grundrisse* and *Capital*. Yet, the concept of totality presupposed by his critical, immanent method which conceptualised capitalism as a self-reproducing, dynamic and contradictory system remained constant in these efforts'.[54] The interpretation presented here modifies this claim on two points. First, it is not the logic of exposition that is resolved differently in the two texts; rather, in one we have the method of enquiry, and in the other the method of exposition. Second, accordingly, the concept of totality is nuanced: in the *Grundrisse*, we witness the totality as the oscillation of categories, whereas in *Capital* we have categorial movement.

If this is correct, the relationship between the method of enquiry and the method of exposition goes further than a simple, undialectical relationship of correction, as some maintain. Callinicos and Ilyenkov, for instance, overlook the threefold character of the method of enquiry introduced by Marx. The thought that the difference of form between these two texts is related to Marx's personal familiarity with the 'different circles of the capitalist hell that is different from the one that corresponds to the law of their own development and is presented in *Capital*'[55] goes particularly off track. Such a perspective can seem acceptable only if the difference between the enquiry and the exposi-

---

54 Grumley 1989, p. 59.
55 Ilyenkov 1982, p. 144; Callinicos 2014, pp. 73–5.

tion, on the one hand, and enquiry, exposition and investigation, on the other, is overlooked. According to this alternative reading, there is no moment of investigation as such, but only the moments of investigation as enquiry and exposition, with the differences textually elaborated on in the last two sections in the previous chapter.

A reference to what comes after the passage in Marx's Afterword quoted above at the beginning of this chapter (see section 1) is illuminating. Marx continues his own quotation from the reviewer Kaufmann:

> Marx only concerns himself with one thing: to show, by an exact scientific investigation [*wissenschaftliche Untersuchung*], the necessity of successive determinate orders of social relations, and to establish, as impeccably as possible, the facts from which he starts out and on which he depends.[56]

This 'scientific investigation', according to the reading presented here, has two moments: enquiry and exposition. Put differently, the method of investigation shows itself as two distinct but also related moments, either as the method of enquiry or as the method of exposition. If this is right, each of these two moments is simultaneously *der Moment* of the investigation, and as such timebound (*Capital* comes after the *Grundrisse*), but also *das Moment* of the investigation, since each is inwardly related to the other:[57] The method of enquiry is one *das Moment* and *der Moment* of investigation; the method of exposition is also one *das Moment* and *der Moment* of investigation. In this way only may one say that 'the contrast between the logical and the historical is a pseudoalternative'.[58] In contrast, a reading that introduces the logical as a prerequisite of the historical makes Marx's methodology too Hegelian.[59]

The method of exposition makes it possible 'that the development of the capitalist mode of [social life] ... can be followed through until it is grasped in its totality.'[60] However, this still does not and cannot provide us with a clear-

---

56 Marx 1976, pp. 100–1. The German text reads: 'Demzufolge bemüht sich Marx nur um eins: durch genaue wissenschaftliche Untersuchung die Notwendigkeit bestimmter Ordnungen der gesellschaftlichen Verhältnisse nachzuweisen und soviel als möglich untadelhaft die Tatsachen zu konstatieren, die ihm zu Ausgangs- und Stützpunkten dienen' (Marx 1962a, p. 26).
57 Marx uses both *das Moment* (e.g., 1983, p. 140: 'soweit nicht das Moment betrachtet wird'; p. 248: 'Das Moment der Lohnarbeit') and *der Moment* (1967, p. 504: 'Aber die Krise ist grade der Moment der Störung und Unterbrechung des Reproduktionsprozesses').
58 Arndt 2012, p. 136 (my translation).
59 See Dussell 2001, p. 210.
60 Rosdolsky 1977, p. 27.

cut, or let us say absolute definition of the categories.[61] In the same vein, the gap between subject and object, thought and being, does not entail a closure.[62] It is rather an incessant process of gradual approximations.

There are some passages in the Introduction elaborating on the crucial question of the relation between thought process and historical process. There is a multitude of possibilities of relations between categorial development and historical development. Since these two are neither homogeneous nor identical, the categories and historical entities overlap, converge, diverge, and occasionally correspond.[63] The result cannot be reduced to positivism but neither to 'historical epistemology'.[64]

In this way, through marking the differences between these two works, this chapter of the book proposed to offer a twofold contribution to the contemporary Marxian studies: it is an attempt toward a solution to a problem that the authors of the *Das Kapital neu lesen* have put forward, namely, the demonstration of an 'inner relation between the method of enquiry and the method of exposition',[65] notwithstanding the difference between these as moments of investigation. On the other hand, it also rebuts the recent claim regarding a rupture between the *Grundrisse* and *Capital*, as discussed in the preceding pages.

On this reading of *enquiry* as equally distinct from but also related to *exposition*, Marx, I think, contributes decidedly to a longstanding problem in the history of philosophy brought forward in different forms by Parmenides, Aristotle, and Hegel.[66] Put simply, to the problem of the starting point as posed by

---

61   Cf. Reichelt 2007, p. 8: '[In *Capital*] categories are defined, in all the clarity that could be wished for, as "objective forms of thought"'. On the absence of ideal definitions in dialectical investigation, see Boveiri 2016b.

62   Cf. Hall 2003, p. 130: 'That is, until the gap between thought and being is closed in practice'. Hall does not seem to fully recognise the drastic consequences of referring to Paul Vilar's paper (1973) to his argument where the latter defends Engels's idea of asymptomatic approximation or progress of thought towards the real.

63   Marx 1973, p. 102: 'To that extent the path of abstract thought, rising from the simple to the combined, would correspond to the real historical process'. Hence, what Marx says in the following passage from *Capital* Volume I must be understood along these lines: 'Reflection on the forms of human life, hence also scientific analysis of those forms, takes a course directly opposite to their real development. Reflection begins *post festum*, and therefore with the results of the process of development ready to hand' (Marx 1976, p. 168).

64   See Hall 2003, p. 132.

65   Hoff, Petrioli et al. 2006, p. 29: 'inneren Zusammenhangs von Forschung und Darstellung' (my translation). This relationship is introduced also as a problem in need of further elaboration by the authors of *Marx's Method in Capital*. See Moseley 1993, p. 12.

66   See Parmenides 2009, pp. 45–59; Aristotle, *Physics* 1.1, 184a16–20 (in Aristotle 2006) and *Metaphysics* Z.3, 1029b3–12 (in Aristotle 1995); and Hegel 1969b, p. 502.

these philosophers and many others, Marx responds that it is essential to first clarify whether it is the question of the method of enquiry or the method of exposition.

In the contemporary literature on the studies of human sciences in general and philosophy in particular, we see recognitions similar to the thesis elaborated on here with regard to the relationship between the method of enquiry and the method of exposition – and this not necessarily by Marxist thinkers or even dialecticians and in different contexts. Here, I limit myself to a few examples. In an appendix to Pierre Bourdieu's groundbreaking sociological study, *Distinction*, we read: 'The order of exposition takes as its starting point the arrival point of [the order of] enquiry'.[67] In *The Conduct of Enquiry: Methodology for Behavioural Science* a similar distinction is recognised as the logic-in-use, the distinction between 'what is actually being done by scientists' and the reconstructed logic which comes thereafter.[68] Such a difference is, I think, more important than what platitude and truism acknowledge. With relation to elaboration on philosophical texts, for instance, a distinction is made between the order of the discovery of the text which is different from the order of comment or elaboration on a text.[69] Even in a handbook of English style, to give another example, one can read: 'Writing, to be effective, must follow closely the thoughts of the writer, but not necessarily in the order in which those thoughts occur'.[70]

Once enquiry and exposition are taken as two moments of the investigation, several difficulties can be clarified, not only in Marx's own works but also in the commentators. In what follows, I discuss some of them. Regarding Marx's works, a good example can be seen in *Capital*. In the opening passage, analysed previously for a different purpose,[71] one reads: 'Our *investigation* [*Untersuchung*] therefore begins with the analysis of the commodity'.[72] Taken literally, this sentence leaves the relationship between investigation, enquiry, and exposition indefinite, for Marx says here that the investigation begins with the analysis of the commodity, but as we have seen above, he also holds that the method of enquiry (*Forschungsweise*) and the method of exposition

---

67 Bourdieu 2007, p. 587, my translation. In the original: 'l'ordre d'exposition ... prend pour point de départ le point d'arrivée [de l'ordre] de recherche'.
68 Kaplan 2009, pp. 10–11.
69 Choulet, Folscheid et al. 2018, p. 62. 'The order of the discovery of the text which is not the order of exposition (of explication or commentary)' (my translation).
70 Strunk and White 2000, p. 26.
71 See section 5 in the previous chapter.
72 Marx 1976, p. 125, emphasis added. The German text reads: 'Unsere Untersuchung beginnt daher mit der Analyse der Ware' (Marx 1962a, p. 49).

(*Darstellungsweise*) should be formally distinguished.[73] According to the reading presented in this chapter, Marx means here that the moment of *exposition* of the investigation (*Untersuchung*) is the beginning of the investigation in *Capital*. This is equally true in Chapter 18 of *Capital* Volume II, when he speaks of the object* of investigation.[74]

As for the commentators, I mention Kosík's standpoint in the *Dialectic of the Concrete*. What is suggested by him in this respect, taken literally and without qualification, is an inconsistent account. On the one hand, we read: '[T]he starting point of investigation must be formally identical with the result'.[75] On the other hand, Kosík also writes: 'The beginning of the exposition and the beginning of the investigation are two different things. The beginning of the investigation is random and arbitrary, the beginning of the exposition is necessary'.[76] The reading presented here suggests a solution for this apparent inconsistency: the beginning of the exposition, that is, the commodity, is identical with the result of the exposition, namely, the capitalist mode as a totality.[77] As stated before, this movement from one cellular totality to the Totality of the capitalist mode of social life is similar to the way a stem cell is taken in science to potentially amount to the body as a whole. There is, then, a movement from the first, the cellular, from the corporeal form, from the commodity, to the capitalist form as a whole. As another commentator, I would also like to mention a passage in Andreas Arndt's influential book *Versuch über den Zusammenhang seiner Theorie*. In his commentary on money as the starting point of the *Grundrisse*, he writes: 'Marx begins in the *Grundrisse* with the investigation [*Untersuchung*] of money theories'.[78] More precisely, one may say that it is the enquiry (*Forschung*) into money theories.

It follows from my position that the claim that enquiry and exposition are two moments of enquiry is untenable.[79] Similarly, I find equally weak a some-

---

73   Marx 1976, p. 102; 1962a, p. 27.
74   'Gegenstand der Untersuchung' (Marx 1963, p. 351), and also 'Gegenstand der Untersuchungen' (Marx 1964, p. 33). The latter phrase was referred to in Chapter 5, section 5.2.
75   Kosík 1976, p. 14.
76   Kosík 1976, p. 16. What Camus says in *Le mythe de Sisyphe* ('Toutes les grandes actions et toutes les grandes pensées ont un commencement dérisoire'; Camus 2013, p. 260) can be just *cum grano salis* correct regarding Marx: it depends on whether we are talking about the *Grundrisse* or *Capital*.
77   Dardot and Laval 2012, p. 326.
78   Arndt 2012, p. 140: 'beginnt Marx in den „*Grundrissen*" mit einer Untersuchung der Geldtheorien[.]' (my translation).
79   Cf. Negri 1991, p. 14.

what mechanistic division of the moments of Marx's project.[80] Moreover, the unified threefold function of the method of enquiry carries with it a criterion for evaluating the enquiry, the application of which goes beyond the analysis of the capitalist mode of social life. It is similar to, but also different from, the famous four steps introduced by Descartes,[81] and this notwithstanding the claim repeated by Marx and Engels that they avoid a recipe or a scheme.[82]

Whereas the threefold function of the method of enquiry may be applied to all investigations (*Untersuchungen*), specifically in enquiry, this is not equally true of the exposition (*Darstellung*). It is incumbent on those who draw a strict (unbridgeable?) gap between nature and science[83] – and hence call for a restriction of the Marxian method to the critique of political economy – to argue against the usage of the threefold dictum with regard to the method of enquiry introduced by Marx. In other words, they should respond to the following question: Why isn't such a threefold function tenable in other enquiries?[84] I think a good answer to this question cannot be given. This is why I think that in putting this forward Marx was attempting to respond to a longstanding and complex question in the history of philosophy that goes beyond the domain of the critique of political economy, namely, the problem of the starting point in philosophical methodology, in the sense of movement from a particular starting point. In so doing, Marx takes up the question: 'With what must the beginning of the science be made?' He responds by suggesting that the answer depends on whether the question is about scientific enquiry or exposition. Such a question, as far as I can see, with the exposition as an a posteriori endeavour, has not been put forward in the history of philosophy, not even by Hegel, who provides us with the a priori derivation of categories in the *Science of Logic*,[85] notwithstanding some similarities.[86] This a priori derivation of the

---

80 Paolucci 2011, p. 62.
81 Descartes 2000, pp. 88–90.
82 Marx and Engels 1978, p. 27; Marx 1962a, p. 25.
83 See Sekine 1997a, p. 3: 'I wish to argue, on the contrary, that nature and society are two altogether different things, and hence that we need different methods to study them' (emphasis added). For a related reading, see Postone 2003.
84 I am not saying that the categories used are universal categories. Hence, I agree to a large extent with Harvey that '[f]or the most part, Marx is emphatic that he is dealing only with the conceptual categories formulated within and appropriate to a capitalist mode of production' (Harvey 2010, p. 111).
85 This has been shown with regard to the metacategory of totality in Chapter 2 above.
86 I thank George Di Giovanni, who kindly confirmed this point, and also for drawing my attention to the importance of Fichte in the relationship between the method of exposition and the method of enquiry. Cf. paragraph 246 in the *Encyclopedia* II (Hegel 1986b, p. 15.), Hegel 2010, pp. 45–55: 'With what must the beginning of science be made?', and

categories, which is characteristic of Hegel's methodology, is exactly what Marx eschews with his introduction of the twofold method of investigation. This has been argued for here in relating this to the metacategory of totality.

As for the apparent inconsistency between the Introduction and the Afterword, the defence of the historical nature of phenomena and the derivation of laws found in the Afterword should be coupled with the logical claim made in the Introduction. The either-or is just faulty. The insertion (so to speak) of history in *Capital* should be read as a concretisation-socialisation-totalisation process achieved by the method of exposition; that is, whereas in the Afterword *Der Moment* is stressed, in the Introduction *Das Moment* is given importance. But seeing beyond *Das Moment*, the logical aspect of each *Gegenstand* to the temporality of that *Gegenstand* is to be coupled with seeing beyond the *Der Moment* of each *Gegenstand* to its inner logic, which does not entail their identity.[87]

4   Conclusion

Every genuine philosopher introduces not only a particular starting point from which to philosophise, but also a particular approach with regard to that starting point.[88] Both characteristics are found in Marx. Not all the implications of his thesis can be discussed here; therefore, I limit myself to a single case. This discussion is connected with the question of limits and barriers in the method of exposition and in the method of enquiry. I begin with a quotation by Frieder Otto Wolf in which he offers his interpretation in this respect:

> For Marx, because of these 'limits of dialectical exposition', which he consciously acknowledges, there is no comparable route stepping through speculative references to general dialectical patterns of thought. Just after the particular individual objects* are 'permeated' in the process of enquiry, that is, after being worked out, through which working out struc-

---

Psychopedis 1992, who ascribes phenomenological *Darstellung* to Hegel's *Philosophy of Right* (p. 5); however, he overlooks the fact that Hegel does not recognise a similar distinction between *Darstellung* and *Forschung*.

87 Compare this with what Engels writes on the introduction to the *Contribution*: 'The logical method of treatment was hence the only appropriate method. But, in fact, it is nothing else other than the historical method, just stripped of the historical form and its disturbing coincidences' (Engels 1971, p. 475, my translation).

88 See Deleuze and Guattari 2005, p. 21: 'Descartes, Hegel, Feuerbach non seulement ne commencent pas par le même concept, mais non pas le même concept de commencement'.

tural causality lets itself be exemplified in the singular objects*, a limited 'dialectical exposition' of the discovered relationships becomes possible for Marx.[89]

In the first place, it is noteworthy to mention that Wolf recognises the need for a distinction between the method of enquiry and the method of exposition. However, he accepts that exposition presupposes enquiry. That said, as a defender of the thesis that 'there is no comparable route stepping through speculative references to general dialectical patterns of thought', Wolf should, along with the viewpoints I criticised previously, *argue* against the application of the threefold function of the method of enquiry generally.

It also follows from this discussion that the treatment of limits and barriers cannot be methodologically the same in the *Grundrisse* and *Capital*. It is therefore necessary to elaborate on the formal difference as proposed by Marx. One aspect of this difference is that when one refers, as Wolf does, to the limits (*Grenze*) of the method of exposition as distinguished from the method of enquiry, one has to speak about the barriers (*Schranke*). Such barriers as found in the *Grundrisse* prepare the path for the method of exposition in *Capital*, where they are thrust into limits. One function of the method of enquiry is then the way it introduces the barriers to be sursumed (*aufgehoben*) in the book where the method of exposition is elaborated on, namely, *Capital*. These barriers cannot be overcome in the method of enquiry, for the inherent characteristics of the method of enquiry still do not disclose their nature; this disclosure needs to be effected in the method of exposition developed in *Capital*.[90]

The development of the totality can finally be comprehended just at this point. The similarity to Hegel's limits and barriers stops at the point where all such limits and barriers are both objective* and social. The forms they bear are,

---

89 Wolf 2006, p. 179, my translation. The original reads: 'Für Marx gibt es – wegen dieser von ihm bewusst beachteten "Grenzen der dialektischen Darstellung" – keine vergleichbare Marscherleichterung durch spekulative Rückgriffe auf allgemeine dialektische Denkfiguren. Allein nachdem im Prozess der Forschung die besonderen singulären Gegenstände "durchdrungen" worden sind, d. h. nachdem herausgearbeitet worden ist, welcher Zusammenhang von strukturaler Kausalität sich an den singulären Gegenständen exemplifizieren lässt, wird für Marx eine begrenzte "dialektische Darstellung" des entdeckten Zusammenhanges möglich.' Admittedly, this reading has its roots in a title-like passage from the *Grundrisse*. See Marx 1983, p. 42: 'Dialektik der Begriffe Produktivkraft (Produktionsmittel) und Produktionsverhältnis, eine Dialektik, deren Grenzen zu bestimmen und die realen Unterschied nicht aufhebt'.

90 Cf. Kosík 1976, p. 16.

for Marx, not vacuous, but real forms. The function of the method of exposition is thus not merely to set forth the research results, nor is it of merely literary value[91] and neither is it a revelation.[92]

Once more, the limits of the method of exposition are the result of the barriers of the method of enquiry, as found in the *Grundrisse*. Such barriers – remembering the barriers in Hegel's *Science of Logic* – carry along with them an *ought* (*Sollen*). In that book, the *ought* is concomitant with the 'barriers'. In Marx's account the 'ought' makes the sursumption (*Aufhebung*) of the barriers of the method of enquiry possible, but also manifests itself in the limits of the method of exposition. The ought of 'Expropriators will be expropriated'[93] goes further than theory.[94] This is itself a sursumption of the judgements of facts, to judgements of value and to judgements of injunction. A description-analysis of the first type of judgements leads to a critique in the second, where an evaluation of the subject matter is offered, which leads in turn to an imperative sentence with an explicit or implicit ought, be it in the form of 'Workers of the world unite' or 'The situation must be transformed'.

What Marx says in the so-called Urtext – 'The dialectical form of exposition is correct, only when it recognises its limits'[95] – must also be taken up and put in relationship with the dual difference presented here, between the limits and barriers on the one hand, and between the method of exposition and the method of enquiry on the other. That is to say, the sentence must be continued with 'and also recognizes its barriers', that is, the barriers which have been already elaborated on in the method of enquiry. A paper commenting on the relationship between the *Grundrisse* and *Capital* has the title 'The Four Levels of Abstraction of Marx's Concept of "Capital": Or, Can We Consider the *Grundrisse* the Most Advanced Version of Marx's Theory of Capital?'[96] The reading proposed here has both a positive and a negative response to this question: As the method of enquiry yes, but not as the method of exposition.

---

91 See Ilyenkov 1982, p. 142.
92 See Bellofiore 2016, p. 56: '*Darstellung* again, is at the same time a "revelation"'. Cf. Hegel 1969b, pp. 65–6, where Hegel draws an analogy between revelation (*Offenbarung*) and a pistol shot.
93 Marx 1962a, p. 791: 'Die Exproprateurs werden exproprüert'.
94 The *Idee des Guten* comes in the last moments of *die Idee des Erkennens*, and the whole *Science of Logic* is the presupposition of the *Philosophy of Right*. See Hegel 1989, p. 32.
95 Marx 1980, p. 90: '[D]ie dialektische Form der Darstellung nur richtig ist, wenn sie Ihre Grenzen kennt'.
96 Fineschi 2013. According to the reading presented here one has to talk about 'moments' not 'levels'.

The thesis proposed by some commentators,[97] that the *Grundrisse* offers *neue Darstellung*, needs further reconsideration. According to the reading presented here, the *Grundrisse* does give us the method of enquiry, and *Capital*, notwithstanding all its shortcomings and points needing development, gives the method of exposition. Given that just the first volume of *Capital* was published by Marx himself and several books were left unwritten even in the forms of notes,[98] it is undoubtedly true that we have no more than the partial realisation of Marx's project. Nonetheless, the partial realisation of the method of exposition in the three volumes of *Capital* does not mean that the totality presented in them is the realisation of a closed totality and a closed realisation of the method of exposition; it is just to affirm that they are the partial realisation of the plan proposed in the *Grundrisse*[99] as the work where method of enquiry is elaborated on (and again, that this is only to the extent expected from notebooks not intended for publication). The richness of these notebooks then is not fully realised in the works where Marx develops his method of exposition. Many books have been written since Marx, on the crises, the changes in the characteristics of the world labour market, etc., and many more are needed.[100] As to the discussion of Marxian totality, the absence of his book on the money market is particularly to be regretted, since according to him it is in the money market that capital posits itself as totality.[101]

The adoption of the approach suggested here leads to a coherent reading of the *Grundrisse* and *Capital* and shows the inner coherence between the method of enquiry and that of exposition, but also raises many questions for further discussion.[102]

The *neue Darstellung* is the Herculean task then left for us.

---

97 Negri 1991, pp. 12–13, 31, and 51.
98 More than that: it is thought that Marx published only about 1/72 of his project! See Dussell 2001, p. 211.
99 Marx 1973, 275.
100 For an elaboration of the paths of further development of Marx's project (*Capital*, critique, and his historical project beyond political economy), see Foster 2018.
101 Marx 1973, p. 275.
102 Callinicos 2018, p. 144: 'The critique of political economy stands before us, massive and unfinished but magnificent, like Michelangelo's slaves in the Accademia in Florence'.

Epilogue

At this stage of the discussion, enough argument has been advanced, I hope, to establish an unambiguous reading of Marx's works regarding the conception of totality and its role in methodological elucidation. It has been established that it is defensible to assert an evolutionary coherence to the Marxian totality. The role of this conception in Marxian methodology and its relationship with the method of inquiry and method of exposition have also been elaborated upon. As we saw in the last chapter, the power of abstraction is realised in two moments: the method of enquiry and the method of exposition.

The conception of dually intertwined totality as a transcategorial metacategory presented here is more promising than the structuralist[1] and poststructuralist accounts in denying the ontological primacy of contingency.[2] Totality is not a category but a metacategory because it is not limited to any specific category. It is transcategorial because its nature is revealed in transition from one category to the other. This conception is also more promising than the competing accounts among Marxist thinkers. It also encompasses the Marxist theory which stresses internal relations.[3] Internal relations are primarily internal relations among the members of wholes. These members are relational entities not in the sense that the characteristics of each one stems from the relationships of that thing with other things, but in the sense that they find their activation through those relations.[4] Taken as an ensemble of relations, each of them is such that it cannot exist without the existence of a totality. The full conception of such a totality is unimaginable without those relations.

This conception of totality is also more promising than the proposed exteriority as an alternative or complementary constituent to totality. In *Towards an Unknown Marx*, Enrique Dussell writes: 'According to Lukács, Kosík or Bloch [totality] is "fundamental" because it is understood as the realm of being which founds entities within its realm'.[5] He forgets to add that totality is also *founded* by its entities. Once this version of totality is adopted, it may be asked

---

1 See Godelier 1967.
2 Postone 2015.
3 For a developed account of the internal relations, see Ollman 2003.
4 Marx 1976, p. 149; discussed above.
5 Dussel 2001, p. 240.

if the introduction of exteriority would be necessary and even helpful. The reason is that the Marxian totality as presented here is, unlike a Hegelian totality, open.[6]

Such openness puts limits on this conception of totality. For instance, it cannot cover those situations where this alien-fetishistic mode of social life does not prevail or is not central – for instance, the situation in Occupied Palestine. It cannot, to give another example, explain the difference between the treatment of Ukrainian and Syrian refugees. But the proposed conception is helpful where this totality is to be grasped as well as those external cases. It is also more promising than the conception which proposes negativity as an alternative to totality.[7] In the conception of totality presented here, negativity is already an inherent characteristic of totality.

That said, there are limits to my argument. Regarding the primary literature, I have limited myself, in principle, to what is found in MEW. To get a broader picture, a further project may reconstruct these discussions with a consideration of *all* the nuances found in MEGA², including the French edition of *Capital* Volume I supervised by Marx.[8] I say *all*, because the reader has witnessed some modest attempts made to integrate the MEGA² version of the much-debated Volume III of *Capital*. Although I do not expect further integration of the nuances in the MEGA² text to invalidate what I believe to be an unambiguous reading of the Marxian Totality presented here, the present work is ultimately to be evaluated in light of that eventual elucidation.

Another problem is the evaluation of the possibility of further integration of the moment of consumption in this social alien-fetishistic contradictory totality, as the moment of singularity, where the human praxis is essentially individual. This entails a challenge for an account of the social totality presented here.

Apart from that, except for a couple of examples,[9] the discussion of totality presented here does not tackle the question of totality in artworks.[10] Although

---

6 Cf. Rockwell 2018, p. 165: 'While Hegel's dialectic was the "totality of reason, a closed ontological system, finally identical with the rational system of history" (Marcuse, 1941/1999, 314), Marx's totality is "the totality of class society, and the negativity that underlies its contradictions and shapes its every content is the negativity of class relations" (Marcuse, 1941/1999, p. 314)'. For a critical review of Rockwell's book, see Boveiri 2021.
7 See Dunayevskaya 2002.
8 See the Appendix 1 for just one example where I have given different versions of such a passage along with my own translation of that French edition.
9 Chapters 3 and 4.
10 In a commentary on one of Paul Cézanne's still life paintings, for instance, we read: 'Each seemingly insignificant element is vital to the overall design'. Murphy 1968, p. 137.

I follow the research on this topic as an amateur,[11] I am not qualified to pass judgement on the meaning of totality with regard to works of art.[12] Nonetheless, I hope that this book will be helpful to a researcher working in that field.

---

11   In Raymond Chandler's *The Big Sleep*, the detective Philip Marlowe says: 'I seem to talk in circles, it just seems that way. It all ties together – everything' (Chandler 1992, p. 223). Another related example may be interesting. During the production of the movie adaptation of Chandler's book, the director Howard Hawks could not figure out whether one character, Owen Taylor, was murdered or committed suicide. They consulted the author, who wrote in a letter: 'They sent me a wire ... asking me, and dammit I didn't know either' (Hiney and MacShane 2000, p. 103). On this, see Jameson 2016. Another work left unconsulted is Lukács's *The Specificity of Aesthetics*; see Lukács 1978a, p. 50.
12   See Best 2020, p. 4 for a promising path in this respect. She demonstrates the pertinence of the conception of totality in the contemporary world notwithstanding the changes that have occurred between Marx's time and the present.

APPENDIX 1

Rereading of a Passage from the French Edition of First Volume of *Capital* Edited by Marx

After the following passage from the Afterword to the second edition of *Capital* Vol. I, which is common in two different French versions:

> Of course, the method of presentation [*Darstellung*] *must differ in form* [*formell*] from that of inquiry [*Forschung*]. The latter has to appropriate the material in detail, to analyze its different forms of development and to track down their inner connection.[1]

We read:

> Erst nachdem diese Arbeit vollbracht, kann die wirkliche Bewegung entsprechend dargestellt werden. Gelingt dies und spiegelt sich nun das Leben des Stoffs ideell wider, so mag es aussehn, als habe man es mit einer Konstruktion a priori zu tun.[2]

> Only after this work has been done can the real movement be appropriately presented [exposed]. If this is done successfully, if the life of the subject-matter is now reflected back in the ideas, then it may appear as if we have before us an a priori construction.[3]

> C'est seulement lorsque cette tâche est accomplie que le mouvement réel peut être exposé en conséquence. Si l'on y réussit et que la vie de la matière traitée se réfléchit alors idéellement, il peut sembler que l'on ait affaire à une construction a priori.[4]

---

1 Karl Marx 1976, *Capital I*, translated by Ben Fowkes, Harmondsworth: Penguin Books, p. 103: 'Allerdings muß sich die Darstellungsweise formell von der Forschungsweise unterscheiden. Die Forschung hat den Stoff sich im Detail anzueignen, seine verschiednen Entwicklungsformen zu analysieren und deren innres Band aufzuspüren'. Karl Marx 1962, *Das Kapital I*, in Karl Marx and Friedrich Engels 1962, Werke 23, Berlin: Dietz Verlag, p. 27.
2 Karl Marx 1962, *Das Kapital I*, in Karl Marx and Friedrich Engels 1962, Werke 23, Berlin: Dietz Verlag, p. 27.
3 Karl Marx 1976, *Capital I*, translated by Ben Fowkes, Harmondsworth: Penguin Books, p. 103.
4 Karl Marx 1993, *Le Capital – Livre Premier*, edited by Jean-Pierre Lefebvre, Paris: Presses Universitaires de France, p. 17.

I have checked with the staff active at the MEGA² project, who have access to Marx's manuscripts. They confirm that the same passage in the version edited and modified by Marx is as follows:

> Une fois cette tâche accomplie, mais seulement alors, le mouvement réel peut être exposé dans son ensemble. Si l'on y réussit, de sorte que la vie de la matière se réfléchisse dans sa reproduction idéale, ce mirage peut faire croire à une construction a priori.[5]

My translation for this latter text is as follows:

> When this task is accomplished, and just then, the real movement can be expounded in its integrity. If one succeeds at this, in a way that the life of the matter reflects itself in the ideal reproduction, this mirage can pretend to be an a priori construction.

---

5   Karl Marx 1982, *Le Capital – Livre premier*, translated by M. Joseph Roy, Moscow: Éditions du Progrès, p. 21.

APPENDIX 2

Some Passages of *Capital III*, in Original for Further Verification

[Note to the reader. The following passages from different versions of what is known as the third volume of *Capital* are not intended to be exhaustive. They are simply presented here to the reader as further verification of the arguments developed in this manuscript.]

∵

Wir haben gesehn, daß der Productionsprozeß im Ganzen betrachtet Einheit von Productions- und Circulationsprozeß ist. Bei der Betrachtung des Circulationsprozesses als Reproductionsprozeß (ch. IV Buch II) wurde dieß näher erörtert. Worum es sich in diesem Buch handelt, kann nicht sein allgemeine Reflexionen über diese 'Einheit' anzustellen. Es gilt vielmehr die konkreten Formen aufzufinden und darzustellen, welche aus dem Proceß des Capitals – als Ganzes betrachtet – hervorwachsen. (In der wirklichen Bewegung der Capitalien treten sie sich in solchen konkreten Formen gegenüber, für die die Gestalt des Capitals im unmittelbaren Productionsprozeß, wie seine Gestalt im Circulationsprozeß nur als besondre Momente erscheinen. Die Gestaltungen des Capitals, wie wir sie in diesem Buch entwickeln, nähern sich also schrittweis der Form, worin sie auf der Oberfläche der Gesellschaft, im gewöhnlichen Bewußtsein der Productionsagenten selbst, und endlich in der Action der verschiednen Capitalien auf einan der, der Concurrenz auftreten.) (Marx 1992b, p. 7)

Im ersten Buch wurden die Erscheinungen untersucht, die der kapitalistische Produktionsprozeß, für sich genommen, darbietet, als unmittelbarer Produktionsprozeß, bei dem noch von allen sekundären Einwirkungen ihm fremder Umstände abgesehn wurde. Aber dieser unmittelbare Produktionsprozeß erschöpft nicht den Lebenslauf des Kapitals. Er wird in der wirklichen Welt ergänzt durch den Zirkulationsprozeß, und dieser bildete den Gegenstand der Untersuchungen des zweiten Buchs. Hier zeigte sich, namentlich im dritten Abschnitt, bei Betrachtung des Zirkulationsprozesses als der Vermittlung des gesellschaftlichen Reproduktionsprozesses, daß der kapitalistische Produktionsprozeß, im ganzen betrachtet, Einheit von Produktions- und Zirkulationsprozeß ist. Worum es sich in diesem dritten Buch handelt, kann nicht sein, allgemeine Reflexionen über diese Einheit anzustellen. Es gilt vielmehr, die konkreten Formen aufzufinden und darzustellen, welche aus dem Bewegungsprozeß des Kapitals, als Ganzes betrachtet, hervorwachsen. In ihrer wirklichen Bewegung treten sich die Kapitale in solchen konkreten Formen gegenüber, für die die Gestalt des Kapitals im unmittelbaren Produktionsprozeß, wie seine Gestalt im Zirkulationsprozeß, nur als besondere Momente erscheinen. Die Gestaltungen des Kapitals, wie wir sie in diesem Buch entwickeln, nähern sich also schrittweis der Form, worin sie auf der Oberfläche der Gesellschaft, in der Aktion der verschiedenen Kapitale aufeinander, der Konkurrenz, und im gewöhnlichen Bewußtsein der Produktionsagenten selbst auftreten. (Marx 1964, p. 33)

∴

[I]st in der Gesellschaft selbst – die Totalität der gesellschaftlichen Productionszweige betrachtet – die Summe der Productionspreisse der producirten Waaren gleich der Summe ihrer Werthe. (Marx 1992b, p. 236)

[I]st in der Gesellschaft selbst – die Totalität aller Produktionszweige betrachtet – die Summe der Produktionspreise der produzierten Waren gleich der Summe ihrer Werte. (Marx 1964, p. 169)

∴

Wenn die *Concurrenz* das Gesellschaftscapital nämlich so vertheilt zwischen die verschiednen Productionssphären, daß die *Productionspreisse* (abstrahirt von der größren oder geringren Portion, worin der Dechet fur fixes Capital in dieselben eingeht) in einer Sphäre = den in diesen Sphären der mittleren Composition, d. h. = K + p, wenn K. der Kostenpreiß, aber *variable* Grösse und p constante Grösse ist, nämlich = der Grösse des Profits p. 100 in jener Sphäre (in jener Sphäre der mittlern Composition Profit zusammenfallend mit dem Mehrwerth) – oder was dasselbe, daß die Profitrate dieselbe in allen Productionssphären (by being equalied to that in those branches of production where the average composition of capital prevails), dann wäre die Summe der Profite in den verschiednen Productionssphären = Summe des Mehrwerths und die Summe der Productionspreisse des gesellschaftlichen Gesammtproducts = Summe seiner Werthe. Es ist aber klar daß die Ausgleichung zwischen den Productionssphären von verschiedner Zusammensetzung (ob diese Verschiedenheit blos auf verschiednem Verhältniß von constantem und variablem Capital, oder auch auf Verschiedenheit der Circulationszeiten beruhe) immer dahin streben muß sie zu equalisiren mit den Sphären von mittlerer Zusammensetzung, sei es nun daß diese exakt der gesellschaftlichen Durchschnittscomposition entsprechen, sei es, daß sie sich derselben annähern. Zwischen den mehr oder minder Annähernden findet selbst wieder Tendenz nach Ausgleichung statt, die der vielleicht idealen, d. h. in der Wirklichkeit nicht vorhandnen Mittelcomposition zustrebt, die Tendenz hat sich um sie herum zu normiren. In dieser Weise herrscht also nothwendig die Tendenz die Productionspreisse zu bloß verwandelten Formen des Werths zu machen oder die Profite in blosse Theile des Mehrwerths zu verwandeln, die aber vertheilt sind, nicht im Verhältniß zum Mehrwerth, der in jeder besondren Productionssphäre erzeugt ist, sondern im Verhältniß zur Masse des in jeder Productionssphäre angewandten Capitals, so daß auf gleich grosse Capitalmassen, wie immer zusammengesetzt, gleich grosse Antheile (aliquote Theile) der Totalität vom gesellschaftlichen Gesammtcapital erzeugten Mehrwerths fallen. (Marx 1992b, p. 248–49)

Die Konkurrenz verteilt das Gesellschaftskapital so zwischen die verschiednen Produktionssphären, daß die Produktionspreise in einer jeden Sphäre gebildet werden nach dem Muster der Produktionspreise in diesen Sphären der mittleren Komposition, d.h. = k + kp' (Kostpreis plus dem Produkt der Durchschnittsprofitrate in den Kostpreis). Diese Durchschnittsprofitrate ist aber nichts andres als der prozentig berechnete Profit in jener Sphäre der mittlem Komposition, wo also der Profit zusammenfällt mit dem Mehrwert. Die Profitrate ist also in allen Produktionssphären dieselbe, nämlich ausgeglichen auf diejenige dieser mittleren Produktionssphären, wo die Durchschnittszusammensetzung des Kapitals herrscht. Hiernach muß die Summe der Profite aller verschiednen Produktionssphären gleich sein der Summe der Mehrwerte, und die Summe der Produktionspreise des gesellschaftlichen Gesamtprodukts gleich der Summe seiner Werte. Es ist aber klar, daß die Ausgleichung zwischen den Produktionssphären von verschiedner Zusammensetzung immer dahin streben muß, sie zu egalisieren mit den Sphären von mittlerer Zusammensetzung, sei es nun, daß diese exakt, sei es, daß sie nur annähernd dem gesellschaftlichen Durchschnitt entsprechen. Zwischen den mehr oder minder Annähernden findet selbst wieder Tendenz nach Ausgleichung statt, die der idealen, d.h. in der Wirklichkeit nicht vorhandnen Mittelposition zu strebt, d.h. die Tendenz hat, sich um sie herum zu normieren. In dieser Weise herrscht also notwendig die Tendenz, die Produktionspreise zu bloß verwandelten Formen des Werts zu machen, oder die Profite in bloße Teile des Mehrwerts zu verwandeln, die aber verteilt sind, nicht im Verhältnis zum Mehrwert, der in jeder besondren Produktionssphäre erzeugt ist, sondern im Verhältnis zur Masse des in jeder Produktionssphäre angewandten Kapitals, so daß auf gleich große Kapitalmassen, wie immer zusammengesetzt, gleich große Anteile (aliquote Teile) der Totalität des vom gesellschaftlichen Gesamtkapital erzeugten Mehrwerts fallen. (Marx 1964, pp. 182–83)

∵

Alle diese Phänomene α), β), γ) *scheinen* ebenso sehr dem durch die Arbeitszeit bestimmten *Werthverhältniß*, als der aus blos unbezahlter oder *Surplusarbeit* bestehenden Natur des *Mehrwerths* zu widersprechen. Es *erscheint* also alles verkehrt in der Concurrenz. Die fertige Gestalt der ökonomischen Verhältnisse, wie sie sich auf der Oberfläche zeigt, in ihrer realen Existenz, und daher auch in den Vorstellungen, und denen der Träger und Agenten dieser Verhältnisse über dieselben, sind sehr verschieden und in der That verkehrt, gegensätzlich zu der *innern wesentlichen*, aber verhüllten *Gestalt*, ihrer unsichtbaren Kerngestalt, und dem ihr entsprechenden *Begriff*. (Marx 1992b, p. 279)

Alle diese Erscheinungen *scheinen* ebensosehr der Bestimmung des Werts durch die Arbeitszeit, wie der aus unbezahlter Mehrarbeit bestehenden Natur des Mehrwerts zu widersprechen. *Es erscheint also in der Konkurrenz alles verkehrt*. Die fertige Gestalt der ökonomischen Verhältnisse, wie sie sich auf der Oberfläche zeigt, in ihrer realen Existenz, und daher auch in den Vorstellungen, worin die Träger und Agenten dieser Verhältnisse sich über dieselben klarzuwerden suchen, sind sehr verschieden von, und in der Tat verkehrt, gegensätzlich zu ihrer innern, wesentlichen, aber verhüllten Kerngestalt und dem ihr entsprechenden Begriff. (Marx 1964, p. 219)

∵

Die wahre Schranke der capitalistischen Production ist das *Capital* selbst, daß das *Capital* und seine Selbstverwerthung als Ausgangspunkt und Endpunkt, als Zweck der Production erscheint; daß die Production Production *für* das Capital und nicht umgekehrt die Productionsmittel blosse Mittel für die Erweiterung und Gestaltung des Lebensprozesses *für* die Gesellschaft sind, welche die Producenten bilden. Die *Schranken*, in denen sich die Erhaltung und Verwerthung der Capitalwerthe, die auf der Basis der Verarmung und Expropriation der grossen Masse der Producenten beruht, bewegen kann, treten daher beständig in Widerspruch mit den Productionsmethoden, die das Capital zu seinem Zweck anwenden muß, und die auf *unbeschränkte* Vermehrung der Production, auf die Production als Selbstzweck, auf unbedingte Entwicklung der gesellschaftlichen Productivkräfte der Arbeit lossteuern. Das Mittel, unbedingte Entwicklung der Productivkräfte der gesellschaftlichen Arbeit geräth in fortwährenden Conflict mit dem beschränkten Zweck, der Verwerthung des vorhandnen Capitals. Wenn die capitalistische Productionsweise daher ein historisches Mittel ist, um die materielle Productivkraft zu entwickeln und den ihr entsprechenden Weltmarkt zu schaffen, ist sie zugleich der beständige Widerspruch zwischen dieser ihrer historischen Aufgabe und den ihr entsprechenden gesellschaftlichen Productionsverhältnissen. (Marx 1992b, p. 324).

Die *wahre Schranke* der kapitalistischen Produktion ist *das Kapital* selbst, ist dies: daß das Kapital und seine Selbstverwertung als Ausgangspunkt und Endpunkt, als Motiv und Zweck der Produktion erscheint; daß die Produktion nur Produktion für *das Kapital* ist und nicht umgekehrt die Produktionsmittel bloße Mittel für eine stets sich erweiternde Gestaltung des Lebensprozesses für die *Gesellschaft* der Produzenten sind. Die Schranken, in denen sich die Erhaltung und Verwertung des Kapitalwerts, die auf der Enteignung und Verarmung der großen Masse der Produzenten beruht, allein bewegen kann, diese Schranken treten daher beständig in Widerspruch mit den Produktionsmethoden, die das Kapital zu seinem Zweck anwenden muß, und die auf unbeschränkte Vermehrung der Produktion, auf die Produktion als Selbstzweck, auf unbedingte Entwicklung der gesellschaftlichen Produktivkräfte der Arbeit lossteuern. Das Mittel – unbedingte Entwicklung der gesellschaftlichen Produktivkräfte – gerät in fortwährenden Konflikt mit dem beschränkten Zweck, der Verwertung des vorhandenen Kapitals. Wenn daher die kapitalistische Produktionsweise ein historisches Mittel ist, um die materielle Produktivkraft zu entwickeln und den ihr entsprechenden Weltmarkt zu schaffen, ist sie zugleich der beständige Widerspruch zwischen dieser ihrer historischen Aufgabe und den ihr entsprechenden gesellschaftlichen Produktionsverhältnissen. (Marx 1964, p. 260)

∵

Es folgt dieß keineswegs *nothwendig* und ist nur behauptet worden, weil der Unterschied zwischen dem *Werth* und dem *Productionspreiß* der Waaren bisher nicht begriffen war.

Wir haben gesehn, daß der *Productionspreiß* einer Waare keineswegs mit ihrem *Werthe* identisch ist, obgleich die Productionspreisse der Waaren in ihrer Totalität betrachtet, nur durch ihren Gesammtwerth regulirt sind und obgleich die Bewegung in den Productionspreissen der verschiednen Waarenarten, all other circumstances remaining the same, ausschließlich durch die Bewegung ihrer Werthe bestimmt ist. Es ist gezeigt worden, daß der Productionspreiß einer Waare *über* oder *unter* ihrem Werthe stehn kann und nur ausnahmsweise mit ihrem Werthe zusammenfällt. (Marx 1992b, 700)

Es folgt dies keineswegs notwendig und ist nur behauptet worden, weil der Unterschied zwischen dem Wert der Waren und ihrem Produktionspreis bisher nicht begriffen war. Wir haben gesehn, daß der Produktionspreis einer Ware keineswegs mit ihrem Wert identisch ist, obgleich die Produktionspreise der Waren, in ihrer Totalität betrachtet, nur durch ihren Gesamtwert reguliert sind, und obgleich die Bewegung der Produktionspreise der verschiednen Warensorten, alle andren Umstände gleichbleibend gesetzt, ausschließlich durch die Bewegung ihrer Werte bestimmt ist. Es ist gezeigt worden, daß der Produktionspreis einer Ware über oder unter ihrem Wert stehn kann, und nur ausnahmsweis mit ihrem Wert zusammenfällt. (Marx 1964, p. 766)

APPENDIX 3

Note on Translation

Aufhebung is one of the most important and the most complex terms in dialectical studies.[1] The term *sursumer* and its derivative *sursomption* were introduced as French equivalents of *aufheben* and *Aufhebung* by Yvon Gauthier. They are also adopted by Gwendoline Jarczyk and Pierre-Jean Labarrière in their French translations of *The Phenomenology of Spirit* and *The Science of Logic*. In this book, I introduce these terms into English as 'to sursume' and 'sursumption'. 'Sublation' and 'sanction' have been in use as English renderings of Hegel's *Aufhebung*. But neither can express the polysemy of the German word, which means retaining, raising, and negating all at the same time.[2] While 'sursumption' may not be an ideal equivalent either, it has the merit that it can be taken as an opposition to subsumption, which Hegelian and Marxian dialectics refute. Moreover, and more related to the discussion of the book, it provides us with the possibility of introducing other derivations used in German and in need of discussion here. Hence, the terms *aufhebbar* and *Aufhebbarkeit* have been translated as 'sursumable' and 'sursumability'.

---

1 Cobben 2006, pp. 110–13.
2 Inwood 1992, p. 283

Bibliography

Works by Marx and Engels

Engels, Friedrich 1971, 'Karl Marx, *Zur Kritik der politischen Ökonomie*', in MEW 13, Berlin: Dietz Verlag, 468–77.

Engels, Friedrich 1975 [1844] 'Outlines of a Critique of Political Economy', in *Marx and Engels Collected Works*, Volume 3, London: Lawrence & Wishart, 418–43.

Engels, Fredrick 1980 [1890] 'Engels to Joseph Bloch, September 21, 1890', in *Marx and Engels Collected Works*, Volume 49, London: Lawrence & Wishart, 33–6.

Engels, Fredrick 1980, *Collected Works*, Volume 49, London: Lawrence & Wishart.

Marx, Karl 1975 [1844] 'Comments on James Mill's *Éléments d'économie politique*', in *Marx and Engels Collected Works*, Volume 3, London: Lawrence & Wishart, 418–43.

Karl Marx 1999, Marx an Kugelmann. London, 27. Juni 1870, in Marx, Karl; Engels, Friedrich (1999), MEW, Band 32, S. 685–86, Berlin: Dietz Verlag.

Marx, Karl 1970, *A Contribution to the Critique of the Political Economy*, translated by S.W. Ryazanskaya, Moscow: Progress Publishers.

Marx, Karl 1975, *Contribution to the Critique of Hegel's Philosophy of Law*, in Karl Marx and Fredrick Engels: Collected Works, Volume 3, pp. 3–129, New York: International Publishers.

Marx, Karl 1976, *Capital I*, translated by Ben Fowkes, Harmondsworth, Middlesex, England: Penguin.

Marx, Karl 1992a, *Capital II*, translated by David Fernbach, Harmondsworth, Middlesex, England: Penguin.

Marx, Karl 1992b, *Ökonomische Manuskripte und Schriften 1863–1867*, in: Marx-Engels-Gesamtausgabe, Abt. II, Bd. 2 (MEGA² II.4.2, Teil 2), Berlin: Dietz Verlag.

Marx, Karl 1991a, *Capital III*, translated by David Fernbach, Harmondsworth, Middlesex, England: Penguin.

Marx, Karl 1977, *Das Elend der Philosophie*, in MEW 4, S. 63–182, Berlin: Dietz Verlag.

Marx, Karl 1968a, 'Auszüge aus Mills "Éléments d'économie politique"', in MEW 40, Berlin: Dietz Verlag, 443–64.

Marx, Karl 1968b, *Doktordissertation: Differenz der demokritischen und epikureischen Naturphilosophie nebst einem Anhange*, in MEW 40, Berlin: Dietz Verlag, 257–373.

Marx, Karl 1968c, *Hefte zur epikureischen, stoischen und skeptischen Philosophie*, in Marx Engels Werke 40, Berlin: Dietz Verlag, 13–256.

Marx, Karl 1968d [1844], *Ökonomisch-philosophische Manuskripte aus dem Jahre 1844*, in Marx Engels Werke 40, Berlin: Dietz Verlag, 465–588.

Marx, Karl 1968e, *Theorien über den Mehrwert*, Dritter Teil, in MEW 26–3, Berlin: Dietz Verlag.

Marx, Karl 1968g, *Aus den dichterischen Versuchen*, in MEW 40, Berlin: Dietz Verlag, 607–12.

Marx, Karl 1987a, *Kritik des Gothaer Programms*, in Marx Engels Werke 19, Berlin: Dietz Verlag, 15–32.

Marx, Karl 1987b, Marx to Engels, 31 July 1865, in Marx Karl, Engels, Fredrick (1987) *Collected Works*, Volume 42, Letters 1864–68, London: Lawrence & Wishart, 172–74.

Marx, Karl 1987c [1879] *Randglossen zu Adolph Wagners "Lehrbuch der politischen Ökonomie"*, in Marx Engels Werke 19, Berlin: Dietz Verlag.

Marx, Karl 1843 letter to Arnold Ruge, Sept. 1843, in *Deutsch-Französische Jahrbücher*, available at: https://www.marxists.org/archive/marx/works/1843/letters/43_09-alt.htm

Marx, Karl 1962b, 'Lohn, Preis und Profit', Marx Engels Werke 16, Berlin: Dietz Verlag, 103–152.

Mrax, Karl 1991b, Marx to Danielson, November 15, 1878, in *Marx and Engels Collected Works*, Volume 45, Letters 1874–1879, London: Lawrence & Wishart, 343–44.

Marx Karl 1979 'The Future Results of the British Rule in India', New-York Daily Tribune, 8 August 1853, in Marx, Karl; Engels, Friedrich (1979) Collected Works, Volume 12, New York: International Publishers, 217–22.

Marx, Karl 1978a, *Critique of the Gotha Program*, *The Marx Engels Reader*, edited by Robert C. Tucker, New York: Norton, 525–41.

Marx, Karl 1978b, Marx an Engels, 16. Januar 1858, in MEW, 29, Berlin: Dietz Verlag, 259–61.

Marx, Karl 1978c [1858], Marx an Ferdinand Lassalle, 22. Februar 1858, in MEW, 29, Berlin: Dietz Verlag, 549–52.

Marx, Karl 1978d, *The Eighteenth of Brumaire of Louis Bonaparte*, *The Marx Engels Reader*, Second edition, edited by Robert C. Tucker, New York: Norton, 594–647.

Marx, Karl 1978e, 'Über Feuerbach', in *Die Deutsche Ideologie*, Karl Marx, and Fredrick Engels, in Marx Engels Werke 3, Berlin: Dietz Verlag, 5–7.

Marx, Karl 1962a [1867], *Das Kapital I, Kritik der politischen Ökonomie*, in *Marx Engels Werke* 23, Berlin: Dietz Verlag.

Marx, Karl 1963a, *Das Kapital II*, in *Marx Engels Werke* 24, Berlin: Dietz Verlag.

Marx, Karl 1963b, *Poverty of Philosophy*, New York: International Publishers.

Marx, Karl 1963c, *The class struggles in France*, 1848–1850, New York: International Publishers.

Marx, Karl 1963d, *Theories of Surplus Value II*, Translated by the Institute of Marxism Leninism, Moscow: Progress.

Marx, Karl, Fredrick Engels 1974, in *Marx Engels Werke* 32, Berlin: Dietz Verlag.

Marx, Karl 1964, *Das Kapital III*, in *Marx Engels Werke* 25, Berlin: Dietz Verlag.

Marx, Karl 2016, *Marx's Economic Manuscript of 1864–1865*, translated by Ben Fowkes, edited by Pierre Moseley, Leiden: Brill.

Marx, Karl 1988, *The Civil War in France: the Paris Commune*, New York: International Publishers.

Marx, Karl and Fredrick Engels 1988, *The Economic and Philosophic Manuscripts of 1844* and *the Communist Manifesto*, translated by Martin Milligan, New York: Prometheus Books.

Marx, Karl; Engels, Friedrich 1999, Gesamtausgabe, MEGA, Band 32, Berlin: Dietz Verlag.

Marx, Karl 1983a, *Grundrisse der Kritik der politischen Ökonomie*, in MEW, Band 42, Berlin: Dietz Verlag.

Marx, Karl 1983b, *Kritik der politischen Ökonomie*, 'Das Kapital' und Vorarbeiten, Band 5, MEGA², II.5, Berlin: Dietz Verlag.

Marx, Karl 1983c, *Mathematical Manuscripts of Karl Marx*, translated by Charles Aronson and Michael Meo, London: New Park Publications.

Marx, Karl 1973, *Grundrisse: Foundations of the Critique of Political Economy*, translated by Martin Nicolaus, New York: Random House.

Marx, Karl 1982, *Le Capital – Livre premier*, translated by Joseph M. Roy, Moscow: Éditions du Progrès.

Marx, Karl 1993, *Le Capital – Livre Premier*, edited by Jean-Pierre Lefebvre, Paris: Presses Universitaires de France.

Marx, Karl 1992c, Marx to Engels on 30 April 1868, in Marx Karl, Engels Frederick *Collected Works*, Volume 43, Letters 1868–1870, London: Lawrence & Wishart, 20–25.

Marx, Karl 1992d, Marx to Joseph Dietzgen, on 9 May 1868, in Marx Karl, Engels Frederick *Collected Works*, Volume 43, Letters 1868–70, London: Lawrence & Wishart, 30.

Marx, Karl 2011, *Manuscrits de 1857–1858 'Grundrisse'*, translated by Jean-Pierre Lefebvre, Paris: Éditions Sociales.

Marx, Karl 1975a [1879] *Marginal Notes on Adolph Wagner's Lehrbuch der politischen Ökonomie*, in *Marx and Engels Collected Works*, Volume 3, London: Lawrence & Wishart, 531–59.

Marx, Karl 1980, *Ökonomische Manuskripte und Schriften 1858–1861*, in Marx-Engels-Gesamtausgabe, Abt. II, Bd. 2 (MEGA II.2), Berlin: Dietz Verlag.

Marx, Karl 1980, *Ökonomische Manuskripte und Schriften 1858–1861*, in Marx-Engels-Gesamtausgabe, Abt. II, Bd. 2 (MEGA II.2), Berlin: Dietz Verlag.

Marx, Karl 2000 [1869], 'On Trade Unions', in *Volksstaat, Nr. 17*, Leipzig in *Karl Marx Selected Writings*, edited by David McLellan, New York: Oxford University Press Inc.

Marx, Karl 1975b, *Texts on Method*, edited and translated by Terrel Carver, Oxford: Blackwell.

Marx, Karl 1975c [1843], 'Comments on the Latest Prussian Censorship Instruction.', in *Karl Marx and Fredrick Engels: Collected Works*, Volume 1, New York: International Publishers, 109–1032.

Marx, Karl 1975d [1902], *The Difference Between the Democritean and Epicurean Philosophy of Nature*, in Karl Marx and Fredrick Engels: Collected Works, Volume 1, New York: International Publishers, 25–105.

Marx, Karl 1967, *Theorien über den Mehrwert*, Zweiter Teil, in MEW 26–2, Berlin: Dietz Verlag.

Marx, Karl 1969, *Theories of Surplus Value I*, translated by the Institute of Marxism Leninism, Moscow: Progress.

Marx, Karl 1971, *Theories of Surplus Value III*, Translated by the Institute of Marxism Leninism, Moscow: Progress.

Marx, Karl 1869, *Volksstaat, Nr. 17* 'Gewerkschaften sind Schulen des Sozialismus' in David McLellan, *Karl Marx Selected Writings*, New York: Oxford University Press, 2000.

Marx, Karl 1968f, *Wages, Price and Profit*, in *Selected Works in One Volume*, London: International Publishers.

Marx, Karl 1981, *Zur Kritik der Hegelschen Rechtsphilosophie*, in MEW 1, pp. 201–337, Berlin: Dietz Verlag.

Marx, Karl 1961c, *Zur Kritik der Politischen Ökonomie*, in MEW 13, pp. 3–160, Berlin: Dietz Verlag.

Marx, Karl 1961, 'Lohnarbeit und Kapital', Marx Engels Werke 6, Berlin: Dietz Verlag, 397–422.

Marx, Karl and Fredrick Engels 1975a, *Collected Works*, Volume 1, New York: International Publishers.

Marx Karl, and Fredrick Engels (1987), *Collected Works*, Volume 42, Letters 1864–68, London: Lawrence & Wishart.

Marx Karl, and Fredrick Engels 1991, *Collected Works*, Volume 45, Letters 1874–79, London: Lawrence & Wishart.

Marx Karl, and Fredrick Engels 1992, *Collected Works*, Volume 43, Letters 1868–70, London: Lawrence & Wishart.

Marx, Karl and Fredrick Engels 1962, *Die heilige Familie oder Kritik der kritischen Kritik. Gegen Bruno Bauer und Konsorten*, in Marx Engels Werke 2, Berlin: Dietz Verlag, 3–224.

Marx, Karl and Fredrick Engels 1972, *Manifest der kommunistischen Partei*, in Marx Engels Werke 4, Berlin: Dietz Verlag, 459–93.

Marx, Karl and Fredrick Engels 1999, Marx Engels Werke 32, Berlin: Dietz Verlag.

Marx, Karl and Fredrick Engels 1975b, *The Holy Family*, in Collected Works, Volume 4, 1844–5, New York: International Publishers, 5–211.

Marx, Karl and Fredrick Engels 1964, *Lettres sur 'le capital'*, présentées par Gilbert Badia, Paris: Éditions Sociales.

Marx, Karl and Fredrick Engels 1968, *Selected Works in One Volume*, London: International Publishers.

Marx, Karl and Fredrick Engels 1945, *The Communist Manifesto*, translated by Samuel Moore, Chicago: Charles H. Kerr & Company.

Marx, Karl and Fredrick Engels 1978, *Die Deutsche Ideologie*, in *Marx Engels Werke* 3, Berlin: Dietz Verlag.

Marx, Karl and Fredrick Engels 1976, *The German Ideology*, in *Marx Engels Collected Works*, Volume 5, New York: International Publishers.

Secondary Literature

Afary, Frida 2012, 'New Persian Translation of Marx's Capital and the Iranian Economy', available at: iranianvoicesintranslation.blogspot.com.

Albritton, Robert and John Simoulidis 2003, *New Dialectics and Political Economy*, New York: Palgrave Macmillan.

Althusser, Louis 1970 [1962], *For Marx*, translated by Ben Brewster, New York: Vintage Books.

Althusser, Louis 2005, *Pour Marx*, Paris: La Découverte.

Althusser, Louis, Étienne Balibar et al. 1965, *Lire le Capital*, Paris: Maspéro.

Anderson, Kevin B. 2009, Interviewed by Ayob Rahmani of *Saamaan-no* (November 2009), Global Discourse [Online], 2: 11, available at: http://global-discourse.com/contents.

Anscombe, Gertrude Elizabeth Margaret 1959, *An Introduction to Wittgenstein's Tractatus*, London: Hutchison University Library.

Aquinas, Thomas 1952, *Quaestiones disputatae de veritate: The Disputed Questions on Truth*, translated by Robert W. Mulligan, Chicago: H. Regnery Co.

Arendt, Hannah 1998, *The Human Condition*, Chicago: University of Chicago Press.

Aristotle 1995, *Metaphysics*, translated by W.D. Ross, Oxford: Clarendon Press.

Aristotle 2006, *Physics, Book I and Book II*, translated by William Charlton, Oxford: Oxford University Press.

Aristotle 1993, *Physics, Book III and Book IV*, translated by Edward Hussey, Oxford: Clarendon Press.

Aristotle 1975, *Posterior Analytics*, translated by Barnes, Jonathan, Oxford: Clarendon Press.

Arndt, Andreas 2007, 'Der Begriff der Materialismus bei Karl Marx', in *Der Materialismus-Streit*, edited by Myriam Gerhard und Walter Jaeschker, Hamburg: Felix Meiner, Vol. 1: 261–74.

Arndt, Andreas, Jure Zovko et al (eds.) 2016, *Hegel-Jahrbuch*, Issue 1, May, De Gruyter.

Arndt, Andreas 1985, *Karl Marx*, Bochum: Bochum Verlangsanstalt.

Arndt, Andreas 2012, *Karl Marx: Versuch über den Zusammenhang seiner Theorie*, Bochum: Germinal Verlag.

Arendt, Hannah 1998, *The Human Condition*, Chicago: University of Chicago Press.
Arthur, Chris 1984, *The Dialectics of Labour: Marx and His Relation to Hegel*, Oxford: Blackwell.
Arthur, Chris 2004, *The New Dialectic and Marx's Capital*, Leiden: Brill.
Asay, Jamin 2020, *A Theory of Truthmaking: Metaphysics, Ontology, and Reality*, Cambridge: Cambridge University Press.
Backhaus, Hans-Georg 1997, *Dialektik der Wertform: Untersuchungen zur Marxschen Ökonomiekritik*, Freiburg: ça ira-Verlag.
Backhaus, Hans-Georg 1974, 1975, 1978, 'Materialen zur Rekonstruktion der Marxschen Welttheorie', *Gesellschaft-Beiträge zu Marxschen Theorie*, 1, 3, 11.
Backhaus, Hans-Georg 1962, 'Zur Dialektik der Wertform.' In: *Beiträge zur marxistischen Erkenntnistheorie*, edited by Alfred Schmidt, Frankfurt: Suhrkamp.
Barnes, Jonathan (ed.) 1984, *The Complete Works of Aristotle*, Princeton: Princeton University Press.
Becker, Carl L. 1955, 'What are Historical Facts?' *The Western Political Quarterly*, Vol. 8, No. 3, 327–40.
Bellofiore, Riccardo 2009, 'A Ghost Turning into a Vampire: The Concept of Capital and Living Labour', in *Rereading Marx: New Perspectives after the Critical Edition*, edited by Riccardo Bellofiore and Roberto Fineschi, New York: Palgrave Macmillan, 178–94.
Bellofiore, Riccardo and Roberto Fineschi 2009, 'Introduction', in *Rereading Marx: New Perspectives after the Critical Edition*, edited by Riccardo Bellofiore and Roberto Fineschi, New York: Palgrave Macmillan, 1–16.
Bellofiore, Riccardo 2016, 'Marx after Hegel: Capital as Totality and the Centrality of Production', in *Crisis Critique*, Volume 3, Issue 3: 30–64.
Bellofiore, Riccardo and Fineschi, Roberto (eds.) 2009, *Rereading Marx: New Perspectives after the Critical Edition*, New York: Palgrave Macmillan.
Bellofiore, Riccardo; Giulio Starosta et al (eds.) 2013, *In Marx's Laboratary. Critical Interpretations of the Grundrisse*, Leiden: Brill.
Berdet, Marc and Thomas Ebke (eds.) 2014, *Actes du colloque Anthropologischer & Aleatorischer Materialismus, Matérialisme anthropologique et matérialisme de la rencontre. Arpenter notre présent avec Walter Benjamin et Louis Althusser*, Philosophische KonTexte Band 4, Berlin: Momo.
Bertalanffy, Ludwig von 1968, *The Organismic Psychology and Systems Theory*, Heinz Werner lectures, Worcester: Clark University Press.
Best, Beverley 2010, *Marx and the Dynamic of the Capital Formation An Aesthetics of Political Economy*, New York: Palgrave Macmillan.
Bidet, Jacques 1984, *Que faire du 'Capital'? Matériaux pour une refondation*, Paris: Klincksieck.
Bidet, Jacques 2004, *Explication et reconstruction du Capital*, Paris: Presses universitaires de France.

Bidet, Jacques 2005, 'La dialectique du Capital: Critique et reconstruction méta/structurelle', in Actes du Colloque 'La dialectique aujourd'hui', organisé par Lucien Sève et Bertell Ollman, Paris: Espaces Marx.

Bidet, Jacques 2008, 'A Key to the Critical Companion to Contemporary Marxism' in *Critical Companion to contemporary Marxism*, edited by Jacques Bidet, and Sathis Kouvelakis, Leiden: Brill, pp. 3–21.

Bidet, Jacques and Kouvelakis, Stathis (eds.) 2008, *Critical Companion to contemporary Marxism*, Leiden: Brill.

Bloch, Ernst 1959, *Das Prinzip Hoffnung*, Frankfurt: Suhrkamp.

Bloch, Ernst 1980, 'Discussing Expressionism' in *Aesthetics and Politics*, edited by Fredric Jameson, London: Verso.

Bloch, Ernst 1996 [1959], *The Principle of Hope*, Cambridge, Mass.: MIT Press.

Blunden, Andy 2017, 'Vygotsky and Activity Theory, The Object in Leontyev, Engeström and Vygotsky', Available at: https://www.ethicalpolitics.org/ablunden/pdfs/Vygotsky_and_Activity_Theory.pdf

Böhm-Bawerk, Eugen von 1926, 'Zum Abschluß des Marxschen Systems', in *Gesammelte Schriften*, edited by F.X. Weiss, Vienna: Leipzig.

Böhm-Bawerk, Eugen von 1949, *Karl Marx and the Close of His System*, New York: Augustus M. Kelley.

Bonefeld, Werner, Richard Gunn and Kosmas Psychopedis 1992, *Opening Marxism*, Volume I, Dialectics and History, London: Pluto Press.

Boudin, Raymond 1993, *Les méthodes en sociologie*, Paris: Presses Universitaires de France.

Bourdieu, Pierre 2007, *La distinction: Critique sociale du jugement*, Paris: Éditions de Minuit.

Bourdieu, Pierre, Jean-Calude Chamboredon et al. 2021, *Le métier de sociologue*, Paris: Éditions HESS.

Boveiri, Kaveh 2013, 'Some Reflections on Social Forum,' *Alterinter*, available at: http://www.alterinter.org/spip.php?article3936, last retrieved, June 1, 2022.

Boveiri, Kaveh 2014, 'Expérience et pauvreté chez Walter Benjamin', in *Anthropologischer & Aleatorischer Materialismus, Matérialisme anthropologique et matérialisme de la rencontre. Arpenter notre présent avec Walter Benjamin et Louis Althusser*, edited by Marc Berdet and Thomas Ebke, Thomas, Berlin: MoMo Berlin Philosophische KonTexte Band 4, 189–96.

Boveiri, Kaveh 2016a, 'Hegel and the Correspondence Theory of Truth in the Science of Logic', in Andreas Arndt, Jure Zovko, Myriam Gerhard (eds.), *Hegel-Jahrbuch*, Volume 2016, Issue 1, May 2016, De Gruyter, 102–7.

Boveiri, Kaveh 2016b, 'On the Absence of Ideal Definitions of Terms in Marx's Works on Political Economy', in *Hegel, Marx, and The Contemporary World*, edited by Kaveh Boveiri, Emmanuel Chaput, et al. (2016), Newcastle upon Tyne: Cambridge Scholars Publishing.

Boveiri, Kaveh 2016c, Review of Harry Harootunian's *Marx after Marx, History and Time in the Expansion of Capitalism*, in *Marx and Philosophy*, December 2016, available at: https://marxandphilosophy.org.uk/reviewofbooks/reviews/2016/2554

Boveiri, Kaveh 2017, 'Zur These eines epistemologischen Bruchs zwischen dem *Kapital* und den *Grundrissen*', in *Materialistische Dialektik bei Marx und über Marx hinaus* edited by Breda Stefano, Kaveh Boveiri et al., Berlin: Freie Universität Berlin.

Boveiri, Kaveh 2018, 'Lukács's Reading of Rosa Luxemburg's Conception of Totality: A Reappraisal', in the Proceedings of the 'International Rosa Luxemburg Conference, Rosa Luxemburg and Her Ideas: Engaging the Left and Changing the World', United Electrical Workers Union, Chicago, April, 26–9, 2018, Available at: http://www.internationale-rosa-luxemburg-gesellschaft.de/Downloads/paper%20Boveiri.pdf

Boveiri, Kaveh 2020, 'On some features of Marx's Method', Review essay on *Marx's Capital, Method and Revolutionary Subjectivity*, by Guido Starosta, published in *Historical Materialism*, available at: http://www.historicalmaterialism.org/book-review/some-features-marxs-method

Boveiri, Kaveh 2021, Review of Russell Rockwell 2018, *Hegel, Marx and the Necessity and Freedom Dialectic: Marxist-Humanism and Critical Theory in the United States*, London: Palgrave Macmillan., in *Marx and Philosophy*, April 2021. available at: https://marxandphilosophy.org.uk/reviews/19040_hegel-marx-and-the-necessity-and-freedom-dialectic-marxist-humanism-and-critical-theory-in-the-united-states-by-russell-rockwell-reviewed-by-kaveh-boveiri/

Boveiri, Kaveh, Emmanuel Chaput et al. (eds.) 2016, *Hegel, Marx, and The Contemporary World*, Newcastle upon Tyne: Cambridge Scholars Publishing.

Breda, Stefano, Kaveh Boveiri et al. (eds.) 2017, *Materialistische Dialektik bei Marx und über Marx hinaus*, Berlin: Freie Universität Berlin.

Brudney, Daniel 1998, *Marx's Attempt to Leave Philosophy*, Cambridge: Cambridge University Press.

Burbidge, John William 2013, *Ideas, Concepts and Reality*, Montreal and Kingston: McGill-Queens's University Press.

Burbidge, John William 2006, *The Logic of Hegel's Logic*, Peterborough: Broadview.

Burns, Tony and Ian Fraser 2000, *The Hegel-Marx Connection*, Basingstoke: Macmillan.

Calkins, Mary Whiton (1903) 'The Order of the Hegelian Categories in the Hegelian Argument', *Mind*, New Series, Vol. 12, No. 47 (Jul., 1903), pp. 317–340

Callinicos, Alex 1978, *The Logic of Capital*, Bookmarks Publication, DPhil Thesis, Oxford: Oxford University Press.

Callinicos, Alex 2014, *Deciphering Capital Marx's Capital and Its Destiny*, London: Bookmarks Publication.

Callinicos, Alex 2018 'Marx's Unfinished but Magnificent Critique of Political Economy', *Science & Society*, Vol. 82, No. 1, January 2018, pp. 139–45.

Camus, Albert 2013, *Œuvres*, Paris: Quarto Gallimard.

Cascardi, Anthony J. 1992, 'Totality and the Novel', *New Literary History*, Vol. 23, No. 3, History, Politics, and Culture (Summer, 1992), 607–627.

Cerutti, Furio 1980, *Totalità, Bisogni, Organizzazione. Ridiscutendo 'Storia e coscienza di classe'*, Florence: La Nuova Italia.

Chakrabarti, Kisor Kumar 1995, *Definition and Induction: A Historical and Comparative Study*, Honolulu: University of Hawai'i Press.

Chandler, Raymond 1992, *Big Sleep*, New York: Vintage.

Choulet, Philippe, Dominique Folscheid et al. 2018, *Méthodologie philosophique*, Paris: Presses Universitaires de France.

Cobben, Paul (ed.) 2006, *Hegel-Lexikon*, Stuttgart: Fromman, pp. 340–1.

Cohen, Gerald Allan 2000, *Karl Marx's Theory of History: A Defence*, Princeton: Princeton University Press.

Cohen, Jean Louise 1982, *Class and Civil Society: The Limits of Marxian Critical Theory*, Amherst: University of Massachusetts Press.

Corredor, L. Eva 1997, *Lukács after Communism: Interviews with Contemporary Intellectuals*, Durham: Duke University Press.

Dardot, Pierre and Christian Laval 2012, *Marx, prénom: Karl*, Paris: Collection NRF Essais, Gallimard.

De Laurentiis, Allegra and Jeffrey Edwards 2013, *The Bloomsbury Companion to Hegel*, London: Bloomsbury.

Deleuze, Gilles ; Guattari, Félix 2005a, *Qu'est-ce que la philosophie?*, Paris: Éditions de Minuit.

Deleuze, Gilles ; Guattari, Félix 2005b, *Capitalisme est schizophrénie, L'Anti-Œdipe*, Paris: Éditions de Minuit.

Descartes, René 2000, *Discours de la méthode*, Paris: Livre de poche.

DeGolyer, Michael 1992. 'The Greek Accent of the Marxian Matrix', in *Marx and Aristotle*, edited by George E. McCarthy, Lanham: Rowman & Littlefield, 107–51.

Di Giovanni, George 2013 'Moment' in De Laurentiis, Allegra and Jeffrey Edwards 2013, *The Bloomsbury Companion to Hegel*, London: Bloomsbury.

Dunayeskaya, Raya 1978 'Critique of Roman Rosdolsky's *The Making of Marx's Capital*: Rosdolsky's Methodology and the Missing Dialectic', available at: http://www.thehobgoblin.co.uk/journal/h62004_RD_Rosdolsky.htm

Dunayevskaya, Raya 2002, *The Power of Negativity: selected writings on the dialectic in Hegel and Marx*, edited by Peter Hudis and Kevin B. Anderson, Lanham, Md.: Lexington Books.

Durkheim, Emile 1915, *Rules of the Sociological Method*, edited by Steven Lukes, New York: Free Press.

Dussel, Enrique 2001, *Towards an Unknown Marx: A Commentary on the Manuscripts of 1861–1863*, London: Routledge.

Elias, Norbert 1991, *Mozart: Sociologie d'un génie*, Paris: Seuil.
Elster, Jon 1985, *Making Sense of Marx*, Cambridge: Cambridge University Press.
Fahey, Charles; C.T. Lenard (et al.) 2009, 'Calculus: A Mathematical Approach', in *The Australian Mathematical Society Gazette*, 36: 258–65.
Ferrer, D., F. Orsini et al. 2020, *A Autobiografia do Pensamento: A Ciéncia da Lógica de Hegel*, Porto Alegre: Editora Fundagao Fénix.
Feuerbach, Ludwig Andreas 1959a, *The Essence of Christianity*, translated by George Eliot, New York: Harper & Row.
Feuerbach, Ludwig Andreas 1959b, *Grundsätze der Philosophie der Zukunft*, in *Sämtliche Werke*, Vol. 11, edited by Friedrich Jodl and Wilhelm Bolin, Stuttgart: Frommann Verlag.
Feuerbach, Ludwig Andreas 1959c, *Vorläufige Thesen zur Reform der Philosophie*, in *Sämtliche Werke*, Vol. 11, edited by Friedrich Jodl and Wilhelm Bolin, Stuttgart: Frommann Verlag, 224–43.
Feuerbach, Ludwig Andreas 1959d, *Zur Kritik der Hegelschen Philosophie*, in *Sämtliche Werke*, Vol. 2, edited by Friedrich Jodl and Wilhelm Bolin, Stuttgart: Frommann Verlag, 159–203.
Fine, Ben; Laurence Harris 1979, *Rereading Capital*, New York: Columbia University Press.
Finelli, Roberto 2009, 'The Limits and Uncertainties of Historical Materialism: An Appraisal based on the Text of Grundrisse (Notebooks III, IV and V)', in *Rereading Marx New Perspectives after the Critical Edition*, edited by Riccardo Bellofiore and Roberto Fineschi, New York: Palgrave Macmillan, 99–111.
Fineschi, Roberto 2013, 'The Four Levels of Abstraction of Marx's Concept of 'Capital'. Or, Can We Consider the Grundrisse the Most Advanced Version of Marx's Theory of Capital?', in: *In Marx's Laboratory. Critical Interpretations of the Grundrisse*, edited by Riccardo Bellofiore, Giulio Starosta et al., Leiden: Brill, 71–100.
Foster, John Bellamy 2018, 'Marx's Open-Ended Critique', *Monthly Review*, https://monthlyreview.org/2018/05/01/marxs-open-ended-critique/#endnote-8-bac
Fox, John 1985, *Understanding Capital: Volume II A Reader's Guide*, Toronto: Progress Books.
Freeman, Alan [Forthcoming], 'Mathematical Foundations of the Value Theory of Finance'.
Fulda, Hans Heinrich 1959, 'Hegels Dialektik als Begriffsbewegung und Darstellungsweise', in *Dialektik in der Philosophie Hegels*, edited by Rolf-Peter Horstmann, Frankfurt: Suhrkamp, 124–76.
Gadamer, Hans-Georg 2006, *Truth and Method*, London, New York: Continuum.
Galindo, Jorge 2006, *Zwischen Notwendigkeit und Kontingenz. Theoretische Selbstbeobachtung der Soziologie*, Wiesbaden: VS Verlag für Sozialwissenschaften.
Gauthier, Yvon 2010, *Hegel: Introduction à une lecture critique*, Quebec City: Presses de l'Université Laval.

Glouberman, Mark 1980, 'Tractatus: Pluralism or Monism?', *Mind*, New Series, vol. 89, 353: 17–36.

Godelier, Maurice 1967, 'System, Structure and Contradiction in *Capital*', *Socialist Register*, Volume 4, 91–119.

Gohlke, Paul 1914, *Die Lehre von der Abstraktion bei Plato und Aristoteles*, Halle: Max Niemeyer.

Goldmann, Lucien 1958, *Recherches dialectiques*, Paris: Gallimard.

Goldmann, Lucien 1968, 'L'Idéologie allemande et les thèses sur Feuerbach', in *L'Homme et la société*, N. 7, 1968. Numéro spécial 150° anniversaire de la mort de Karl Marx, 37–55.

Goldmann, Lucien 1970, *Marxisme et sciences humaines*, Paris: Gallimard.

Goldstick, Dan 2009, *Reason, Truth, and Reality*, Toronto: University of Toronto Press.

Goldstick, Dan 2000, 'Correspondence', in *The Proceedings of the Twentieth World Congress of Philosophy*, Analytic Philosophy and Logic, 6: 195–197.

Goldstick, Dan 2020, 'Logical form', *Philos Forum*, 51: 411–412.

Goldstick, Dan and Frank Cunningham 1978, "Activism and Scientism in the Interpretations of Karl Marx's First and Third Theses on Feuerbach", in *Philosophical Forum*, Volume 8, Nos. 2–4, 269–287.

Gramsci, Antonio 1971, *Selections from Prison Notebooks*, Quentin Hoare and Geoffrey Nowell Smith (Translators, Editors), New York: International Publishers.

Grumley, John Edward 1989, *History and Totality: Radical Historicism from Hegel to Foucault*, London: Routledge.

Halbwachs, Maurice 1937, 'Le point de vue sociologue'. Extrait de *X-Crise*. Bulletin n° 34, 1937. Texte de 2 conférences faites au Centre polytechnicien d'études économiques.

Hall, Stuart 2003, 'Marx's Notes on Method: A "Reading" of the "1857 Introduction"', *Cultural Studies*, 17:2, 113–49.

Harris, Henry Silton 1997, 'Hegel's Correspondence Theory of Truth', in *Hegel's Phenomenology of Spirit: A Reappraisal*, Garry, K., Browning, 11–22.

Harvey, David 1999, *The Limits to Capital*, London: Verso.

Harvey, David 2010, *A Companion to Marx's Capital*, London: Verso.

Harvey, David 2010, *The Enigma of Capital: and the Crises of Capitalism*, New York: Oxford University Press.

Hegel, Georg Wilhelm Friedrich 1980a, *Enzyklopädie der philosophischen Wissenschaften im Grundrisse*, Erster Teil Die Wissenschaft der Logik Mit den mündlichen Zusätzen, Hegels Werke in Zwanzig Bänden, 8. Auf der Grundlage der Werke von 1832–1845 neue edierte Redaktion Eva Modenhauer und Karl Markus Michel, Frankfurt am Main: Suhrkamp.

Hegel, Georg Wilhelm Friedrich 1980b [1907], *Phänomenologie des Geistes*, in Hegels Werke in Zwanzig Bänden, 3. Auf der Grundlage der Werke von 1832–1845 neue edierte Redaktion Eva Modenhauer und Karl Markus Michel, Frankfurt am Main: Suhrkamp.

Hegel, Georg Wilhelm Friedrich 1986b, *Enzyklopädie der philosophischen Wissenschaften im Grundrisse*, Zweiter Teil Die Naturphilosophie Mit den mündlichen Zusätzen, Hegels Werke in Zwanzig Bänden, 9. Auf der Grundlage der Werke von 1832–1845 neue edierte Redaktion Eva Modenhauer und Karl Markus Michel, Frankfurt am Main: Suhrkamp.

Hegel, Georg Wilhelm Friedrich 1983, *Die Philosophie des Rechts*, Francfort: Suhrkamp.

Hegel, Georg Wilhelm Friedrich 1955, *Hegel's Lectures on the History of Philosophy*, volume two, translated by E.S. Haldane, and H. Francis Simson, New York: The Humanities Press Inc.

Hegel, Georg Wilhelm Friedrich 1986a, 11. *Jenaer Schriften* (1801–1807) in Hegels Werke in Zwanzig Bänden, Auf der Grundlage der Werke von 1832–1845 neue edierte Redaktion Eva Modenhauer und Karl Markus Michel, Frankfurt am Main: Suhrkamp.

Hegel, Georg Wilhelm Friedrich 1969a, *Hegel's Science of Logic*, translated by A.V. Miller, Atlantic Highlands, N.J.: Humanities Press International.

Hegel, Georg Wilhelm Friedrich 2010, *Hegel's Science of Logic*, translated by Di Giovanni, George, New York: Cambridge University Press.

Hegel, Georg Wilhelm Friedrich 1985, 'On the Essence of the Philosophical Criticism in the Present State of Philosophy', in *Between Kant and Hegel*, edited by H.S. Harris, Albany: State University of New York Press.

Hegel, Georg Wilhelm Friedrich 1985, 'On the Relationship between Skepticism to Philosophy', in *Between Kant and Hegel*, edited by H.S. Harris, Albany: State University of New York Press.

Hegel, Georg Wilhelm Friedrich 1977, *The Difference between Fichte's and Schelling's 'System der Philosophie'*, translated by Walter Cerf and H.S. Harris, Albany: State University of New York Press.

Hegel, Georg Wilhelm Friedrich 1975 [1830], *The Hegel's Logic, Being Part One of the Encyclopaedia of the Philosophical Sciences*, translated by John Niemeyer Findlay, Oxford: Clarendon Press.

Hegel, Georg Wilhelm Friedrich 1952 *Hegel's Philosophy of Right*, translated by T.M. Knox, Oxford: Clarendon Press.

Hegel, Georg Wilhelm Friedrich 1989, *Grundlinien der Philosophie des Rechts, oder Naturrecht und Staatswissenschaft im Grundrisse*, in: Werke, Bd. 7, Frankfurt: Suhrkamp.

Hegel, Georg Wilhelm Friedrich 1977 [1807], *The Phenomenology of Spirit*, translated by A.V. Miller, Oxford: Oxford University Press.

Hegel, Georg Wilhelm Friedrich 1969b, *Wissenschaft der Logik I*, Hegels Werke in Zwanzig Bänden, 5, Auf der Grundlage der Werke von 1832–1845 neue edierte Redaktion Eva Modenhauer und Karl Markus Michel, Frankfurt: Suhrkamp.

Hegel, Georg Wilhelm Friedrich 1969c, *Wissenschaft der Logik II*, Hegels Werke in Zwanzig Bänden, 6. Auf der Grundlage der Werke von 1832–45 neue edierte Redaktion Eva Modenhauer und Karl Markus Michel, Frankfurt: Suhrkamp.

Heidegger, Martin 1967, *Sein und Zeit*, Tübingen: Max Niemeyer.

Heidegger, Martin 1975 *Reden und andere Zeugnisse eines Lebensweges: 1910–1976, Gesammtausgabe, 1, Veroffentlichte Schriften*, Frankfurt: V. Klostermann.

Henrich, Dieter 1982 'Logische Form und reale Totalität', *Hegels Philosophie des Rechts*, Dieter Henrich, und Rolf-Peter Hortsmann (eds.), Stuttgart: Klett-Kotta, 428–50.

Heinrich, Michael 1996/1997, "Engels' Edition of the Third Volume of Capital and Marx's Original Manuscript", in: *Science and Society*, Vol. 60, No. 4, Winter 1996–7, 452–66.

Heinrich, Michael 2012, *An introduction to the three volumes of Karl Marx's Capital*, translated by Alexander Locascio, New York: Monthly Review Press.

Heinrich, Michael 2016, '"Capital" after MEGA: Discontinuities, Interruptions, and New Beginnings', in *Crisis and Critique*, Volume 3, issue 3, 93–138.

Heinrich, Michael and Fred Moseley, *Marx's Abstract Theory of Value and Money in Volume 1 of Capital* (A debate), https://www.youtube.com/watch?v=9OuQtocg81c

Henry, Michel 1976 *Marx I, une philosophie de la réalité*, Paris: Gallimard.

Henry, Michel 1976, *Marx II, une philosophie de l'économie*, Paris: Gallimard.

Hilferding, Rudolf 1949, 'Böhm-Bawerk's Criticism of Marx', in Eugen von Böhm-Bawerk, *Karl Marx and the Close of his System*, New York: Augustus M. Kelley, 120–96.

Himmelweit, Susan and Simon Mohun 1978, 'The Anomalies of Capital', in *Capital and Class*, 2: 67, 68–105.

Hiney, T. and F. MacShane (eds.) 2000, *The Raymond Chandler Papers*, New York: Atlantic Monthly Press.

Hoff, Jan; Alexis Petrioli et al (Editors) 2006, *Das Kapital neu Lesen. Beiträge zur radikalen Philosophie*, Berlin: Westfälisches Dampfboot.

Hoffmeister, Johannes 1932, *Goethe und der deutsche Idealismus: Eine Einführung zu Hegels Realphilosophie*, Leipzig: Felix Meiner Verlag.

Horvath, Ronald J., and Kenneth D. Gibson, 1984, 'Abstraction in Marx's Method', *Antipode*, 16 (1): 12–25.

Houlgate, Stephen 2006, *The Opening of Hegel's Logic, from Being to Infinity*, West Lafayette: Purdue University Press.

Hume, David 2007, *Dialogues Concerning Natural Religion and Other Writings*, edited by Dorothy Coleman, New York: Cambridge University Press.

Ilyenkov, Evald Vassilievich 1979, *Die Dialektik des abstrakten und konkreten im 'Kapital' von Karl Marx*, Berlin: Das europäische Buch.

Ilyenkov, Evald Vassilievich 1982 *The Dialectics of the Abstract and the Concrete in Marx's "Capital"*, translated by S. Syrovatkin, Moscow: Progress Publishers.

Inwood, Michael 1992, *A Hegel Dictionary*, Oxford: Blackwell Publishers.

Jacoby, Russell 1981, *Dialectic of Defeat*, Cambridge: Cambridge University Press.

Jameson, Fredric 1980, *Aesthetics and Politics*, London: Verso.
Jameson, Fredric 1990, *Late Marxism: Adorno, or, the Persistence of the Dialectic*, London, New York: Verso.
Jameson, Fredric 2009, *Valences of the Dialectic*, London, New York: Verso.
Jameson, Fredric 2011, *Representing Capital: a Commentary on Volume One*, London, New York: Verso.
Jameson, Fredric 2016, *Raymond Chandler: The Detections of Totality*, Verso, London; New York.
Jay, Marti 1977, 'The Concept of Totality in Lukács and Adorno', *Telos*, Volume 7, 117–37.
Jay, Martin 1984, *Marxism and Totality: The Adventures of a Concept from Lukács to Habermas*, Berkeley: University of California Press.
Johnston, M. William 1967, 'Karl Marx's Verse of 1836–1837 as a Foreshadowing of His Early Philosophy', *Journal of the History of Ideas*, Vo. 28, No. 2 (Apr–Jun. 1967), 259–68.
Kant, Immanuel 1968, *Kritik der reinen Vernunft*, Berlin: Reclam.
Kant, Immanuel 1998, *Critique of Pure Reason*, Cambridge: Cambridge University Press.
Kaplan, Abraham 2009 [1964], *The Conduct of Enquiry: Methodology for Behavioural Science*, New Brunswick, New Jersey: Transaction Publisher.
Kervégan, Jean-François 2007, *L'effectif et le rationnel: Hegel et l'esprit objectif*, Paris: Vrin.
Kervégan, Jean-François 2017, 'La liberté du concept', *Studia Hegeliana*, Volume III, 71–88.
Kervégan, Jean-François 2018, *The Actual and the Rational: Hegel and Objective Spirit*, Chicago: University of Chicago Press.
Klemperer, Klemens von 1968, *Germany's New Conservatism: Its History and Dilemma in the Twentieth Century*, Princeton: Princeton University Press.
Kosík, Karel 1966, *Dialektika konkrétního; studie o problematice člověka a světa*, Prague: Academia.
Kosík, Karel 1976, *Dialectic of the Concrete*, translated by Karel Kovanda and James Schmidt, Dordrecht: D. Reidel.
Kosík, Karel 1978, *La dialectique du Concret*, translated by Roger Dangeville, F. Paris: Maspero.
Kosík, Karel 1986, *Die Dialektik des Konkreten: Eine Studie zur Problematik des Menschen und der Welt*, translated by Marianne Hoffman, Frankfurt: Suhrkamp.
Krahl, Hans Jürgen 1970, 'Bemerkungen und Verhältnis von Kapital und Hegelshcer Wesenslogik', in *Aktualität und Folgen der Philosophie Hegels*, edited by Oskar Nagt, Frankfurt: Suhrkamp.
Kroeger, Adolph Ernst 1872, 'The Difference Between the Dialectic Method of Hegel and the Synthetic Method of Kant and Fichte.' *The Journal of Speculative Philosophy*, April 1872, Vol. 6, No. 2 (April, 1872), Penn State University Press, 184–7.

Kuhn, Thomas 1970, *The Structure of Scientific Revolutions*, Chicago: University of Chicago Press.
Labica, Georges 1987, *Karl Marx Les 'Thèses sur Feuerbach'*, Paris: Presses Universitaires de France.
Labriola, Antonio 1980, *Socialism and Philosophy*, St. Louis: Telos Press.
Lafontant, Jean 2008, 'Quelques éléments de la sociologie générale' in *Initiation thématique à la sociologie*, edited by Jean Lafontant, Simon Laflamme, Quebec City: Édition Prise de Parole, Cognitio.
Lafontant, Jean and Simon Laflamme 2008, *Initiation thématique à la sociologie*, edited by Jean Lafontat, Simon Laflamme, Quebec City: Édition Prise de Parole, Cognitio.
Lamb, David 1992, 'Teleology: Kant and Hegel' in *Hegel's Critique of Kant* edited by Stephen Priest, Hampshire: Greg Revivals, 173–84.
Lebowitz, Michael A. 2009, *Following Marx: Method, Critique and Crisis*, Leiden: Brill.
Lebowitz, Michael A. 1998, 'Review of Feston Shortall's, in *The Incomplete Marx*', *Historical Materialism Volume 3* (Iissue 1), 173–88.
Leibniz, Wilhelm Gottfried 1881, *La Monadologie*, Paris: C. Delagrave.
Lemieux, Cyril 2010, 'Problématiser', in *L'enquête sociologique*, edited by Serge Pugnam, Paris: Presses Universitaires de France, 27–51.
Lenin, Vladimir Ilyich 1952, *Materialism and Empirio-Criticism*, Moscow: Foreign Language Publishing House.
Lenin, Vladimir Ilyich 1961, *Philosophical Notebooks*, in *Lenin Collected Works*, Vol. 38, Moscow: Progress Publishers.
Lenin, Vladimir Ilyich 1976, Collected Works, Volume 38, Moscow: Progress Publishers.
Levine, Norman 2002, 'Hegel and the 1861–1863 Manuscripts', in *Rethinking Marxism*, 14, 4: 47–58.
Levine, Norman 2005, 'Marx's First Appropriation of Hegel', *Critique*, 36–7: 125–6.
Levine, Norman 2009, 'Hegelian Continuities in Marx', *Critique*, 37, 3: 345–70.
Levins, Richard 1998, 'Dialectics and System Theory', *Science & Society*, 62, 3, Dialectics: The New Frontier (Fall), 375–99.
Lewontin, Richard Charles 2000, *The Triple Helix: Gene, Organism, and Environment*, Cambridge, Mass.: Harvard University Press.
Lobkowicz, Nicholas 1968, 'Abstraction and Dialectics', in *The Review of Metaphysics*, 21, 3 (Mar.): 468–90.
Locke, John 1999, *An Essay Concerning Human Understanding*, Philadelphia: Pennsylvania State University.
Lukács, Georg 1970a, *Geschichte und Klassbewußtsein, Studien über marxistische Dialektik*, Darmstadt and Neuwied: Hermann Luchterhand Verlag.
Lukács, Georg 1970b, 'The Dialectic of Labour: Beyond Causality and Teleology', *Telos* 6, 162–83.

Lukács, Georg 1971a, *History and Class Consciousness*, translated by Rodney Livingstone, Cambridge, Mass.: MIT Press.

Lukács, Georg 1971b, *The Theory of Novel*, Cambridge, Mass.: MIT Press.

Lukács, Georg 1975, *The Young Hegel*, translated by Rodney Livingstone, Cambridge, Mass.: MIT Press.

Lukács, Georg 1978a, *The Ontology of Social Being, 1. Hegel, Hegel's False and His Genuine Ontology*, Translated by David Fernbach, London: Merlin Presss.

Lukács, Georg 1978b, *The Ontology of Social Being, 2. Marx, Marx's Bacic Ontological Principles*, translated by David Fernbach, London: Merlin Presss.

Lukács, Georg 1980 [1938], 'Realism in Balance' in *Aesthetics and Politics*, edited by Fredric Jameson, translated by Rodney Livingstone, London: Verso, 28–59.

Lukács, Georg, John Rees et al. 2002, *A Defence of History and Class Consciousness: Tailism and the Dialectic*, translated by Esther Leslie, London and New York: Verso.

Luxemburg, Rosa 1961, *The Russian Revolution and Leninism or Marxism*, Chicago: University of Chicago University Press.

Luxemburg, Rosa 2013, *Complete Works, Volume 1*, edited by Peter Hudis, translated by David Fernbach, Joseph Fracchia, and George Shriver, London: Verso.

Macherey, Pierre 2008, *Marx 1845: Les 'THÈSES' sur Feuerbach*, Paris: Éditions Amsterdam.

MacKinnon, Catharine 1987, *Feminism Unmodified*, Cambridge, Mass.: Harvard University Press.

Mandel, Ernst 1975, *Late Capitalism*, London: NLB.

Maney, Mark, E. 2003, *Capital as Organic Unity, The Role of Hegel's Science of Logic in Marx's Grundrisse*, Dordrecht: Springer.

Marcuse, Herbert 1941, *Reason and Revolution*, Oxford: Oxford University Press.

Marcuse, Herbert 2007, *One Dimensional Man*, London and New York: Routledge.

Mattick, Jr., Paul, 1993, 'Marx's Dialectic' in *Marx's Method in Capital, A Reexamination*, edited by Fred Moseley, New Jersey: Humanities Press, pp. 115–134.

McLellan, David 2000, *Karl Marx: Selected Writings*, New York: Oxford University Press Inc.

McNally, David 2010, *Monsters of the Market Zombies, Vampires and Global Capitalism*, Leiden: Brill.

McTaggart, Ellis 1999, *Studies in the Hegelian Dialectic*, Kitchener: Batoche Books.

Milton, John 1918, *Areopagitica*, Cambridge: Cambridge University Press.

Milward, Bob 2000, *Marxian political economy: Theory, History and Contemporary Relevance*, London: Macmillan.

Molière 1971, *L'avare*, Paris: Nouveaux Classiques Larousse.

Mortensen, Chris 2012 'Change and Inconsistency', in The Stanford Encyclopedia of Philosophy, edited by Edward N. Zalta, available at: http://plato.stanford.edu/archives/win2012/entries/change/.

Moore, Willis 2005, 'Structure in Sentence and in Fact', in *Essays On Wittgenstein's Tractatus* edited by Irving M. Copi, and Robert, W. Beard, New York: Macmillan, 87–93.

Moseley, Fred (ed.) 1993, *Marx's Method in Capital, A Reexamination*, New Jersey: Humanities Press.

Moseley Fred (ed.) 2005, *Marx's Theory of Money: Modern Appraisals*, New York: Palgrave Macmillan.

Moseley, Fred 2014, 'The Universal and the Particulars in Hegel's Logic and Marx's Capital' in *Marx's Capital and Hegel's Logic: A Reexamination*, edited by Fred Moseley and Tony Smith, Leiden: Brill, 115–139.

Moseley, Fred 2015, *Money and Totality. A Macro-Monetary Interpretation of Marx's Logic in Capital and the End of the 'Transformation Problem'*, Leiden: Brill.

Moseley, Fred and Martha Campbell (eds.) 1997, *The New Interpretations of Marx's Method*, Atlantic Islands: Humanities Press.

Mosely, Fred and Tony Smith 2014, *Marx's Capital and Hegel's Logic: A Reexamination*, Leiden: Brill.

Moseley Fred, Micahel Heinrich debate 2021, Marx's Abstract Theory of Value and Money in Volume 1 of *Capital*
https://www.youtube.com/watch?v=9OuQtocg81c

Murphy, Richard W. 1968, *The Wolrd of Cézanne*, New York: Time-Life Books.

Murray, Patrick 1988, *Marx's Theory of Scientific Knowledge*, Atlantic Highlands, New Jersey: Humanities Press International.

Murray, Patrick 2005, 'Money as Displaced Social Form: Why Value cannot be Independent of Price?', in *Marx's Theory of Money: Modern Appraisals*, edited by Fred Moseley, New York: Palgrave Macmillan.

Musgrave, Alan 1981, ''Unreal Assumptions' in Economic Theory: The F-Twist Untwisted', *Kyklos*, Volume 34, Issue 3, 377–387.

Negri, Antonio 1991, *Marx beyond Marx: Lessons on Grundrisse*. Harry Cleaver, translated by Michael Ryan and Maurizio Viano, edited by Jim Fleming, New York: Autonomedia.

Norman, Richard; and Sean Sayers 1980, *Hegel, Marx and Dialectic: A Debate*, Atlantic Highlands, New Jersey: International Humanities Press.

Oakley, Allen 1983, *The Makings of Marx's Critical Theory: A bibliographical Analysis*, London: Routledge & Kegan Paul.

Ollman, Bertell 1993, *Dialectical Investigations*, New York: Routledge.

Ollman, Bertell 2003, *Dance of the Dialectic, Steps in Marx's Method*, Urbana: University of Illinois Press.

Onnsach, Ernst-Otto 2006, 'Objektivität', in: (u.a.) hersg. (2006) *Hegel-Lexikon*, edited by Paul Cobben, Stuttgart: Fromman, 340–341.

Paolucci, Paul 2001, 'Classical Sociological Theory and Modern Social Problems: Marx's

Concept of the Camera Obscura and the Fallacy of Individualistic Reductionism.' *Critical Sociology*, 27, 1: 617–67.

Paolucci, Paul 2005, 'Assumptions of the Dialectical Method: The Centrality of Labour for Human Species, Its History, and Individuals.' *Critical Sociology*, 31, 3: 559–81.

Paolucci, Paul 2007, *Marx's Scientific Dialectics*, Leiden: Brill.

Paolucci, Paul 2011, *Marx and the Politics of Abstraction*, Leiden: Brill.

Paolucci, Paul P. 2019, *Marx's Experiments and Microscopes Modes of Production, Religion, and the Method of Successive Abstractions*, Leiden: Brill.

Pareto, Vilfredo 1902, *Les Systèmes socialistes*, vol. 2. v. Paris: Girad & E. Brière.

Parmenides 2009, *The Fragments of Parmenides, A Critical Text With Introduction and Translation the Ancient Testimonia and a Commentary*, translated by H.A. Coxon, Las Vegas: Parmenides Publishing.

Pascal, Blaise 1963, *Pensées, in Œuvres Complètes*, Paris: Seuil.

Patterson, C., Thomas 2009, *Karl Marx, Anthropologist*, New York, Oxford: BERG.

Piaget, Jean 1950, *Introduction à l'épistémologie génétique*, Volume 3, Paris: PUF.

Plato 1997, *Complete Works*, edited by John M. Cooper, Indianapolis: Hackett.

Plekhanov, Georgiĭ Valentinovich 1956, *The development of the monist view of history*, translated by Andrew Rothstein, Moscow: Foreign Languages Publishing House.

Plekhanov, Georgiĭ Valentinovich 1980, *Fundamental Problems of Marxism, with an Appendix of His Essays: The Materialist Conception of History, The Role of the Individual in History*, translated by Julius Katzer, New York: International Publishers.

Polanyi, Karl 1934, 'Othmar Spann: The Philosopher of Fascism', *New Britain*, 3, 53: 6–7.

Ponzio, Augusto 2002, *Individuo umano, linguaggio e globalizzazione nella filosofia di Adam Schaff*, Milan: Mimesis.

Postone, Moishe 1978, 'Necessity, Labor, and Time: A Reinterpretation of the Marxian Critique of Capitalism', *Social Research*, 45, 4, Marx Today (Winter 1978): 739–88.

Postone, Moishe 2003, *Time, Labor, and Social Domination, A Reinterpretation of Marx's Critical Theory*, Cambridge: Cambridge University Press.

Postone, Moishe 2015, *Capitalism, Temporality, and the Crisis of Labor*. Available at: https://www.youtube.com/watch?v=HgMvTGO1j-k

Postone, Moishe, Capital, Class 3, https://www.youtube.com/watch?v=Op8rotGX1xw

Postone, Moishe, Capital, Class 6, https://www.youtube.com/watch?v=A09GkOJoRKY&t=1891s

Postone, Moishe and Helmut Reinicke 1974, 'On Nicolaus "Introduction" to the *Grundrisse*', in *Telos*, 130–48.

Priest, Stephen (ed.) 1992, *Hegel's Critique of Kant*, Hampshire: Greg Revivals.

Prokopczyk, Czelaw 1980, *Truth and Reality in Marx and Hegel*, Amherst: University of Massachusetts Press.

Proudhon, Pierre-Joseph 1888, *The Philosophy of Poverty*, translated by Benjamin Tucker, Boston: Benj. R. Tucker.

Psychopedis, Kosmas 1992, 'Dialectical Theory: Problems of Reconstruction', in *Opening Marxism, Volume 1, Dialectics and History*, edited by Werner Bonefeld, Richard Gunn and Kosmas Psychopedis Gunn, Richard; Psychopedis, Kosmas, London: Pluto Press, 1–53.

Pugnam, Serge (ed.) 2012 *L'enquête sociologique*, Paris: Presses Universitaires de France, Quadrige.

Reichelt, Helmut 1996, 'Warum hat Marx seiner dialektische Methode versteckt?', in *Beiträge zur Marx-Engels Forschung*, Berlin: Argument Verlag.

Reichelt, Helmut 2001a, 'Die Marxsche Kritik ökonomischer Kategorien. Überlegungen zum Problem der Geltung in der dialektischen Darstellungsmethode im "Kapital"', https://kenkubota.de/archiv/www.metzger-riehn.de/kt/ReicheltGeltung.pdf

Reichelt, Helmut 2001b, *Zur logischen Struktur des Kapitalbegriffs bei Karl Marx*, Freiburg im Breisgau: ça ira

Reichelt, Helmut 2007 [2001], 'Marx's Critique of Economic Categories: Reflections on the Problem of Validity in the Dialectical Method of Presentation in *Capital*', *Historical Materialism*, 15: 3–52.

Reuten, Geert 1993, 'The Difficult Labour of A theory of Social Value: Metaphors and Systematic Dialectics at the Beginning of Marx's Capital' in *Marx's Method in Capital, A Reexamination*, edited by Fred Moseley, New Jersey: Humanities Press, 89–114.

Ricardo, David 1817, *On the Principles of Political Economy and Taxation*, London: John Murray.

Rideell, John (tr.) 2015, *To the Masses, Proceedings of the Third Congress of the Communist International 1921*, Chicago: Haymarket Books.

Rockwell, Russell 2018, *Hegel, Marx and the Necessity and Freedom Dialectic: Marxist-Humanism and Critical Theory in the United States*, London: Palgrave Macmillan.

Rosdolsky, Roman 1969, *Zür Entstehungsgeschichte des Marxschen Kapital*, Frankfurt: Europäischer Verlagsanstalt.

Rosdolsky, Roman 1977, *The Making of Marx's "Capital"*, London: Pluto Press.

Rosental, Mark Moiseevič 1957, *Die Dialektik in Marx' 'Kapital'*, Berlin: Dietz Verlag.

Russell, Bertrand 1956, *Portraits from Memory and Other Essays*, London: Allen & Unwin.

Sartre, Jean-Paul 1963, *Search for a Method*, translated by Hazel E. Barnes, New York: Alfred A. Knopf.

Sartre, Jean-Paul 1976 [1960], *Critique of Dialectical Reason*, translated by Alan Sheridan-Smith, edited by Jonathan Ree, London: Verso.

Sayer, Derek 1979, *Marx's Method: Ideology, Science, and Criticism in 'Capital'*, New Jersey: Humanities Press.

Sayer, Derek 1987, *The Violence of Abstraction: The Analytical Foundations of Historical Materialism*, Oxford: Blackwell.

Schaff, Adam 1999, 'Structurelle Arbeitslosigkeit – das soziale Grundproblem unserer Epoche', "La disoccupazione strutturale e la grande trasformazione", in Ponzio, Augusto (2002), *Individuo umano, linguaggio e globalizzazione nella filosofia di Adam Schaff*, Milan: Mimesis, 253–266.

Schelling, Friedrich Wilhelm Joseph 2012, *Further Presentations from the System of Philosophy* (1802), in *The Philosophical Rupture between Fichte and Schelling*, translated and edited by Michael G. Vater and David W. Wood, Albany: State University of New York Press.

Schelling, Friedrich Wilhelm Joseph 2007a, *Historical-critical Introduction to the Philosophy of Mythology*, translated by Mason Richey and Markus Zisselsberger, Albany: State University of New York Press, 154–5.

Schelling, Friedrich Wilhelm Joseph 2007b, *The Grounding of Positive Philosophy: The Berlin Lectures*, translated by Bruce Matthews, Albany: State University of New York Press.

Schelling, Friedrich Wilhelm Joseph 1989, *The Philosophy of Art*, Douglas W. Stott, Minneapolis: University of Minnesota Press.

Schelling, Friedrich Wilhelm Joseph 1980, *The Unconditional in Human Knowledge: Four Early Essays (1794–1796)*, translated by Fritz Marti, London: Associated University Presses, Bucknell University Press.

Schelling, Friedrich Wilhelm Joseph 1927a, *Werke, Band I.*, Munich: München Beck.

Schelling, Friedrich Wilhelm Joseph 1927b, *Werke, Band II*, Munich: München Beck.

Schmidt, Alfred 1970, *Beiträge zu marxistischen Erkenntnistheorie*, Frankfurt: Suhrkamp.

Schmidt, Alfred 1993, *Der Begriff der Natur in der Lehre von Marx*, Hamburg: Europäische Verlagsanstalt.

Schmidt, Alfred 1971, *The Concept of Nature in Marx*, translated by Ben Fowkes, London: LNB.

Sciabarra, Chris Mathew 1995, *Marx, Hayek, and Utopia Progressive Education at the Crossroads*, Albany: State University of New York Press.

Sekine, Thomas T. 1997a, *An Outline of the Dialectic of Capital, Volume I*, Palgrave London: Macmillan Press.

Sekine, Thomas T. 1997b, *An Outline of the Dialectic of Capital, Volume II*, Palgrave London: Macmillan Press.

Sekine, Thomas T. 1998, 'The Dialectic of Capital: An Unoist Interpretation', in *Science & Society*, 62, 3: 434–5.

Sève, Lucien 1967, 'The Structural Method and the Dialectical Method', *International Journal of Sociology*, Summer – Fall, 2, 2/3, *Structuralism and Marxism: A Debate*, 195–240.

Sève, Lucien 2014, *Penser avec Marx aujourd'hui. Tome 3 'La philosophie'?*, Paris: La Dispute.

Sextus Empiricus 1976, *Outlines of Pyrrhonism*, translated by R.G. Bury, Cambridge, Mass.: Harvard University Press.

Sheehan, Helena 1993, *Marx and the Philosophy of Science*, Humanities Press, Atlantic Highlands.

Shortall, Felton C. 1994, *The Incomplete Marx*, Avebury: Aldershot.

Smith, Adam 1970, *The Wealth of Nations*, Penguin Books, England.

Smith, Tony 1990, *The Logic of Marx's Capital: Replies to Hegelian Criticisms*, Albany: State University of New York Press.

Smith, Tony 1993a, *Dialectical Social Theory, from Hegel to Analytical Marxism and Postmodernism*, Albany: State University of New York Press.

Smith, Tony 1993b, 'Marx's Capital and Hegelian Dialectical Logic' in *Marx's Method in Capital, A Reexamination*, edited by Fred Moseley, New Jersey: Humanities Press, 15–33.

Spann, Othmar 1939, *Kategorienlehre*, Jena: Gustav Fischer Verlag.

Spinoza, Baruch 1985, *Collected Works of Spinoza, vol. 1*, Edwin Curley, (Editor and Translator) Princeton: Princeton University Press.

Stahl, Titus 2016, 'Georg [György] Lukács', *The Stanford Encyclopedia of Philosophy* (Summer 2016 Edition), Edward N. Zalta (ed.), URL = https://plato.stanford.edu/archives/sum2016/entries/lukacs/

Starosta, Guido 2016, *Marx's Capital, Method and Revolutionary Subjectivity*, Leiden: Brill.

Strunk, William Jr. and E.B. White 2000, *Elements of Style*, London: Macmillan.

Sullivan, Peter M. 2000, 'The totality of facts', *Proceedings of the Aristotelian Society*, New Series, 100: 175–92.

Taylor, Charles 1995, *Hegel*, Cambridge: Cambridge University Press.

Texier, J. 1982, 'Le privilège épistémologique du présent et la nécessité du moment génétique dans les Grundrisse de K. Marx', *La Pensée*, 225: 40–52.

Thatcher, Margaret 1987, No Such Thing as Society, in an interview in *Women's Own*, available at http://www.margaretthatcher.org/document/106689.

Theunissen, Michael Von 1975, 'Begriff und Realität, Hegels Aufhebung des Metaphysischen Wahreitsbegriffs', in *Denken im Schatten des Nihilismus*, edited by Alexander Schwan, Darmstadt: Wissenschaftliche Buchgesellschaft, 164–95.

Theunissen, Michael von 1980, *Sein und Schein, Die kritische Funktion der Hegelschen Logik*, Frankfurt: Suhrkamp.

Thomas, Peter 2002, 'Philosophical Strategies: Althusser and Spinoza', *Historical Materialism*, 10, 3: 71–113.

Thomasson, Amie 2013, 'Categories', The Stanford Encyclopedia of Philosophy (Fall 2013 Edition), edited by Edward N. Zalta, available at: http://plato.stanford.edu/archives/fall2013/entries/categories/.

Tilly, Charles 1993, *The Logics of Social Structures*, Cambridge: Cambridge University Press.

Tran, Duc Thao 2012, *De Husserl à Marx, Phénoménologie et matérialisme Dialectique*, Paris: Édition Delga.
Tudor, Lucien 2012, The German Conservative Revolution & Its Legacy, *Countercurrents*, available at: https://counter-currents.com/2012/08/the-german-conservative-revolution-and-its-legacy/
Tudor, Lucien 'Othmar Spann: A Catholic Radical Traditionalist' available at: https://www.academia.edu/7629964/Othmar_Spann_A_Catholic_Radical_Traditionalist
Uchida, Hiroshi 1988, *Marx's Grundrisse and Hegel's Logic*, London: Routledge.
Vaught, Underwood, Ansley 2008, *The Specter of Spinoza in Schelling's 'Freiheitschrift'*, Pennsylvania: Villanova University.
Vilar, Pierre 1973, 'Marxist history, A History in the Making: Towards a Dialogue with Althusser', *New Left Review*, 1/80, July August.
Von Neuman, John and Oscar Morgenstern 1953, *Theory of Games and Economic Behavior*, Princeton: Princeton University Press.
Vygotsky, Lev Semyonovich 1986, *Thought and Language*, translated and edited by Alex Kozulin, Cambridge, Mass.: MIT Press.
Vygotsky, Lev Semyonovich 1986, *Thought and Language*, Cambridge, Mass.: MIT Press.
Wasjulin, Wiktor Alekseyevich 1987, 'Das Historische und Logische in der Methodologie von Karl Marx', in *Jahrbuch des Institut für Marxistische Studien und Forschungen*, 238–44.
Weston, Thomas 2012, 'Marx on the Dialectics of Elliptical Motion', in *Historical Materialism*, 20, 4: 3–38.
Westphal, Kenneth R. 1997, 'Harris, Hegel, and the Truth about the Truth', in *Hegel's Phenomenology of Spirit: A Reappraisal*, edited by Garry, K. Browning, 23–9.
Westphal, Kenneth R. 1998, 'Hegel's Solution to the Dilemma of the Criterion', *History of Philosophy Quarterly*, 5, 2: 173–88.
Westphal, Kenneth R. 2003, *Hegel's Epistemology, A Philosophical Introduction to the Phenomenology of Spirit*, Indianapolis: Hackett.
Winfield, Richard Dien 1976, 'The Logic of Marx's Capital', *Telos* 27, 111–139.
Wittgenstein, Ludwig 1922, *Tractatus Logico-Philosophicus Logisch-philosophische Abhandlung*, London: Kegan Paul. Available at: http://people.umass.edu/klement/tlp/
Wittgenstein, Ludwig 1929, 'Some Remarks on Logical Form', *Proceedings of the Aristotelian Society, Supplementary Volume*, 9, Knowledge, Experience and Realism, 162–71.
Wittgenstein, Ludwig 1958, *Philosophical Investigations*, translated by Gertrude Elizabeth Margaret Anscombe, Oxford: Blackwell.
Wolf, Dieter 2016, 'Abstraktionen in der ökonomisch-gesellschaftlichen Wirklichkeit und in der diese Wirklichkeit darstellenden Kritik der politischen Ökonomie', available at: http://www.dieterwolf.net/wp-content/uploads/2016/02/Abstraktion.pdf.
Wolf, Frieder Otto 2006, 'Marx' Konzept der 'Grenzen der dialektischen Darstellung',

in *Das Kapital neu Lesen. Beiträge zur radikalen Philosophie*, edited by Jan Hoff and Alexis Petrioli et al, Berlin: Westfälisches Dampfboot, 159–88.

Zelený, Jindřich 1980, *The Logic of Marx*, translated and edited by Terrell Carver, Oxford: Blackwell.

Žižek, Slavoj (ed.) 2002, *Revolution at the Gates: Selected Writings of Lenin from 1917*, London: Verso.

Index

Abstract xi, 23, 35, 41, 57, 67, 68, 75, 91, 93, 94, 99, 100, 105, 106, 107, 108, 109, 110, 118, 118n, 121, 126, 128, 128n, 128n222, 137, 138, 146, 148, 149, 150, 158
Abstract principle, the method of 42
Abstraction 7, 42, 48, 59, 71, 74, 74n, 85, 86, 89, 90, 92, 95, 99, 104, 106, 107, 108, 112, 118, 127, 154, 166
   Aristotelian 89
   empty 102
   erroneous 99
   false 126
   Hegel's (Hegelian) 89, 91, 92
   Inference of the 92
   Lockean empiricist 89
   Marxian 71, 92, 99, 100, 101, 118
   Power of 71, 86, 89, 130, 166
   Real 59, 74, 75
   reductive 128n
Afary, Frida 80n
Althusser, Louis 30n, 76, 102n, 103n, 123n, 144, 150, 150n
Arendt, Hannah 60n
Aristotle 22, 22n, 107n, 158, 158n
Arndt, Andreas 87n, 92n, 99, 99n102, 100n, 142n, 157n, 160n
Arthur, Chris 62n, 108n
Asay, Jamin 48n
Aufhebbar 177, see sursumption
Aufhebbarkeit 177, see sursumption
Aufheben 177, see sursumption
Aufhebende 94, see sursuming
Aufhebung 18n, 31, 134, 164, 177, see sursumption

Backhaus, Hans-Georg 154n
Bellofiore, Riccardo 79n, 80n, 106n, 116n, 119n, 164n
Best, Beverley 168n
Bidet, Jacques 3, 3n, 144, 144n, 148, 148n, 149, 149n
Big Sleep 168n
Bloch, Ernst 38, 64n, 68, 166
Blunden, Andy 49
Boudin, Raymond 44n

Bourdieu, Pierre 95n, 159n
Burbidge, John William 57n

Callinicos, Alex 3n, 25n, 25n67, 25n68, 117n, 122n, 136n, 137n, 144n, 149, 149n, 149n25, 150, 150n, 150n28, 150n30, 151, 155n, 156, 156n, 165n
Camus, Albert 74n, 160n
Capital viii, ix, 1, 2, 3, 32, 45, 45n, 61, 76, 77, 78, 79, 80, 80n, 80n9, 81, 88, 89, 96, 98, 99, 101, 101n, 101n108, 102, 107, 107n, 110, 119n, 120, 121, 122, 122n, 123, 123n, 124, 126, 127, 128, 128n, 130, 131, 132, 133, 134, 136, 136n, 136n267, 136n268, 137, 137n, 140, 140n288, 140n289, 141, 142, 143, 144, 145, 146, 147, 148, 148n, 149, 149n, 150, 150n, 151, 153, 153n, 154, 155, 156, 157, 158, 158n, 158n64, 158n66, 159, 160, 160n, 162, 163, 164, 165, 165n, 167, 169, 169n, 169n3, 169n4, 170, 171
Category 5, 18n, 26, 27, 27n, 29, 30, 32, 33, 34, 35, 37, 37n, 38, 39, 44n, 59, 85, 101, 101n, 107, 111, 112, 116, 117n, 122, 123, 124, 127, 131, 133, 153, 154, 155, 156, 158, 166
   Categorial development 158
   Categorial movement viii, 3, 18, 37, 38, 39, 77, 85, 107n, 120, 122, 122n, 123, 128, 132, 136, 141–42, 150, 153, 155, 156
   Metacategory 26, 27, 39, 120, 123, 161n, 162, 166
Cerutti, Furio 3n, 41n
Chandler, Raymond 168n
Concrete vii, 22, 25, 26, 33, 35, 41, 42, 43, 44, 45, 46, 47, 55, 57, 58, 63, 68, 78, 92, 93, 99, 100, 101, 104, 105, 109, 121, 128, 137, 138, 140, 146, 148, 149, 150, 156, 171
Concreteness 64
Dialectic of the Concrete 1, 2, 11, 41n, 51n, 160
Pseudo-concrete vii, 42, 45, 46, 52n, 62, 63n, 64, 74, 99, 101
Concretisation 41, 42, 58, 67, 92, 99, 120, 121, 122, 123

Dardot, Pierre 65n, 87n, 91n, 139n, 160n
Deleuze, Gilles 8n, 104n, 162n
Descartes, René 4, 161, 161n, 162n

Di Giovanni, George   19n, 21n, 27n, 161n
Dunayeskaya, Raya   117n
Durkheim, Emile   14
Dussel, Enrique   126n, 166n

Elias, Norbert   10, 10n
Engels, Friedrich

Feuerbach, Ludwig Andreas   viii, 2, 46, 49, 52, 56, 57, 61, 62, 64, 75, 83, 91, 95, 96, 130, 132, 133, 141, 162n
Fichte   81, 81n, 82, 161n
Finelli, Roberto   79n, 116n, 118n, 118n185, 119n
Fineschi, Roberto   79n, 153n, 154, 154n, 154n48, 154n49, 164n
Foster, John Bellamy   165n
Freeman, Alan   70n

Gadamer, Hans-Georg   54n
Gauthier, Yvon   22n, 47n, 89n, 112n, 115n, 177
Guattari, Félix   8n, 104n, 162n
Goldmann, Lucien   96, 96n, 97
Goldstick, Dan   6n, 48n
Gramsci, Antonio   32n, 152n
Grumley, John Edward   29n, 31n, 33n, 38n, 87n, 92, 156

Halbwachs, Maurice   88n
Hall, Stuart   98n, 98n95, 103n, 103n119, 140n, 142n, 158n, 158n65
Harvey, David   97n, 129n, 139n, 161n
Hegel, Georg Wilhelm Friedrich   iii, vii, ix, x, 2, 4, 8, 12n, 13, 13n, 16, 17, 17n, 18, 18n, 18n7, 18n8, 18n9, 18n10, 18n11, 18n12, 18n13, 18n14, 18n15, 18n16, 18n17, 19, 19n , 19n19, 19n20, 19n21, 19n22, 19n23, 19n24, 20n, 20n25, 20n26, 20n27, 20n28, 20n29, 20n30, 20n31, 21, 21n, 21n33, 21n34, 21n35, 21n36, 22, 22n, 22n39, 22n40, 22n41, 22n42, 22n43, 22n44, 23, 23n47, 23n48, 23n49, 23n50, 23n51, 23n52, 23n53, 23n54, 24, 24n, 24n56, 24n57, 24n58, 24n59, 24n60, 25, 25n, 25n62, 25n63, 25n64, 25n65, 25n66, 25n67, 26, 26n71, 26n72, 26n74, 27, 27n, 27n76, 27n79, 27n80, 28, 29, 30, 30n, 32, 34n, 36, 38, 38n, 39, 41, 44, 44n, 45n, 46, 47, 48, 51, 54, 56, 56n, 57n, 63n, 64, 67, 72, 76, 76n, 81, 81n, 82, 83, 83n, 84, 84n, 85, 85n, 86, 88, 89, 89n, 91, 98, 99, 100, 102, 104, 105, 105n, 105n128, 112, 113n, 114, 114n, 115, 115n, 116, 116n, 119, 120, 120n, 123n, 128n, 129n, 130, 131n, 142n, 144, 144n, 146, 146n, 148, 148n, 149, 150, 150n, 151, 153n, 154, 155, 155n, 157, 158, 158n, 161, 161n, 162, 162n, 162n89, 163, 164, 164n, 164n95, 167, 167n, 177
   Owl of Minerva   83, 105
   Phenomenology of Spirit   13, 22n, 26, 63n, 83, 89, 155
   Philosophy of Right   27, 83, 105, 162n, 164n
   Science of Logic (Wissenschaft der Logik)   2, 17, 18n, 21, 21n, 25, 26, 27, 32, 85, 89, 93, 120n, 146, 155, 161, 164, 164n, 177
Heidegger, Martin   58n
Heinrich, Michael   78n, 80n, 136n, 136n266, 151n
Houlgate, Stephen   19n, 25n, 27n
Hume, David   91n

Ilyenkov, Evald Vassilievich   101n, 101n109, 104n, 105, 105n, 116n, 141n, 151, 151n, 151n33, 156, 156n, 164n
Inwood, Michael   37n, 56n, 177n

Jacoby, Russell   47n, 56n
Jameson, Fredric   1n, 44n, 46n, 47n, 49n, 57n, 104, 168n
Jay, Marti   3, 29n

Kant, Immanuel   x, 8, 17, 17n, 27, 39, 41n, 50, 81, 81n, 82n, 85
Kaplan, Abraham   159n
Kosík, Karel   vii, x, 1, 3, 4, 4n, 5, 6, 8, 9, 9n, 10, 11, 11n, 12n, 13, 14, 16, 17, 17n, 21n, 28, 33n, 35n, 36, 37, 37n, 38, 40, 41, 41n, 41n3, 41n4, 42, 42n, 42n6, 42n7, 42n8, 42n9, 42n10, 42n11, 43, 43n, 43n13, 43n14, 43n16, 44, 45, 45n, 46n, 47, 47n, 48, 50, 51, 51n, 52, 52n, 53, 53n, 55, 55n, 55n52, 55n53, 56, 57, 57n, 58, 58n, 58n65, 58n66, 58n67, 59, 59n, 59n69, 59n70, 59n71, 60, 60n, 60n73, 60n74, 60n75, 61, 61n, 61n77, 62, 62n80, 62n81, 62n82, 63, 64, 65, 65n, 65n92, 65n93, 65n94, 66, 66n, 66n96, 66n98, 66n99, 67, 67n, 68, 68n, 68n102, 69, 69n,

INDEX 203

Kosík, Karel (cont.) 69n105, 69n106, 69n109, 70, 70n, 71, 71n, 71n117, 71n118, 72, 73n, 74n, 74n127, 75, 75n, 76, 76n, 76n132, 77, 77n, 77n135, 78n, 81, 90, 105, 113n, 120n, 126n, 142, 142n, 152, 152n, 160, 160n, 160n77, 163n, 166
Kroeger, Adolph Ernst 26n

Labriola, Antonio 69, 69n, 69n108
Laval, Christian 65n, 87n, 91n, 139n, 160n
Leibniz, Wilhelm Gottfried 4n, 87
 Monad 87
Lemieux, Cyril 152n
Lenin, Vladimir Ilyich 24, 29, 30, 32n, 47n, 54n
Lobkowicz, Nicholas 101n
Locke, John 89
Lukács, Georg 2, 3n, 27, 28, 28n, 29, 29n, 29n4, 29n5, 30, 30n, 30n7, 30n9, 30n10, 30n11, 30n12, 31, 31n, 32, 32n, 32n21, 32n22, 32n23, 32n24, 33, 33n, 33n26, 33n27, 33n28, 33n30, 33n31, 33n32, 34, 34n, 34n34, 34n36, 35, 35n, 35n41, 35n42, 35n43, 36, 36n, 37, 37n, 37n52, 37n53, 38, 38n, 38n55, 38n56, 38n57, 38n58, 39, 39n, 39n61, 39n62, 39n63, 41, 43n, 54n, 58, 58n, 58n67, 61, 62, 64, 65n, 75, 84, 84n, 100, 166, 168
Luxemburg, Rosa 32n, 100, 138

Macherey, Pierre 97, 97n
MacKinnon, Catharine 55n
Mandel, Ernst 150, 150n, 150n31
Marcuse, Herbert 55, 55n, 167n
McLellan, David 80n, 82n, 82n16, 83n, 84, 84n, 84n27, 84n28, 85, 85n33, 86n, 86n38, 88
McTaggart, Ellis 18n
Meta-methodology 84
Method x, 5, 18, 26, 30, 30n, 32, 33, 33n, 34, 35, 37, 42, 64, 79, 82, 99, 121, 128, 130, 142, 144, 145, 145n, 146, 147, 149, 153n, 154, 156, 158, 161, 162
Method of exposition viii, 3, 3n, 77, 78, 78n, 142, 144, 145, 145n, 150, 151, 154, 155, 156, 157, 158, 159, 161n, 162, 163, 164, 165, 166

Method of enquiry viii, 3, 77, 78, 78n, 144, 145, 145n, 150, 151, 152, 153, 153n, 154, 156, 157, 158, 159, 161, 161n, 162, 163, 164, 165, 166
Method of investigation 3, 70, 151, 153, 157, 162
Methodology vii, ix, x, xi, 3, 29, 65, 82, 83, 84, 89, 141n, 145, 151, 157, 161, 162, 166
Milton, John 84n
Molière 57n
Moment 2, 3, 3n, 6, 18, 19, 20, 21, 22, 23, 23n, 24, 25, 26, 31, 32, 33, 35, 43, 57n, 59, 60, 63, 67, 71, 72, 74, 77, 87, 89, 89n, 100, 101, 102, 103, 103n, 105, 106, 108, 109, 110, 111, 112, 113, 114, 117, 119, 120, 121, 122, 123, 124, 125, 127, 128, 132, 135, 136, 138, 139, 141, 150, 152, 152n, 153, 155, 157, 158, 159, 160, 161, 164n, 164n97, 166, 167, 171
 submoment 153
 das and der 89, 101, 157, 157n, 162
Momentum, 89, 130
Moseley, Fred 3, 106, 106n, 106n134, 106n135, 110n, 136, 136n, 158
Murphy, Richard W. 167n

Negri, Antonio 153n, 160n, 165n

Object 50, 52, 53, 55, 56, 58, 59, 62, 102, 125, 158
Objective 22, 28, 42, 43, 43n, 46n, 50, 51, 52, 53, 55, 56, 57, 59, 60, 60n, 62, 113, 114, 129n, 130, 141, 158n
Objectively 33, 35, 47, 49, 55, 141
Objectivity vii, 23, 24, 25, 30, 43, 47, 48n, 49, 50, 51, 52, 53, 54, 55, 55n, 56n, 57, 57n, 72, 116, 129
Objectivise 55
Objectivation 50, 55, 56, 59
Object* [Gegenstand] 51, 52, 53, 54, 55, 56, 76n, 87, 89, 95, 102, 103, 122, 125, 132, 133, 146, 160
Objective* [Gegenständlich] 51, 53, 56, 57, 62n, 63, 65, 66, 67, 69, 71, 81, 87, 91, 106, 117, 119, 128, 129, 163
Objectively* 119, 129, 130
Objectivity* [Gegenständlichkeit] 51, 56, 63, 65, 72, 129, 129n, 130, 131
Objectification 51, 52, 55, 56, 59, 60, 74n, 114
Objectual 50, 52, 58, 59, 62, 73

Objectuality 50
Ollman, Bertell 26n, 30n, 34n, 83n, 166n

Paolucci, Paul 14, 14n, 70n, 161n
Pareto, Vilfredo 34n
Parmenides 26, 44, 158, 158n
Pascal, Blaise 71, 71n, 72
Patterson, Thomas C. 87n
Plato 26
Plekhanov, Georgiï Valentinovich 69, 69n
Polanyi, Karl 15, 15n
Postone, Moishe 103n, 112n, 130n, 138n, 161n, 166n
Proudhon, Pierre-Joseph 90, 90n, 136
Psychopedis, Kosmas 162n

Reichelt, Helmut 85n, 120n, 121n, 154n, 154n46, 158
Ricardo, David 100, 103
Rockwell, Russell 167
Rosdolsky, Roman 110n, 116, 117, 119, 144, 144n, 147, 148, 148n, 149n, 157
Russell, Bertrand 5, 9, 9n, 31n

Sartre, Jean-Paul 60n, 75n
Schelling, Friedrich Wilhelm Joseph 1, 4, 11, 11n, 12, 12n, 12n29, 12n30, 12n31, 12n32, 13, 13n, 13n37, 12n38, 12n39, 15, 47
Schmidt, Alfred 76n, 120n
Sciabarra, Chris Mathew 72n
Sève, Lucien 34, 34n, 35, 35n
Sextus Empiricus 48, 48n
Smith, Adam 109, 125
Smith, Tony 123, 128n, 129n, 148, 148n, 153n
Spann, Othmar 1, 4, 11, 13, 13n, 15, 15n
Spannian 14
Spinoza, Baruch 13, 83, 83n, 90
Stahl, Titus 38n
Starosta, Guido 106n, 126n, 132n, 145n
Strunk, William Jr. 159n
Sursumable 177
Sursumable, Unsursumable 87
Sursuming 46, 94
  self- 18
Sursumability 177

Sursume 20, 21, 24, 31, 45, 46, 62, 63, 64, 67, 74, 89, 94, 163, 177
Sursumer 177
Sursumption 18, 31, 97, 134, 164, 177, 212
Sullivan, Peter M. 10n

Taylor, Charles 17n
Thatcher, Margaret 14, 14n, 129n
The 1844 Economic and Philosophical Manuscripts viii, 2, 76, 78, 86, 118, 118n, 131
The Holy Family 92
The German Ideology viii, 2, 46, 46n, 64, 65n, 84, 91, 93, 96, 98, 100, 152
The Grundrisse viii, ix, 1, 2, 3, 35, 36, 37n, 55, 76, 76n, 77, 78, 80, 89n, 98, 99, 106, 106n, 107, 107n, 110, 116n, 117n, 118, 118n, 119, 120, 120n, 121, 122, 122n, 123, 125, 126, 127, 129n, 134, 137, 143, 144, 145, 147, 148, 148n, 149, 149n, 150, 152, 152n, 152–53n38, 153, 154, 155, 156, 157, 158, 160, 160n, 160n79, 163, 163n, 164, 165
'Theses on Feuerbach' viii, 2, 49, 50n, 52, 56, 57, 61, 62, 75, 83, 91, 96, 97, 132, 133, 141
Theunissen, Michael 27n, 81n
Tilly, Charles 27n
Totality
  abstract 43
  bad 43, 99
  Empty 42, 43, 68, 99
  False 43, 99
  as totalisation 6, 8, 26, 30, 42, 60, 62, 64, 65, 103, 110, 114, 120, 121, 122, 123, 132, 141, 162
  as detotalisation 110
  moments of 91, 100, 103
Tran, Duc Thao 53n
Tudor, Lucien 15n

Vygotsky, Lev Semyonovich 155n

Weston, Thomas 119n
Wittgenstein, Ludwig 1, 4, 5, 5n, 6, 6n, 7, 7n, 8, 8n, 9, 9n, 10, 10n, 47
Wolf, Dieter 152n
Wolf, Frieder Otto xi, 162

www.ingramcontent.com/pod-product-compliance
Lightning Source LLC
Chambersburg PA
CBHW070621030426
42337CB00020B/3878